MW00830041

Administrative Traditions

Administrative Traditions

Understanding the Roots of Contemporary Administrative Behavior

B. GUY PETERS

OXFORD
UNIVERSITY PRESS

OXFORD
UNIVERSITY PRESS

Great Clarendon Street, Oxford, OX2 6DP,
United Kingdom

Oxford University Press is a department of the University of Oxford.
It furthers the University's objective of excellence in research, scholarship,
and education by publishing worldwide. Oxford is a registered trade mark of
Oxford University Press in the UK and in certain other countries

First Edition published in 2021

Impression: 1

Published in the United States of America by Oxford University Press
198 Madison Avenue, New York, NY 10016, United States of America

British Library Cataloguing in Publication Data
Data available

Library of Congress Control Number: 2020952084

ISBN 978-0-19-829725-3

DOI: 10.1093/oso/9780198297253.001.0001

Printed and bound by
CPI Group (UK) Ltd, Croydon, CR0 4YY

Preface

Contemporary political and administrative systems may be described as "modern" or "post-modern," and they are the products of a number of political and managerial changes over the past few decades. These contemporary systems, however, also reflect their pasts. This book is an attempt to understand how the underlying ideas and traditions of an administrative system affect its contemporary structure and behavior. But it is also important to understand how change can occur in institutionalized political systems, and, further, how their pasts affect their present and their future.

The idea of administrative traditions developed in this book is conceived as an approach to comparative public administration. By enumerating the basic elements of these traditions we have a framework for comparing administration. The focus in this volume is on the consolidated democracies of Europe, North America, and the Antipodes, but the same criteria can be used to understand public administration in a variety of other settings. I have demonstrated the utility of these dimensions of traditions to some extent in the later chapters of this book, but they could be used more extensively and intensely for the cases discussed here, as well as for other administrative systems.

This book in finally appearing after an extremely long time in development. I would like to have finished it much sooner, as I am sure Oxford University Press would also have liked. That said, I am also sure that the manuscript is better because of the extra time spent in thinking through some issues. The basic concepts are little changed from when I began on the project a decade ago, but some parts of the book have changed significantly from the original plan. Perhaps the greatest change has been in the way in which I have treated the effects of colonialism on public administration in Africa. I am still not an expert on African government and administration, but I believe the current presentation is vastly improved over the rather simplistic conceptions I was planning to use initially.

Over the very long time that it required to complete this book, a number of friends and colleagues have provided useful comments that have helped. I wish to express my thanks to Martin Painter with whom I did an edited book on traditions a decade ago. And thanks also to Philippe Bezes, Daniel Carelli, Tom Christensen, Wolfgang Drechsler, Joao Guedes-Neto, Maximilian Nagel,

Amaury Perez, Maxfield Peterson, Lou Picard, Conrado Ramos, and Eckhard Schröter. Numerous others have been subjected to talks on the subject and have provided useful, and generally polite, comments. I am sure there are others with whom I have discussed these ideas that I am leaving out, and to them I apologize. And as always, special thanks to Jon Pierre whose counsel and friendship have helped this and many other projects. And thanks to Sheryn who has had to endure a decade of angst and grumbling, and for helping manage the bibliographic and indexing tasks.

Contents

List of Tables   viii

1. Understanding Comparative Bureaucracy   1
2. The Administrative Tradition Approach to Public Bureaucracy   23
3. The Napoleonic Tradition   54
4. The Germanic Tradition   75
5. The Scandinavian Tradition   94
6. The Anglo-American Tradition   116
7. The European Union as a Distinctive Tradition?   139
8. Other Administrative Traditions   154
9. Transferring Traditions: The Colonial Experience   178
10. Persistence and Change in Public Administration   194

References   215
Index   251

List of Tables

1.1. Heady's configuration of civil service systems   8

1.2. Public confidence in the Civil Service and Parliament, 2010–14   16

1.3. Dimensions of organizational culture   18

1.4. Elements of administrative traditions   21

2.1. Beck's patterns of administrative culture (with applications)   24

2.2. Civil servants as members of parliament   34

2.3. Average public service motivation by region   37

3.1. Proportion of respondents belonging to one or more groups (2016)   64

3.2. Trade union density (2018)   65

4.1. State traditions in Germany   80

4.2. Own Source Revenues   89

5.1. Control of government, 1917–2019 (number of years)   102

5.2. Declining organizational participation   113

8.1. European and Asian administrative traditions   162

8.2. Dimensions of organizational culture   167

8.3. Levels of professionalization of civil service systems in Central and Eastern Europe, and Western Europe   174

9.1. Sources of failure in African public administration   186

9.2. Comparison of civic and affective spaces of communication   188

9.3. Relationship of formal and informal institutions   190

9.4. Measures of administrative performance of countries based on colonial background   191

10.1. Administrative traditions and administrative reforms: levels of compatibility   210

1

Understanding Comparative Bureaucracy

No matter how democratic and participatory a political system may be it will always require some form of bureaucracy to implement decisions and to monitor public compliance with its laws (see Gormley and Balla 2013; Cook 2014). A well-functioning public bureaucracy is essential for the rule of law, one of the criteria commonly utilized to measure good governance (Besancon 2003). In contemporary states the bureaucracy does far more than simply implement programs, and is a major locus for both policymaking and of adjudication (See Seerden and Stroink 2002; Page 2010; Kerwin and Furlong 2019), not to mention a major source of policy advice for political leaders (Brans et al. 2006). As well as providing policy advice to its nominal political masters the manner in which public administrative functions within different national settings directly or indirectly influences the policy choices made in those countries. And in developing and transitional governments the bureaucracy is a crucial factor in development (Evans and Rauch 1999), providing expertise and stability in often troubled political systems.

Although crucial to the success of public governance, the public bureaucracy has been studied perhaps less by contemporary political scientists than have other components of the public sector.[1] The relative dearth of research on the public bureaucracy is especially evident in comparative terms (Pollitt 2015 but see, inter alia, Pierre 1995; Burns and Bowornwathana 2001; Heady 2001; Peters 2018a). This relative absence of interest in comparative bureaucracy may be a function of the bureaucracy appearing rather dull when compared to political parties and elections, or even legislatures. Further, the managerial concerns of much of the contemporary public administration community fail to emphasize the important political and policy dimensions

---

[1] There is, of course, a thriving academic field of public administration but it has become increasingly divorced from political science and comparative politics, especially in the United States (see Torfing et al. forthcoming). The failure of these two bodies of literature to speak to one another weakens both significantly. Much of contemporary political science ignores 95 percent of the employees of government, and public administration often ignores the political environment within which it functions.

Administrative Traditions: Understanding the Roots of Contemporary Administrative Behavior. B. Guy Peters, Oxford University Press (2021). © B. Guy Peters. DOI: 10.1093/oso/9780198297253.003.0001

of the public bureaucracy, emphasizing instead the quotidian management of public organizations.

This book will compare the public bureaucracy as a component of governance in the public sector of contemporary political systems. This analysis will be an attempt to locate these institutions within their state traditions or "families" (Dyson 1980; Heper 1987; Castles 1993) but also demonstrates that public bureaucracies have distinguishing features of their own that may operate somewhat independently of the states within which they function. Silberman (1993), for example, emphasized rationality as a central feature of bureaucracies regardless of the national setting, although that rationality functions differently in different settings. The argument to be made in this book is that although each national administrative system is distinctive,[2] they are also part of a number of families that share common inheritances, common structures, and common values. Those values concern how to administer public policy, the role and character of the public service, and their relationship with other institutions in government—especially the political executive.

In addition, I will be focusing on the extent to which the patterns that are observed in contemporary administrative systems represent an inheritance of ideas and structures from the past. The fundamental argument here, not dissimilar to some of the ideas of historical institutionalism, is that once patterns of administration or policy have been established they tend to persist. Other patterns of administration may be layered on top of those basic patterns, or those pre-existing patterns may be redefined over time (see Mahoney and Thelen 2010a) but some basic values and practices of the system will persist, and may reassert themselves later if they are replaced by newer alternatives.[3]

Finally, we will be interested in the role that administrative traditions play in shaping reform. Although administrative reforms have been an enduring feature of the public sector, their pace and intensity has been perhaps greater for the past several decades. The strength of the ideas of New Public Management (NPM) (see Christensen and Laegreid 2010) and the several alternatives to that prospective paradigm for public administration (see Peters 2017) are also discussed. A number of studies have argued that Continental European systems have been very different from Anglo-American systems in reacting to

---

[2] And in some cases, especially federal systems, there are marked differences among sub-national administrative systems. See Johns et al. (2006).

[3] For example, while New Zealand was the "poster child" for New Public Management (Boston 1996), after some years many of the values of the underlying Westminster system reasserted themselves (Gregory 2003; Chapman and Duncan 2007; but see also Lodge and Gill 2011).

these ideas (see, for example, Kickert 1997; Torres 2004) but even within those very broad categories of countries there are major differences.[4] As I examine administrative traditions I will attempting to understand and explain how the history of the systems explains their future and their likelihood of responding to pressures for reform.

Comparing Public Bureaucracies

The fundamental task of comparative politics is to describe and explain differences and similarities among political systems, whether the systems in question are countries, *Länder*, communes, or whatever. The object of the explanation can be whole systems, or it may be components (institutional or territorial) of those systems. Indeed, explaining differences in institutions, or in roles such as those of the political executive, may be a less demanding exercise, simply because the nature of the institution and its tasks will control some sources of difference among the explicand, and hence produce somewhat less variability than might be found for whole political systems (LaPalombara 1968). Even when scholars seek to develop "mid-range theory," again whether based on institutions or on subsets of nations (Heisler 1978; Herbst 2014) for comparison there are still an almost infinite number of possible explanations for observed differences, and the task of comparative explanation remains difficult.

Although the task of comparison is difficult, it is also necessary. Even while there is a significant increase in using experimental methodologies for studying political phenomena, the best way to study political institutions, and perhaps the especially the public bureaucracy, is through comparative analysis. For these complex institutions, it is important to examine how they function as formal, and informal, organizational structures and not just to examine the individual behaviors of the members. The logic of New Institutionalism (March and Olsen 1989) which argues that individuals have their preferences shaped by their membership in the institution rather than being exogenous to the institution, is crucial for understanding how these organizations work.

This book is an attempt to provide a description and new explanation for differences among the public bureaucracies across a range of countries. I will focus on the industrialized democracies of Europe, North America, and the

---

[4] For example, the United States and Canada adopted relatively little of the NPM model, while the United Kingdom and the Antipodes did so extensively. See also Horton (2011).

Antipodes. The creation of public bureaucracies has been one of the first stages in the process of modernizing the state (Torstendahl 1991). Indeed, part of the logic for Max Weber having created his Ideal Type model of bureaucracy (Eliason 2000; Jann 2003) was to identify the goals of, and processes for, a gradual professionalization and bureaucratization of the German state.

In addition to these developed Western democracies, I will also give some attention to other administrative traditions. Given the limitations of space these discussions may appear superficial, but the intention is to demonstrate that the general model of administrative traditions is applicable in a wide range of cases, and is not peculiarly Western. Therefore, I will spend some time examining the Confucian and Islamic traditions, as well as the development of contemporary public administration in Latin America. Finally, I will examine how the four dominant traditions in European and North American administration have been transmitted to their former colonies, as well as to the bureaucracy of the European Union.

Bureaucracies may be one of easier institutions in the public sector to compare, given that they all must do approximately the same things and they tend to be organized in relatively similar ways. This relative similarity can be contrasted with the differences among parliaments, for example, in which some are genuine transformative, policymaking organizations, others are arenas in which the executive discusses its policies and is held accountable, and others are merely rubber stamps for a hegemonic political party or controlled by the prime minister and cabinet (see Poguntke and Webb 2007; Savoie 2008). Although they may perform their tasks rather differently, the tasks of the bureaucracy are similar, even when the focus is expanded to include bureaucracies in less-developed and authoritarian regimes (see Gandhi 2008; Hyden 2013).

Although the range of variation among bureaucracies appears to be less than for most other institutions and actors in the public sector, there is still substantial variation, and a great deal of work to do in order to provide convincing explanations for the observed differences. For example, there are marked differences in personnel systems and the ways in which people are recruited, rewarded, and sanctioned within the public bureaucracy (Van der Meer et al. 2015). These differences begin with the fundamental one between job and career systems, e.g., systems in which public servants are hired to perform a certain job or are hired for their potential for a career in the system (Mendez 2019). That fundamental difference permeates personnel systems and type of personnel who are recruited to government. Similarly, ideas of how, and how much, public servants should be rewarded for performing their tasks varies substantially across governments (Hood et al. 2002; Brans and Peters 2012).

We also need to understand the structural features of the public sector when we attempt to understand administrative traditions. The public sector in all advanced political systems is composed of a large, and increasingly large, number of different types of organizations that are linked through a variety of instruments such as finance, law, and personnel systems (Seidman 1999; Verhoest et al. 2016). The development of common, coordinating instruments is becoming more important as adoption of the ideas of NPM has tended to produce somewhat greater heterogeneity among organizations in the public sector (Peters 2015). Governments are now more diverse, have more complex internal management relationships, and more diverse mechanisms for internal control (Hood et al. 2004), and also are more involved with organizations in the private sector that require new forms of accountability and control.

Scholars also have attempted to explain the role that individual public servants, especially senior public servants, play in the process of governance and policymaking (Aberbach et al. 1981). This role in policymaking continues to be one of the most common issues raised concerning the role of bureaucrats in government (Page 2010), both by practitioners and by scholars. At the extreme, it has been argued that political leaders are at the mercy of their senior public officials who control information and are able to shape the decisions that are made by politicians (De Graaf 2011).[5] The contrary claim is also advanced, with bureaucrats sometimes believing themselves to have their latitude for independent, and even legally mandated, action severely constrained by political interference. And in those circumstances civil servants may pursue mechanisms to resist the control (O'Leary 2013; Olsson 2016).

Some of the differences in the role of bureaucrats in governing are a function of the individuals involved in the relationships between minister and civil servant, but some also are a function of the tradition within which those individuals perform their tasks. Some traditions tend to assume, or at least attempt to create, a clear separation between politicians and civil servants, with the further assumption that political leaders should direct policy. Other traditions assume much greater integration of political and administrative roles in policymaking. Likewise, policy areas requiring high levels of scientific

---

[5] One can find this claim in many memoirs of senior public servants, perhaps most famously in the diaries published by Richard Crossman (1966); see also Fenton (2006).

or technical expertise may provide civil servants more room for influence when confronting generally less expert political leaders.

We also need to understand the behavior of individual public servants as they make decisions about how to conduct themselves within government (Brehm and Gates 1997; Le Grand 2003). Although the major emphasis in studies of public bureaucracies has been on the senior levels of these organizations, there are thousands and even millions of public employees who do the day-to-day work of government. It can be argued that the emphasis on the upper echelons of the service tends to ignore the decision-making role of those other levels, and especially the officials at the bottom in regular conflict with clients. These "street-level bureaucrats" (Lipsky 2010; Meyers and Nielsen 2011; Zacka 2017) make thousands of decisions each day and may be all that the average citizen ever sees of the public sector. To some extent the behavior of these lower echelon employees is structured as much by the nature of the tasks as by the discretion available to the individual public servant (Hupe et al. 2015), although even the most mechanical tasks may be affected by differences among traditions.

Explaining Bureaucratic Behavior

Just as there are numerous differences among administrative systems that need to be explained, there are also a number of possible ways of explaining them. In this section I will outline five alternative explanations for behavior within public organizations. Some of these explanations depend on the behavior of individuals within the structures, while others are based more on the properties of the institutions themselves. All of these explanations are especially important in this book for explaining differences in the behavior of individuals and organizations across political systems. I will be arguing that although these explanations all have some utility, the concept of administrative traditions which I develop in this book provides a more powerful way of conducting that comparative analysis (see also Capano 2003; Painter and Peters 2010b).

Formal, Legal Explanations

One common pattern of explanation in public administration is to utilize formal, legal differences among countries to explain both the nature of the public sector and what happens within it. This has been the dominant approach to bureaucracy, going back to scholars such as Max Weber (Anter 2005) and Woodrow Wilson (1887). Weber clearly intended his rational legal conceptions about bureaucracy to be an Ideal Type against which to compare real-world organizations, but many scholars, and seemingly also many practitioners themselves, have taken the ideas somewhat more literally (for a discussion, see Page 1989; Peters 2010a).

In some political systems the legalistic norms usually associated with a Weberian bureaucracy remain dominant, and have been able to resist attempts to move toward more flexible and managerial conceptions of what the civil servant is meant to do while in office. But even in highly legalistic administrative systems there is always an informal organization that co-exists with the formal norms and may either support that formal system of organization, or perhaps undermine it (Rainey and Steinbauer 1999). Therefore it is insufficient to just look at the formal administrative rules and regulations, just as comparative politics scholars have long found it insufficient to examine only constitutions and legal systems.

A number of typologies and taxonomies of bureaucracy have been advanced to attempt to capture the formal differences among administrative systems. Some, such as the classic analyses of Blau and Scott (2003), Seidman (1999), and Perrow (1972) have been based on the nature of organizations themselves, and the tasks that they perform within the bureaucracy. Others have been based on the nature of entire bureaucratic systems. For example, Ferrell Heady (2001) has classified administrative systems, largely on the basis of his inspection of the cases, in both historical and contemporary systems in five categories: classic, "civic culture" types, successful modernizers, communist, and undeveloped (Table 1.1). Likewise, Metin Heper (1987) developed an extensive classification system for bureaucracies based on types of polities and the definition of the state.

These typologies and taxonomies are useful as far as they go, but also have substantial weaknesses. Perhaps most importantly they can lump together a range of administrative systems that are broadly similar but also have substantial differences. For example, the Heady taxonomy tends to lump together all four of the administrative traditions among democratic systems discussed in this volume, while I will be attempting to demonstrate that they are different in a number of important ways.[6] Further, typologies based on the nature and tasks of organizations tend to ignore the public nature of public administration, and the role of other state institutions in affecting their behavior.

---

[6] Any attempt at classification and comparison across political systems will involve some overgeneralization, but this seems an extreme example.

Table 1.1 Heady's configuration of civil service systems

	Ruler trustworthy	Party controlled	Policy receptive	Collaborative
Relation to political regime	Rule responsive	Single-party responsive	Dominant party responsive	Military responsive
Socioeconomic context	Traditional	Planned or corporatist	Pluralist competive	Corporatist or planned
Focus on personnel management	Chief executive or ministry by ministry	Chief executive or ministry by ministry	Independent agency	Chief executive or ministry by ministry
Qualification requirements	Patrimony	Party patronage or party loyalty	Professional performance	Bureaucratic determination
Sense of mission	Compliance or guidance	Compliance or cooperation	Policy or constitutional responsiveness	Cooperation or guidance

Source: Heady (1996).

As well as the legal foundations of different administrative systems, the formal structures of the public sector also affect the nature, and performance, of the public bureaucracy (see Egeberg 2013). For example, an administrative system organized through autonomous or semi-autonomous agencies will function very differently from one with pyramidal structures within larger cabinet departments. Likewise the degree of horizontal differentiation of government, and the presence or absence of coordinating organizations in the center, will also have significant effects of the performance of the bureaucracy (see Bouckaert et al. 2010).

While these structural differences are usually discussed in terms of the efficient provision of public services, the effects on policy choices may be more important. Lester Salamon (1981) argued that the search for efficiency through reorganization was largely futile, but the institutional designer could alter policy choices based on the location of the organization relative to other organizations. For example, moving the U.S. Coast Guard from the Department of Treasury to the Department of Transportation to the Department of Homeland Security emphasized very different parts of its complex mission. Internally the organization was largely unchanged, but its priorities were altered by these reorganizations.

Politics and the Political Process

Another possible explanation of the behavior of bureaucrats is that public officials and their organizations are engaged in a political process. That political process should not be conceived as a partisan political conflict, although certainly discussions of politicization of the bureaucracy demonstrate that political parties are concerned with who is administering public policy (Rouban 2011; Panizza et al. 2019). Most of the political activity of bureaucracy is organizational, with senior civil servants attempting to maintain and enhance the position of their organizations, through budgetary or policy-making processes, or in relationships with client groups within society.

To this point we have been implicitly discussing the bureaucracy as a single entity, although in practice the more appropriate way to think of the public bureaucracy is as a collection of organizations, each having some demonstrable interests of its own. These organizations are often in competition with one another over scarce resources as well as in conflict over the content of public policy. One task of senior managers in such a decentralized administrative system is to fight his or her corner and ensure that the organization receives the financial and other resources required to survive, to be effective, and to shape public policy in desired directions. This type of activity is intensely political, even if it does not involve political parties or politicians.

But the bureaucracy may have some collective interests as well. For example, the civil service as a whole has an interest in higher salaries and benefits, and may organize into labor unions in order to bargain for those benefits. Further, especially in political systems with strong political control, the bureaucracy may also have a collective interest in increasing their own autonomy and having more control over their careers. The bureaucracy has potential power as an institution in almost any political system but in one such as the European Union with relatively weak political institutions, this institution may border on being dominant (see Chapter 7).

Economics and Rational Action

Economics, and its fundamental assumptions of individual rationality and utility maximization, also provides a set of possible explanations for the behavior of bureaucracy. The basic assumption of this approach has been that bureaucrats are rational actors and attempt to maximize their own utility through their positions in the public sector. For example, William Niskanen (1971; for a critique, see Blais and Dion 1991) has argued rather famously that bureau chiefs, meaning senior managers in the public bureaucracy, are able to use their control of information in order to extract larger budgets from their "sponsors," meaning the legislature. The monopoly position of bureaus enables them to control information available to control organizations, so that the obvious remedy has been to create competition as in the agency model associated with NPM.

Other economic models focus more on the behavior of lower level public employees who attempt to exploit their positions in the bureaucracy for either gain, or perhaps for greater leisure (Brehm and Gates 1997; Frank and Lewis 2004; see also Pierre and Peters 2017). Other economic models of the behavior of individual public administrators focus on problems of delegation and principal–agent relationships, as well as the effective flow of information within public sector hierarchies themselves (Gailmard and Patty 2012).

Economic models of bureaucracy also address the nature and behavior of the organizations that comprise the public sector. The principal–agent model can be seen as a description of organizations, as well as of the behavior of individuals (Przeworski 1999; Verhoest et al. 2014). Likewise, studies of the politics of bureaucracy emphasize the extent to which organizations, as well as the individuals within them, will pursue self-interest through a political process.[7]

---

[7] This may appear to anthropomorphize organizations, but it is also clear that there are collective interests within the organization, as well as a commitment of actors within and without the organization to the goals of the organization.

All economic models of bureaucracy, however, assume that individual members of the organizations are rational, self-interested actors and that their individual behavior will largely determine the behavior of the organizations. Further, organizations are at times anthropomorphized and assumed to act in a rational manner. That reliance on the assumption of rationality is perhaps difficult to accept when one considers the evidence available on the behavior of civil servants in their roles in government. These assumptions are especially difficult for comparative analyses of bureaucratic behavior. As discussed above there are different administrative cultures that shape the behavior of individuals within their organizations. Further, in Western administrative systems there are marked differences between contract- and trust-based administrative systems (Bouckaert 2012). And even within individual organizations in individual governments there may be marked differences in the ways in which individuals perceive their jobs and the tasks of being a public administrator.

Institutional Theory

We can also conceptualize bureaucracies as institutions, and indeed bureaucracies are one of the dominant institutions in any political system. Therefore, institutional theories can provide important explanations for the behavior of those structures. The difficulty with that statement is that there are a number of alternative versions of institutional theory, all of which have something to say about bureaucracies (see Peters 2018a). While each of these approaches to institutional theory provides some insights into the manner in which institutions function, the absence of a single institutional perspective does weaken the approach when compared to other, simpler, approaches such as rational choice.

In the first version of the New Institutionalism to emerge, March and Olsen (1989) argued that institutions have a "logic of appropriateness" that shapes the behavior of structures and their members. As in many theories of organizations (see Selznick 1957) membership in an institution provides the individual with a set of symbols, myths, and values that shape their behavior.

This approach, depending on ideas, bears a strong resemblance to the administrative culture argument discussed throughout the book. Discursive institutionalism (Schmidt 2010; see also Hay 2006 on constructivist institutionalism) is also based on ideas but emphasizes the extent to which institutions are defined by discourses, both internally and externally. However, unlike the more sociological nature of March and Olsen's New Institutionalism, the discursive model assumes that discourses defining the institution are often in flux, and are modified by the individuals involved and by the need to adapt to changing circumstances (Alasuutari 2015), and changing needs of communicating with the environment.

A third version of institutional theory, historical institutionalism (Steinmo et al. 1992), depends on the notion of "path dependency" to explain behaviors. The assumption is that when an institution adopts policies and patterns of behavior at its "formative moment" it will persist in those patterns until there is some strong force that deflects them from that pattern. These "punctuated equilibria" of change are not predictable and involve significant transformations of the institutions and its policies. Later developments in historical institutionalism have emphasized a range of more gradual mechanisms for change such as layering and displacement (Mahoney and Thelen 2010b). Historical institutionalism may appear an especially apt explanation for bureaucratic behavior when examining administrative traditions.

Finally, rational choice institutionalism conceptualizes institutions as sets of rules (Ostrom 1990), incentives, or veto points (Tsebelis 2002) that will shape the manner in which individuals will behave as they pursue their self-interest. From a rational choice perspective institutions can also be seen as sets of principal–agent relationships in which principals attempt to gain compliance from the agents to whom they have delegated powers (see Shepsle 2006). There is an associated assumption that agents will always, or at least frequently, attempt to shirk their duties in order to receive their salary while making the least possible contribution to the goals of the organization.

In all of these various approaches to institutionalism, however, there is an attempt to understand the bureaucracy as a collectivity, with the direction of causation going from the institution to the individual.[8] That is, by being a member of an institution the individual acquires values, or a commitment to a particular pattern of public policy, and therefore is different than he or she was before joining the institution. And even if he or she does not have a changed perspective, the formal rules and incentives will shape behaviors while functioning within the institution. The rational individual may therefore attempt to use those incentives to pursue their individual goals.

Bureaucracies are one of the clearest examples of a public sector institution, and have been analyzed as such in a number of settings (see Eisenstadt 1964; Silberman 1993). Bureaucracies are relatively permanent structures, and have

---

[8] Rational choice versions of institutionalism combine the latter two elements and assume that rational individuals are functioning in an environment of rules and incentives devised to shape their behavior. Further, in this view, institutions are highly malleable and by changing the structure of rules individual behavior can also be easily changed. Institutions are not defined by values but by more flexible factors such as incentives designed into the structures.

some control over the recruitment and socialization of their members. Public bureaucracies also tend to conform to the normative conceptualization of an institution, having values and routines that shape not only internal behavior but also policy preferences of the members (Goodsell 2014). Alternatively, the rational choice version of institutionalism provides a good description of the way in which rules within the bureaucracy, as well as those governing its relationship with other institutions, shape behaviors.

The Individuals

The several explanations for bureaucratic behavior mentioned above focus on the nature of the structures and organizations that comprise the public bureaucracy. But those structures are inhabited by individuals, and those individuals also affect the manner in which the bureaucracy functions. The rational choice approach is based on the behavior of individuals, but assumes that they will all act rationally and therefore their behavior can be shaped by the incentives and disincentive within the organizations.

We could argue that this level of explanation for behavior is indeed the most important for the performance of the bureaucracy. Although we may at times anthropomorphize institutions and organizations, ultimately it is the individuals within them who make the decisions. Further, individuals within the bureaucracy are in day-to-day contact with citizens, and interactions between the representatives of the state and its citizens may define not only the quality of services provided but also how citizens regard the state and the government (Dubois 2010; Auyero 2012).

Several factors are important for explaining the behavior of individuals within the public bureaucracy. The first is the social composition of that army of bureaucrats responsible for managing the affairs of state. There is a long history of studying the socioeconomic, ethnic, and gender composition of bureaucracies (Kingsley 1944; Peters et al. 2015). The assumption, albeit without an overwhelming level of empirical support, is that these social characteristics will influence the decisions made by public servants. And even if the evidence supporting differences of behavior is based on these characteristics, there is a strong normative argument in favor of making the bureaucracy representative.

In addition to the social background of the administrative elite, their education and socialization are also important for understanding their performance in office (Armstrong 1973). Several classic distinctions in the education and careers of civil servants, such as the distinction between specialists and generalists, and the emphasis on law in the formation of administrative elites, emphasize the extent to which the social backgrounds of those elites may be less significant than the common training and experience that they share within government. But these distinctions also show how different that career development can be across countries.

Scholars and practitioners of public administration have also been concerned about the degree of political involvement in the selection and retention of public services (Grindle 2012; Panizza et al. 2019). As mentioned above, there is another large literature on the role that patronage has played in the selection of officials. Forms of patronage range from a few top advisors being appointed on political grounds to almost the entire public sector being hired for political reasons. In all political systems there is a felt need by political leaders to have people they can trust near them in government. And in this case there is substantially more evidence that the selection of individuals does matter for policy.

I will discuss administrative cultures in a following section, but the public bureaucracy is embedded in the broader culture of society as well. A number of anthropological accounts of public administration, especially in developing societies, point to the importance of understanding links between bureaucratic behavior and national cultures (Blundo and Le Meur 2009; Gupta 2012). Even for more developed societies, the use of anthropological theories and methods has provided insights into the way in which bureaucracies function (Hood 2000; Rhodes 2011).

Finally, the attitudes of individual public servants will influence their behavior while in the bureaucracy. Perhaps the most important attitudinal factor is their "public service motivation," or perhaps lack of it (Vandenabeele 2008). Are members of the public bureaucracy motivated by the importance of providing a service and making good policy decisions, or are they in government for other purposes, such as having a secure job with a reasonable level of pay? The answers to these questions do vary across countries, and even across organizations within a single country, but the good news for the public is that there is strong evidence which demonstrates that most public servants are in their jobs for more than remunerative reasons.[9]

The Citizens

As is generally the case, the discussion to this point has concentrated on the structures and behaviors of the occupants of positions in the public sector,

---

[9] Although I am discussing this as a personal attribute of members of the bureaucracy, they may gain some of that public service motivation as a result of socialization once they join an organization in the public sector.

and especially in the public bureaucracy. But anyone attempting to understand the behavior of bureaucrats must also understand the behavior of their clients—the public. These two sets of actors are engaged in continual contact at the "street level" (Hupe 2019). Just as the behavior of bureaucrats can shape the perceptions of citizens about the nature of government and the state, so too can the behavior of citizens send signals to public officials about how governance can and should be performed.

The most important element of the signals sent by citizens to government is the level of trust that citizens have. If citizens do trust their government, and the public administrators implementing the laws of that government, then implementation becomes substantially easier for those administrators. On the other hand, if citizens believe that officials are corrupt and only seeking benefits for themselves, they will resist, usually covertly, the actions of those bureaucrats. This may be through tax evasion, lack of cooperation in criminal proceedings, or a host of other ways to deny the legitimacy of the state and its agents.

The interactions between citizens and state actors have options for virtuous or viscous spirals. If there is an encounter (Kahn et al. 1976; Van de Walle 2018) between members of these two groups and it is positive—the bureaucrat acts appropriately and the citizen respects the authority and professionalism of the public servant—then each will go into subsequent meetings with positive expectations, And the effects of the opposite pattern of interactions is also predictable. These interactions between street-level bureaucrats and citizens are then important not only for the delivery of services but also for creating expectations about the behavior of the groups.

There is some evidence about the manner in which citizens think about a public bureaucracy. The World Values Survey has been measuring the confidence that citizens have in the civil service (see Van de Walle 2007). As shown in Table 1.2 the level of confidence expressed by citizens is highly variable, even within geographical and economic groups—almost twice as many Swedish respondents than Italians expressed confidence in the civil service. The most extreme cases of distrust come from less-developed political systems but there are a number of more advanced political systems in which the civil service is far from respected by the public. The level of confidence in the civil service is, however, often higher than confidence in political institutions such as parliament, and is more than double confidence in Congress in the United States.

Table 1.2 Public confidence in the Civil Service and
Parliament, 2010–14
(Percentage responding "Great Deal" and "Quite a Bit")

	Civil Service	Parliament
Algeria	33.4	22.0
Argentina	16.1	24.9
Australia	43.7	28.3
Egypt	32.4	25.3
Germany	54.2	53.5
Ghana	54.2	56.3
India	50.4	46.3
Japan	31.8	19.8
South Korea	48.1	25.5
Mexico	21.0	25.5
Netherlands	33.4	32.6
Peru	14.7	12.0
Philippines	65.8	58.7
Poland	19.5	11.0
Singapore	76.3	75.5
Sweden	50.6	59.3
United States	45.1	20.2

Source: World Values Survey (http://www.worldvaluessurvey.org/wvs.jsp).

Administrative Cultures

We can also argue that public bureaucrats behave the way they do because of political and administrative cultures (see Peters 2001b: ch. 2; for a general review, see Howlett 2003). All social and political systems have sets of values that shape the behavior of the individuals within them, but understanding the avenues through which culture affects behavior is difficult. As scholars have argued (e.g., Elkins and Simeon 1979) culture is often the residual variable— if all other explanations fail then it must be culture. Or, as Anechiarico (1998: 29) argued:

… administrative culture is not an autonomous, causal factor in the public sector. Administrative culture is both the sum of historical and political factors and an indicator of contemporary interaction of political and structural factors.[10]

---

[10] In this conceptualization administrative culture looks very much like Vickers' (1968) concept of the "appreciative system," which involves an interaction between norms of the organization and its environment, creating an evolving set of norms.

While perhaps amorphous, it is also clear that culture—including ideas about good administration and good governance—does matter. In addition to the interest in administrative culture in the public sector, the private sector has also discovered the importance of cultures for making globalized industries function properly (Chanlat et al. 2013). It is clear that firms operating in one culture will be managed differently, and employees will behave differently, and those differences must be recognized and accommodated.

The link of culture to public administration also can be difficult to identify (see Fisch 2008). In the case of public bureaucracies individual behavior will be shaped in part by general values in the political culture—hierarchy, trust, loyalty, and participation, among others (see Pye 1965). For example, political systems that are more hierarchical are less likely to give their civil servants any significant autonomy from the political leadership than are more open societies. Likewise, in political systems that are highly trustful, the bureaucracy, and government more generally, may be given substantial latitude for action (Gualmini 2008).

The behavior of individuals within government bureaucracies is also shaped in part by general ideas about management and organizations existing in their society (see Ott and Baksh 2005; Hofstede et al. 2010). In Hofstede's original model of organizational culture six dimensions, expressed as dichotomies, define how organizations function (Table 1.3). While developed primarily for private sector organizations, this model is also relevant for the public sector. For example, the means-oriented versus goals-oriented dimension can be seen as a contrast between the procedural orientation associated with "bureaucracy" versus more policy-oriented forms of administration and management that have emerged within the public sector.

As Hofstede's work on organization culture has developed over time, a second version of the dimensions of culture has emerged (also shown in Table 1.3), now being advocated as the way to understand national cultures. As they have evolved, these dimensions appear more oriented toward management styles than the patterns of behavior for individuals within the organization, and they provide a wider range of alternatives for thinking about how organizations and their leaders perform.

In addition to the Hofstede model of organizational culture the GLOBE model of organizational culture (see House et al. 2009); Table 1.3; see also Trompenaars and Hampden-Turner 1993) also identifies a number of dimensions of organizational culture, several focusing on various distinctions between individualism and collectivism. In addition, Minkov (2011) provides yet another set of dimensions for organizational cultures (see also Table 1.3).

Table 1.3 Dimensions of organizational culture

a. Hofstede
  Means-oriented vs. goals-oriented
  Internally-oriented vs. externally-oriented
  Easy-going vs. strict work discipline
  Open vs. closed system
  Local vs. professional
  Employee-oriented vs. work-oriented

b. *GLOBE*
  Performance orientation
  Future orientation
  Assertiveness orientation
  Social collectivism
  In-group collectivism
  Humane orientation
  Power distance
  Gender egalitarianism
  Uncertainty avoidance

c. Minkov
  Industry vs. indulgence
  Monumentalism vs. flexutility
  Hypometria vs. prudence
  Exclusionism vs. universalism

Sources: Hofstede et al. (2010); Minkov (2011).

All of these largely inductive studies represent attempts to determine the existence of patterns of belief about organizations and management within cultures, as well as something about the consequences of those cultural differences. These studies of organizational culture also say something about the orientations of society as a whole.[11]

These rather sweeping characterizations of national cultures, and their cultures of management within organizations, especially that of Hofstede, have been subject to a number of criticisms (e.g., McSweeny 2002; Jones 2007). One of the standard critiques questions the extent to which a country can be characterized as having a single culture, especially when we are aware that individual organizations have their own distinctive cultures. Further, Hofstede's evidence for drawing these conclusions about culture were drawn from a single type of organization in the private sector, and hence may not be applicable more broadly. And finally, the dimensions extracted may be time as well as organizationally biased. As management theory changes, so too will

---

[11] For another classification based on dichotomies, see Beck (2008).

the ideas being implemented in organizations in many parts of the world (see Chapter 9).

Despite the critiques and the assumptions built into these models of culture, they do raise several important points for attempting to understand public organizations. One important point is the contrast between collective and individualistic values, whether the collectivity in question is social or within the organization itself. Another dimension that appears is some assessment of the degree to which hierarchy is accepted within organizations. These studies of the cultures within organizations are also concerned with commitments to performance as opposed to commitment to other values such as leisure (meaning also time with family, for example). This value may be increasingly relevant for the public sector as performance management becomes common within the public sector. As I begin to work my way through the more historical and descriptive discussion of administrative traditions, some of the points developed there can be substantiated by using the information from these various empirical studies.

The Hofstede model of organizational culture, as well as the several other models, focuses on national patterns, as indeed I will be in the discussion of administrative traditions. But although there are such patterns, it is also important to remember that individual organizations may have their own distinctive cultures. For example, the uniformed services in the public sector tend to have distinctive patterns of beliefs and practices; organizations that are committed to particular policy goals will develop their own internal cultures that support those goals (Goodsell 2011); and some organizations simply develop and maintain strong belief patterns and working patterns.

Also, there have been studies of administrative cultures that are more specific to the public sector. For example, Sisson (1959) discussed the "spirit" of British administration, but in terms that might well be seen as an administrative culture. Several authors have attempted to define the administrative cultures of former British colonies in South Asia (see, e.g., Sharma 2000). Jorge Nef (1998) has provided an interesting discussion of administrative culture in Latin America. This listing of examples could be extended, but although these discussions of individual administrative cultures are interesting they are also extremely particularistic and do not provide dimensions that can be used to analyze administrative behavior considered more generally.

The danger, therefore, in focusing on administrative cultures at a national level, is that we commit the ecological fallacy and assume that the behavior of individuals (or even individual organizations) will be determined by the national pattern (Brewer and Venaik 2014; see also Dunham 1999). Even when those patterns are identified empirically, and not just through anecdote, the danger of excessive generalization remains very apparent. Thus, while national cultures may establish expectations about behavior they should not be taken as empirical reality and there is a need to investigate just how well actual organizations match the expectations.

Following on from the above, there is also an expectation that employees in the public sector are different from those in the private sector. They are assumed to have more commitment to service and be less motivated by money than are employees in the private sector. One examination of these basic human values, however, found very little difference between the sectors in these values, and also relatively little difference between countries (Beck 2008). The subtle differences observed may be important and be associated with differences in behaviors, but there may also be more commonality in those values than is often assumed.

Organizations in the public sector may share in some of the values of general managerial culture, but will also have values that are distinctive. There will be some particular values of the public administration itself—a "public service motivation"—that may be the most immediate influence on the behavior of the public bureaucracy (Vandenabeele 2008). Whatever the source of those values, the fundamental argument is that the mental images that the people within government have of public administration will have a major impact on their behavior in their positions. We hope that most of these employees will indeed be motivated by public service, and most evidence is that they are, but there are no guarantees.

Finally, I should note that administrative culture is an important dependent variable, as well as an independent variable explaining individual behavior. For example, in administrative systems which grant individual organizations, or perhaps the civil service as a whole, substantial autonomy from political control, those organizations are more likely to develop a strong organizational culture that is distinct from the general cultural patterns. The military, as a uniformed bureaucracy, may be the best example of that development of alternative cultures. Likewise, the level of external connection of the organization with clients and other stakeholder groups may lead to higher levels of cultural divisions within the organization, as "street-level bureaucrats" become more committed to serving their clients rather than defending the formal procedural norms of the organization (Zacka 2017; Hupe 2019).

Elements for Explaining Administrative Behavior and Administrative Traditions

The above discussion of alternative explanations for administrative behavior covers a great deal of territory in public administration. All of these explanations can contribute to an understanding of how public bureaucracies function, but each has its weaknesses and its blind spots. Those that focus attention on structure tend to ignore or to devalue individual agency, while those focusing on agency may give insufficient attention to structure. Therefore, I am seeking a more comprehensive pattern of explanation in the form of administrative traditions.

Table 1.4 presents a way of integrating some of the forms of explanation for administrative behaviors with the ideas for patterns of public administration. This table is intended so show that in order to understand how public administration functions in different settings, it is crucial to understand a number of factors involved in the ways in which bureaucracies function in different settings. Some of the factors involved are more relevant for some aspects of behavior than for others. For example, behavioral and procedural elements will be more important for understanding patterns of control within the bureaucracy than will institutional variables. But all these elements must be understood in order to have a full understanding of the ways in which public sector organizations function, and how they relate to society and to politics.

The numerous possible explanations for comparative behavior within the public bureaucracy, and the complexity of interactions among those explanations, appear to require some attempt to simplify the pattern of explanation. In this book I will be attempting to do so through the use of administrative traditions as a means of bringing together a number of these explanatory

Table 1.4 Elements of administrative traditions

	Ideational	Institutional	Procedural	Behavioral
Administrative/society relationships				
Administrative/political relationships				
Nature of administrative work				
Patterns of control				
Coherence				

Source: Nørgaard and Winding (2007).

elements. This then requires identifying salient features of patterns of administration that differentiate them from one another, and then attempting to develop models of the different patterns of behavior. I will do this through the development of various administrative traditions, as something approaching ideal types against which to compare the behaviors of real-world administrative systems.

All these mechanisms for explaining bureaucratic behavior in the public sector have their utility and provide insights into the functioning of public organizations. In this volume, however, I will be arguing that behavior can also be understood through the inheritance of values and structures—administrative traditions. These traditions contain some of the elements discussed above, such as culture and values, but they represent more or less coherent packages that define appropriate behavior for individuals and for organizations. These traditions represent the default options toward which the designers and managers of institutions will revert when faced with challenges or unusual demands for public governance. Further, administrative traditions are linked to more general conceptions of governance, and to state traditions, and therefore are not just matters that might be considered strictly administrative.

Chapter 2 will develop the concept of administrative traditions in much greater detail. That chapter will be arguing that by developing a set of analytic dimensions we can understand the behavior of administrative systems, and to some extent the individuals within them. These dimensions will, in the remainder of the book, be applied to primarily Western administrative systems, and they are able to differentiate among the Continental European systems that are often lumped together as being essentially similar (see Hammerschmid et al. 2007). In addition, although the emphasis will be on administrative systems in Western countries, these dimensions may have more general applicability. That is, I will be arguing that these dimensions will be useful for understanding a wide range of administrative systems within the public sector.

The argument being advanced here is not causal in any formal sense (see Peters 2020). Rather, the argument is more that these underlying administrative traditions establish a context within which certain types of behaviors are more probable than are others. As will be noted in the chapters on each of the four traditions to be developed in this book, there are numerous paradoxes and contradictions within these patterns. But at the same time the traditions do provide an excellent starting point for understanding governance and public administration in these countries, and create a platform for understanding public administration more generally.

2

The Administrative Tradition Approach to Public Bureaucracy

The preceding chapter has presented a number of alternative explanations for observed differences in public administration across countries. These possible explanations are at a variety of levels, ranging from micro-level explanations based on the ideas and behavior of individuals to macro, institutional explanations. All of these explanations have some utility but in this chapter I will be advancing the argument on behalf of a more encompassing explanation. As intimated in Chapter 1, this chapter and the remainder of the book will focus on the concept of *administrative traditions* and their utility as an approach to comparing public bureaucracies.

Administrative traditions provide one way of creating a more comprehensive explanation of the structure and behavior of public bureaucracies. By administrative tradition we mean an historically based set of values, structures, and relationships with other institutions that defines the nature of appropriate public administration within a society. There may not be an exact replication of the historical pattern of administration in the contemporary administrative system but there are still demonstrable influences of those "legacies" that continue to influence public bureaucracies and their members (see Meyer-Sahling 2009).

This concept of administrative traditions is an attempt to bring together a number of characteristics of administrative systems and to demonstrate how these elements fit together to create more or less coherent institutions. These characteristics are, as intimated above, in part inherited from the past but they also contain a series of overlays of more contemporary adaptations to changed circumstances and requirements. The administrative traditions within the con-solidated democracies can be grouped into several broad patterns, although each country will have its own particular interpretation of the tradition to which it belongs. Even with those differences within the tradition, however, these pat-terns provide a means of understanding and interpreting public administration. The same pattern of similarities along with specificities can be observed in the other administrative traditions to be discussed.

Administrative Traditions: Understanding the Roots of Contemporary Administrative Behavior. B. Guy Peters, Oxford University Press (2021). © B. Guy Peters. DOI: 10.1093/oso/9780198297253.003.0002

The idea of an administrative tradition combines some of the elements of explanation discussed in the previous chapter. For example, traditions contain some elements of an administrative culture, but yet do not depend entirely, or even primarily, on cognitive explanations (Table 2.1). Further, the concept of administrative tradition has some elements of institutionalism but neither is it entirely structuralist in its view of how individuals and organizations will behave. In particular, the concept of state tradition has some affinity with historical institutionalism in that it assumes that there is a persistent pattern of behavior that continues to influence the nature of administration in the contemporary period. There is also a strong sense that administrative structures are embedded in the broader political system and are engaged in a political process, but administrative traditions should be considered distinct from state traditions, as we will discuss at greater length below.

Although the concept of tradition sounds entirely historical and somewhat static, I will be arguing that despite their formation in the past, and development over decades and indeed centuries, traditions do have contemporary relevance and continue to influence patterns of behavior in public bureaucracies. Further, although their roots are generally seemingly quite stable, traditions are also dynamic. This dynamism is seen in part by the adaptations made by individual countries to basic patterns as they confront new challenges and integrate new ideas. Further, the traditions themselves have changed over time. They have had to adjust to the vastly increased administrative workload produced by the welfare state—which is also the modern administrative state (Metzger 2017). Further, they have had to adjust first to mass democratization and then more recently to reinterpretations of democracy that permit greater individual and group influence over decisions by government. Thus, there is both continuity and change and that mixture is in part why this concept is so appealing as a mechanism for comparison and explanation.

Table 2.1 Beck's patterns of administrative culture (with applications)

Style of Communication	Implicit	Explicit
Role of time	Polychron	Monochron
Orientation of action	Individual	Mission
Differentiation	Uniformity	Variety
Style of discourse	Disagreement	Consent
Power distance	High	Low
Problem-solving	Circular	Linear

Source: Beck (2008).

It is important to emphasize that administrative traditions should be differentiated from political culture, or even administrative culture (see Anechiarico 1998; Peters 2001b), although the traditions do contain some cultural elements. The notion of tradition involves what people, especially political and administrative elites, think about administration, but it also involves a number of legal and structural features of public administration, as well as the relationship between state and society as state actors engage in the administration of policies. The concept of tradition also is more oriented toward the political elite and their involvement in governing while much of the literature on political culture is oriented toward the mass public, and that on organizational culture within individual organizations.

Administrative traditions might also be thought to be just a restatement of the concept of "style" used to describe policymaking in European and other states (Richardson 1982; Van Waarden 1995; Howlett and Tosun 2019). While this concept may appear to be a strong candidate for subsuming the idea of tradition in comparing administrative systems, there are also some crucial differences. One is that the idea of style tends to focus on the state as an entity rather than on administration, and on policymaking rather than implementation.[1] As I will point out, the public bureaucracy does have a definite role to play in the policymaking process but policymaking as conceptualized by scholars such as Richardson involves a number of other factors.

That being said, the concept of policy style does focus attention on the manner in which deeply embedded patterns of policymaking influence contemporary policy choices, and that basic idea is not dissimilar to that of an administrative tradition. For example, the Howlett and Tosun (2019: 13) version of policy styles links the degree of openness of the policymaking system with the relative strength of elite and mass-level actors. Each of these modes of governing would assign a different role to the public bureaucracy and those roles help define the administrative tradition.

Knill (1999) has used the term "administrative tradition" when examining the reactions of European Union countries to the policy initiatives coming from the EU. Despite a focus on implementation of EU directives, Knill's definition (more implicit than explicit) comes closer to policy styles than it does to what I mean by administrative traditions. He discusses the degree of

---

[1] Richardson (1982) defines style as different systems of decision-making reflecting different procedures for making societal decisions. Those styles reflect the extent to which governments attempt to anticipate problems as well as the extent to which they involve a range of social actors in the decisions.

congruence between policies coming from Brussels and those developed within the individual countries. While almost certainly different types of policy may require different forms of administration for effective implementation, in this analysis I will focus more closely on the patterns of administration themselves and less on the content of the policies.

Historians rather naturally have had to grapple with the question of legacies and the role that the past plays in contemporary behavior within governments. For example, Adelman (1999; see also Daly 1968) has attempted to understand the complex legacies of past colonialism, as well as conscious institutional choices, that have shaped the state and public administration in Latin America. Although often less interested in the impact of the past on contemporary public administration than on the nature of the earlier state traditions themselves, these studies do help demonstrate how the persistence of patterns occurs, and recurs, within the state.

Elements of Administrative Traditions

The brief attempt at a stipulative definition of administrative tradition presented above may not be entirely successful in helping to differentiate tradition from other concepts, or to identify it in operation within an administrative system with which we are familiar. One way of making that task more manageable is to discuss some of the central features of these traditions. We will discuss these characteristics in a rather brief form here and then develop them more completely when I discuss the four traditions that I will argue characterize public administration in Western, developed democracies. These elements do not define the traditions per se, but they do provide insight into their nature and the avenues of influence over administrative behavior. And although based on the experiences of Western, developed democracies these same elements of administrative traditions can be useful in understanding public administration in a wider range of administrative systems.

State and Society I

The first element of administrative traditions is the relationship between state and society. This relationship is a crucial defining characteristic of state traditions (Dyson 1980; Migdal 2009) but also has substantial relevance for the conduct of public administration. Although there are certainly more subtle characteristics of states and their traditions to be discussed in the separate chapters on the various administrative traditions (see also Peters 2020), we can begin with a rather stark dichotomy between organic and contractarian conceptions of the relationship between state and society. In the former conception, the state is assumed to be linked organically with society and the two entities have little meaning apart from each other. This almost metaphysical conception of the state and its role in governance can be contrasted with the contractarian notion in which the state arose from a conscious social and political contract, expressed through a constitution or other constitutive arrangements, between the society and the institutions that will govern them (Stacy 2002).

In the contractarian conception the state is not a natural entity; rather, it is a human construct and thus also highly malleable.[2] The contracting partners in these relationships are not identifiable actors but rather the more encompassing entity of society, and the contract is more implicit than explicit. That said, once the contract is created there is an identifiable entity—the state apparatus—that may be seen as party to the contract. The willingness of society to reject that apparatus is usually limited to throwing a sitting government out of office, but the Jeffersonian concept of changing institutions frequently does appear to be alive in many settings.

Although defining the nature of the public sector in general, the nature of relationships between state and society also have direct impact on the manner in which public administration is likely to be conducted. In particular the organic conceptions tend to ascribe less of an autonomous role to society and to citizens with the state than having the obligation to defend the society. In that role the state and its administrators know relatively few bounds in their actions, and a state-centric conception of governance is a natural consequence (Peters and Pierre 2016). There will be prescribed procedures for the exercise of that power, but the power itself is inherent in the very nature of the state with this conception of their role relative to society. In organic states, executives tend to have greater decree powers and greater ease in declaring a state of emergency than do executives in contractarian societies.

---

[2] The contractarian conception of the state, and of the mutability of state institutions in this conception of the state, is presented clearly in the American Declaration of Independence, claiming that natural law gives members of society the right to make changes in the governing order. Somewhat paradoxically, the natural instinct after gaining independence was to write a constitution that itself seemed to be intended to be difficult to alter, albeit not immutable.

In contrast to the organic conception, the contractarian conception of the state assumes that the state grew out of a conscious compact with the citizens and therefore is to some extent subordinate to society. This conception of the state, and its perhaps ephemeral nature, can be seen clearly in the works of British political philosophers such as Thomas Hobbes and John Locke. In such a view the powers of the state, and especially those of the individuals who administer the laws made by other state institutions, have more narrowly circumscribed ranges of action. In a contractarian conception any residual rights tend to lie with the citizens, while in the state-centric view they rather naturally lie with the state.

These alternative conceptions of the state can be related to the role of the public bureaucracy. For example, Christoph Knill (1999) has argued that there are two fundamental types of bureaucracy, and these types are related to patterns of administrative reforms. For Anglo-American regimes with a contractarian conception of the state, the public bureaucracy is merely an instrument and hence can easily be reformed. For more organic political systems the bureaucracy is intimately connected with that organic state and hence any reforming activity is to some extent altering the fundamental nature of the state itself.

In the extreme, either of these conceptions of the state may present problems for governing. The contractarian state lays itself open to claims by disgruntled citizens of having violated their contract and hence being illegitimate. For example, militia groups occupying government buildings in Oregon in 2016 justified their actions using the contractarian concept (although they almost certainly did not understand that they were doing so; see Stack 2016). On the other hand, more organic conceptions of the state make reform difficult, given the interconnectedness of the various elements of the state, and the direct connection between state and society. And when change does occur within an organic state, it is more likely to be extreme.[3]

The above discussion of the nature of the state and its importance for defining the operations of the public sector is based on some perhaps familiar political theory. That theory may not, however, appear to have direct relevance for public administration. Another way to cast this distinction is to attempt to assess the autonomy of the state (Nordlinger 1981). The question of state autonomy assumes that the state as an entity has interests and preferences that are different from social actors. That assumption is inherent in several

---

[3] The swings between authoritarian and very democratic regimes throughout French history is a good example of this pattern of change.

traditions of state theory. This understanding of the state is perhaps clearest in classic Weberian notions of the state but also appears in pluralist conceptions about the state.[4] Even if we are not willing to accept the state as some anthropomorphized entity with preferences of its own, it is clear that individual organizations within the bureaucracy do have those interests and attempt to advance them through their actions. Further, these organizations tend to think they are pursuing a public interest.

The constraints on state autonomy arise most importantly for my concerns here from society.[5] For example, Peter Katzenstein (1987) has argued that the German state is only semi-sovereign, constrained as it is both by law and by links to society. In all corporatist or corporate pluralist states the close links with civil society may constrain the autonomy of the state, while at the same time providing it with other sources of policy capacity. Indeed, the extreme relationship between state and society in these political systems tends to define the nature of the state (see Christensen 2003). Michael Mann (1984) refers to these linkages between state and society as "infrastructural power," especially as they tend to enhance the capacity of the state for control of society.

The impact of social actors on the autonomy of the state is not entirely the result of pressure politics of corporatist bargaining. States often delegate authority to non-state actors in order to utilize their expertise in technical policy areas (see Green 2016), or states may want to avoid potential blame for failed policies (Hood 2011). Thus, it may be in the long-term interest of states to reduce their own autonomy in the short-run and let social and market actors make and implement public policies on its behalf.

The state also is embedded in an international system—both the market and a system of international public bodies such as the International Monetary Fund and the World Trade Organization. For the members of the European Union, including most of the countries central to the analysis of this book, that transnational influence over state behavior is especially significant, given the number of policy areas over which national governments do not have complete control. While the loss of autonomy of contemporary states may be overstated (see Weiss 1999), it is clear that contemporary

---

[4] For example, Theodore Lowi's treatise on interest group liberalism in the United States was based to a great extent of the assumption that the American State (yes there is one! See Skowronek 1982) had been captured by interest groups who were then utilizing the power of the state for their own purposes rather than for the public interest.

[5] Although not addressed directly in this analysis, Marxist theories of the state assume that the autonomy of the state, especially the bourgeois state, is constrained by class interests (see Jessop 1982).

governments do not have the type of sovereignty of which Jean Bodin wrote (see Jacobsson et al. 2016).

Finally, the autonomy of the state is also constrained by law and by constitutions. As Katzenstein noted for Germany, the presence of constitutional constraints on the use of power, especially in combination with a strong legalistic culture (see Chapter 4) may reduce the capacity of the incumbents of public offices to make decisions. Those state actors may not be able to do anything they might like, but must follow both substantive and procedural rules about governing. Thus, the United Kingdom, with a more flexible constitution that imposes fewer strict restrictions of State action, can be more autonomous that many other democratic countries.[6]

Law vs. Management

A second feature that defines administrative traditions is the choice between management and law as defining the fundamental tasks of administrators. This is another rather stark dichotomy and will require some subsequent refinement when discussing individual cases. Even in the dichotomous form, however, this concept does capture an important dimension of difference among administrative systems. One way of defining the principal role of the public administrator is to consider him or her as charged with administering public law. This legalistic conception of public administration assumes that the law is clear and readily understandable and that all the individual administrator must do is to apply the law to the cases at hand. Good administration in this Weberian world of administration is therefore using the law appropriately and effectively, and not surprisingly most administrators in these legalistic administrative systems are trained as lawyers, and think of themselves as lawyers (Capano 2003; Bogumil and Jann 2009).

Of course, the simplicity of the task of applying the law declines at the higher levels of the hierarchy of the public sector, and at those higher levels policymaking and policy advice become more significant activities in the role of the civil servant. Further, political issues, rather than "mere administration," become more important the higher one rises in the administrative hierarchy. That said, there is still a formal and legal responsibility for public servants

---

[6] The commitment of parliamentary sovereignty is one of the reasons that voters supported the Brexit campaign in 2016. Restrictions coming from the European Union and the European Court of Justice were seen by the proponents of the Leave campaign to be undermining the capacity of the British government to make its own policy decisions, and preserve their contract with society.

regardless of the level of the structures at which they function. And the policy advice provided by civil servants may be shaped more by legal concerns than in other administrative systems.

The alternative view of the role of the public administrator is that of the manager. This view of the job of a civil servant does not deny the importance of following the law. It does, however, argue that the first responsibility of the senior public servant is to get things done, and to make the organization with which he or she is charged perform as well as possible in implementing the laws that are on the statute books. At this point, the two conceptions of the role of the civil servant merge to some extent, given that managerial efforts are directed at implementing the law, with management skills being the means to achieve that end. Still, as much of the implementation literature (Pressman and Wildavsky 1973; Houck 2002) emphasizes, the law is the beginning point rather than the ending point for managerialist public administration and laws to some extent evolve through implementation (Wildavsky and Browne 1983).

The emphasis on management in some administrative traditions does not imply that these managers are somehow acting illegally. Rather, the question is what is the primary definition that the administrators, and especially the higher level administrators in an organization, have concerning their jobs and also how are they evaluated? The emphasis on management can also be linked to conceptions of accountability (see below). A strictly legalistic basis for accountability is not readily compatible with a managerialist conception of managers, while more politicized conceptions of accountability, or perhaps even performance-based ideas about accountability, may make little sense in a more legalized environment.

Cutting across these two major conceptions is the role of senior public servant as policy advisor. One may question the extent to which this role is a relatively modern invention, arising as the public sector expanded in response to demands first of warfare and then of welfare. The role of providing policy advice expanded to meet these demands at the same time that they began to overwhelm the capacity of politicians to cope with the demands for policymaking (Rose 1976b). The role of policy advisor has some degree of congruence with both of the above mentioned dominant roles On the one hand, knowledge of existing laws and the capacity to draft future law is certainly one important aspect of policy advice. On the other hand, policy advice is generally more than legal drafting; it is advising not only how thing can be done and but also on the possible social, economic, and even political consequences of those policy choices. Those consequences may be expressed in both substantive and political terms, thereby linking advice from bureaucrats to the political arena rather directly.[7]

All of the above having been said, the managerialist conception of the role of the public servant is becoming more widely diffused than in the past. The ideas of New Public Management (NPM) (Hood 1991; Bouckaert and Pollitt 2009) have been diffused widely, in part to meet the challenges posed by the expanded role of the state. In addition, these ideas have become "ideas in good currency," and have penetrated even the German and French systems (and similar systems; see Ongaro 2009) that have resisted managerialist ideas in the past.[8] These shifts in the perceived role of the senior public service will also have an impact on the relationship between politics and administration, the next of these characteristics to be discussed.

Despite the strength and pervasiveness of managerialist ideas, the fundamental differences among administrative systems may well persist. While these ideas have indeed penetrated Continental European systems it has been primarily at the level of local government rather than at the level of the state itself (Wollmann 2001). Even within the Anglo-American tradition there have been marked differences in the acceptance of the ideas of NPM. Although the American system, and to some extent that of Canada, have been amenable to management ideas for decades, NPM did not have the impact it did in the United Kingdom and the Antipodes.[9] NPM was not needed because these countries had "old public management" already operating.

There are, of course, other conceptions of the job of being a public administrator that could be held by members of the bureaucracy. For example, they may consider themselves to be primarily responsible for providing services to the public, and care little about the formalities of law and management. When the political leaders of a country are pursuing illiberal programs, civil servants may consider themselves guardians of the constitution (Johnson 2017). Or in authoritarian regimes civil servants may consider themselves representatives of the dominant political party. Still, the difference between law and management does provide a useful basis for understanding much of the internal functioning of public organizations.

---

[7] For a discussion of the political and substantive elements of policy success or failure, see Bovens et al. (2001).

[8] That said, the cameralist background of administration in Germany did contain elements similar to contemporary managerialism.

[9] Managerial ideas appeared in the 1930s in the United States with the Brownlow Committee, and later with the Hoover Commissions. In Canada, Royal Commissions such as Glasco and Lambert also espoused managerial conceptions of administration.

Administration and Politics

A third dimension of administrative traditions to some extent involves specification and elaboration of the first two. This dimension is based on the relationship that is assumed to exist between politicians and their civil servants (Aberbach et al. 1987; Peters 1987). The basic question for this dimension is the extent to which public servants are expected to be autonomous from political pressures, administering the law *sine ira ac studio*. The alternative conception of the role of civil servants, and especially civil servants toward the top of the administrative hierarchy, are expected to be politically sensitive, if not politically active, in making and executing law. While public administrators should be responsive to their political "masters" they should also be responsible to law, and civil servants therefore may be caught between conflicting demands.

Further, there is the question of the extent to which administrative and political careers are separate, and whether separation of the careers is considered important for proper public administration. In some countries, for example, the parliament contains a large number of career public servants who are simply on leave while they pursue their political careers (Table 2.2). These civil servants can return to their civil service careers once their political adventures are over, and having those political contacts is rarely detrimental to the subsequent administrative career; indeed the effect is often quite positive.[10]

Just as the question of the dominance of law or management defines one aspect of the role of civil servants in governing, so too does the question of the how political and administrative leaders are supposed to work together in governing. In all administrative traditions there is a conception, albeit developed somewhat later in some systems, that some part of the civil service should be apolitical and be charged simply with administering the law in as fair and impartial a manner as possible. So, the spoils system and the political machines that once allocated public jobs from the highest to the lowest in the United States is now considered largely unthinkable (Ingraham 1995) and the idea of merit has been thoroughly institutionalized. There are still numerous political appointments in the executive branch, but most of the American public bureaucracy is managed through the merit system. That having been

---

[10] For example, in Germany over half of the *Bundestag* are public civil servants (considered broadly), while in Austria roughly one-third are career bureaucrats (Braendle and Stutzer 2010). In France, over 30 percent of parliamentarians are public servants, often from the *grands corps*, and the percentage would be much higher if teachers are included (see Cotta and Tavares de Alameda (2007).

Table 2.2 Civil servants as members of parliament

Europe	Total Public Service	Higher Civil Service
Denmark	42	2
Finland	46	22
France	41	7
Germany	39	11
Hungary	17	7
Italy	22	7
Netherlands	46	21
Norway	33	8
Portugal	26	9
United Kingdom	19	4
Latin America	Total Public Service	
Argentina	19	
Bolivia	7	
Brazil	15	
Chile	12	
Colombia	17	
Costa Rica	13	
Ecuador	16	
El Salvador	12	
Guatemala	4	
Honduras	4	
Mexico	16	
Nicaragua	13	
Panama	8	
Uruguay	4	
Venezuela	16	

Sources: Cotta and Tavares de Alameda (2007); Neto (2018).

said, there is some point of proximity to political leaders in most administrative systems where it is clear that appointments have to take into account politics as well as policy and administrative capabilities..

To some extent the role of senior civil servants is always political. Even if they are not partisan appointments and efforts are made to make them anonymous to parliament and the public (Hood and Lodge 2006) these officials inherently are doing jobs that are important for the success of the government of the day. Given that importance, the government of the day will want to have some form of control over these officials. That control may be extremely overt, the capacity to name their own officials for example, or it may be subtle, having senior officials moved sideways, with the news being announced in the most oblique manner possible. The incompatibility of a minister and a civil servant may have nothing to do with party political preferences, but simply be differences in personality or "mindset."[11] Still, there are marked differences in the extent to which civil servants are politicized and in their vulnerability to dismissal or forced retirement if there are changes in the governing political party.

The degree of politicization of the civil service is widely argued to be increasing, even in countries that have prided themselves on a strong merit system and the political neutrality of public service (Peters and Pierre 2004a; Neuhold et al. 2013). Likewise, NPM devalues the concept of a career, neutral civil service in favor of a more temporary and perhaps more politically attuned public service. The diffusion of ideas is in some ways reducing the distinctiveness of administrative traditions but these traditions are also proving themselves to be very resilient. It may well be, in fact, that over time the challenges to traditions posed by NPM may reinforce rather than erode traditions. There is some evidence of a backlash against these ideas and some restatement of older ideas about what constitutes appropriate levels of political involvement in the recruitment of public servants and in the execution of the law.[12]

Even with the general trend toward more politicization of the civil service, there are marked differences in the extent to which political involvement of civil servants is tolerated, or even expected, even in European political systems. In general, Southern European administrative systems permit or require a more politicized public service, as do those in Central and Eastern Europe (Mazur and Kopychinski 2020). The shift toward politicization has been perhaps especially evident in those countries in Central and Eastern Europe that have elected populist governments.

Administration and Service

In English we often refer to the people who work in the public bureaucracy as "civil servants" or "public servants." The language used in other cultures— *fonctionnaire*, *tjensteman*, or *Beamte*, for example—do not contain that assumption of service to the public. The training and the culture within these

---

[11] For example, when Margaret Thatcher argued she wanted civil servants "like us," that did not necessarily mean members of the Conservative Party. Rather, it seemed to mean that she wanted civil servants interested in getting things done rather than in playing what she considered to be the usual games of bureaucratic politics. Further, she may have wanted civil servants who were small "c" conservatives as much as big "C" Conservatives.

[12] I will discuss some of this counter-reformation in the four chapters on the particular traditions.

public bureaucracies may emphasize public service, but the language does not.[13] This linguistic issue is, however, more than just that and raises crucial questions about the nature of public administration in the country. S. N. Eisenstadt (1964) argued that members of the bureaucracy had three possible orientations: service to others, passive tool (of the state), and self-aggrandizement. These alternative orientations may say a great deal about the nature of public bureaucracy.

Tobin Im (2014) speaking of Asian public administration, describes this as the difference between administration and service. The administrative version of public administration emphasizes dealing with citizens in a proper and legal manner, but nothing more. Just as already discussed with the law versus management dichotomy, the bureaucrat acts according to the law and administers the program. For bureaucrats not at street level some of the same questions may arise. For example, Im points out in Korean bureaucracy that there is an ethos of extreme specialization in which one bureaucrat is responsible for a task, with little or no sense of a larger picture of service to the public. This is in contrast to the increasing use of teams and collaboration in the public sector in many countries (Athanasaw 2003).

An emphasis on service implies that the task of the public servant is to fulfill the legal obligations of public programs, and perhaps to do more. In this conception of the role played by public employees the individual has some commitment to the public and should attempt to find ways of making programs work for their recipients (Pepinsky et al. 2017). This means that the service role of public bureaucrats is especially important at street-level (Hupe 2019). At the lower levels of public bureaucracy, employees have the opportunity to provide direct service to members of the public and the orientation to public service may be especially important in finding ways that government may indeed be of service to its "customers."

Placing the word "customers" in quotation marks emphasizes some of the differences between the NPM, market-based, approach to the public, and a conception of the role of public bureaucrats in serving citizens. The idea of serving customers in NPM implies that there is only, or at least primarily, an economic connection between the public servant and the individual receiving the service. Providing services to citizens, or even clients for a professional, implies that the individual receiving the service has more rights and is the primary focus of the "transaction." Providing services to citizens implies a

---

[13] One important exception is the concept of *service public* in France, meaning the activities of the state on behalf of the public.

Table 2.3 Average public service motivation by region

Eastern Europe	4.46
Northern Europe	4.67
Western Europe	4.85
Australasia	5.00
Asia	5.04
Northern America	5.30
Southern Europe	5.41
South and Central America	5.44

Source: Vandenabeele and Van de Walle (2008).

much more central position for that citizen when compared to the role of a customer.

The concern with public service on the part of public employees has sparked a major research program on "public service motivation" on the part of those employees (see Horton 2008; Table 2.3). The basic question is the extent to which members of the public bureaucracy are indeed motivated to accept, and maintain, employment in the public sector because they are interested in providing a service to their fellow citizens. While the evidence is that most people in private employment are in those positions for the money, financial motivations appear less important in government.[14] The evidence is that most public sector employees work for government either because of the opportunity for service, or because of the characteristics of their colleagues and the workplace.

The extensive literature on public service motivation does not, however, provide a uniform picture of the role of this source of motivation (Pandey and Stazyk 2008). There are marked differences based on country, age, profession, and other characteristics of public employees. For example, Vandenabeele and Van de Walle (2008; see also Table 2.1) found significant differences in public service motivation among the regions of the world, with Southern Europe having the highest average scores and the countries of Central and Eastern Europe having the lowest (see also Chapter 7).

As well as having importance for recruiting and retaining public employees, service orientation also affects styles of administrative reform, and even fundamental policy choices. For example, as countries have been faced with "permanent austerity" over the past several decades, their options have been to reduce services and save money, or to maintain services and find ways of

---

[14] That is probably a good thing, given that salaries in the public sector are lower than in the private sector, especially for more highly qualified individuals.

making the services more efficient, or perhaps even raise taxes.[15] Many countries have chosen to reduce services but others, such as the Scandinavians, have opted to maintain or even improve services (see Greve et al. 2019).

In summary, variation in the commitment to public service provides another important dimension that defines administrative traditions and administrative behavior. This dimension appears deeply rooted in the traditions of administration, as shown by some of the more extreme examples such as Russia (see p. 155), but it also may be dimension that is more malleable than many, and the attitudes and behavior of bureaucrats may be altered through training and changing ideas about the nature of governing and the role of bureaucracy (Denhardt and Denhardt 2003).

The Career

Implied in the above discussion of politics and administration is a conception of a civil service career being at least partially distinct from both political and private sector careers. One feature that has tended to differentiate administrative traditions is the extent to which there is a distinct career in public bureaucracy, and the extent to which individuals tend to remain within administrative positions for their entire working life. Historically, one element of the formation of state bureaucracy was its differentiation both from the household of the monarch and from the private sector (Armstrong 1973). The further differentiation of the bureaucracy led to the creation of separate legal categories for public servants, most clearly identifiable in Germany and other countries copying the German administrative style with the category of *Beamten* for senior level public servants—other public employees are employed under general labor law.

Further, within the civil service itself, there are marked variations in the definition of career and the manner in which individuals are recruited, promoted, rewarded, and managed in the course of their careers (see Eymeri-Douzanes 2001). For example, in the German case mentioned above, recruitment to the administrative elite tends to occur at the inception of a career, and is typically the full career for the individual. Likewise, in France, the senior civil service is trained by government through the Ecole nationale

---

[15] This is obviously a simplification of the real options available to governments, but does illustrate the importance of the service orientation.

d'administration and the successful graduates of that school are recruited into the *grands corps* of the state.

In other cases, many members of the higher civil service may begin their careers outside government and then are recruited into the public sector. In most cases, this later recruitment is temporary, and individuals come and go from public service, as with the political executives in the United States or relatively open labor markets in the Scandinavian countries. Finally, there are instances in which individuals leave the public sector relatively early in their working life and go into the private sector. The most notable case of this pattern is *pantouflage* in France (Rouban 2010),[16] in which many members of the administrative elite leave the public sector to take important positions in the private sector (see p. 39).

The importance of having a distinct civil service career arises primarily in the creation of an institutional identity and esprit de corps for the civil service, and as a protection against undue influence from political forces. But having a more open civil service career structure also enables governments to bring in needed talent horizontally from the private sector, and to remain in closer contact with society. This dimension of administrative traditions is obviously linked with the preceding discussion of politicization of administration, but has an independent impact on the nature, and performance, of the public bureaucracy.

State and Society II

We have already discussed one aspect of the relationship between state and society that is relevant at the most macro level of analysis. There is also another important aspect of this relationship that is more directly relevant for the day-to-day operations of government and public administration. This is defined by the role that societal actors can legitimately play in making and implementing public policies. Some state, and administrative, traditions accord a legitimate position to societal interests, and have attempted to integrate interest groups into the policy process as aids to state power. Further, given their connections with important segments of society, the involvement

---

[16] In Japan, the practice of amakudari, or the "descent from Heaven" (and a similar pattern in South Korea and Taiwan) involves senior civil servants retiring early from government and taking well-remunerated positions in public or quasi-public corporations (see Nakamura and Dairokuno 2003). This is part of the overall compensation package for a lifetime of work in the public sector.

of these social groups in policymaking is also an alternative source of legitimation for the state, and an alternative form of democracy. For example, corporatist arrangements (Schmitter 1974; Molina and Rhodes 2002) for interest intermediation provide a limited range of interest groups with the right to take part in policymaking, with the expectation that they will trade that right to participate for some complicity in the decisions taken.

While formal corporatist arrangements are the most familiar form of involvement of social actors with the state, there are other forms of legitimate interactions between social actors and the public sector. While strict, tripartite versions of corporatism tend to limit the number of actors involved, corporate pluralism (Rokkan 1967; Binderkrantz and Christensen 2015) involves a much wider range of actors. The same is true for networks and for other forms of contemporary interactive governance (Torfing et al. 2012) in which multiple actors are involved in making and implementing policy. In all these forms of interest intermediation the bureaucracy's capacity to act autonomously is restrained, while those constraints would be less apparent for pluralist systems.

The alternative conception of the role of societal interests in relationship to government is that they to some extent undermine the authority of the state, and represent an unwarranted incursion into the prerogatives of state action (McConnell 1966; McFarland 2004). Or even if interest groups do not undermine the authority of the state, they may be seen as dividing society and undermining the capacity of government to pursue the public interest. Political systems operating with these negative conceptions of interest groups and their relationship to the state tend to limit access to interest groups and those groups must expend a good deal of political energy in the politics of access. In almost any democratic system it is difficult to exclude interests entirely, so the question becomes which interests and under what circumstances will they be admitted into the policymaking arena. At the extreme, authoritarian systems have created their own unions or their own associations to (presumably) represent the interests of segments of society (see Anderson 1970; Cai 2014). Even in democratic regimes governments may be involved in fostering and legitimating interest groups that support the general policy thrusts of the state, and perhaps the government of the day.[17]

---

[17] One useful classification of the way in which the state promotes, or at least acknowledges more or less official interest groups is found in Joseph LaPalombara (1965). The links may be based on common policy concerns—*clientela*—or based on partisan affinities or ideologies—*parantela*. See also Braun (2012).

The above discussion is largely of the state as an entity and its relationships with societal interests. There is also a specific administrative element involved in this dimension. First, perhaps the principal point of contact between societal interests and the state is the public bureaucracy. Most people (professionals as well as the general public) tend to think about interest groups lobbying and attempting to influence legislative decisions, but many more administrative decisions are made in the public sector than legislative decisions (Baldwin 1996; Kerwin and Furlong 2019). Advice about new legislation often comes from the bureaucracy, and therefore participation on advisory committees (Balla and Wright 2001) or in other opportunities to shape the views of bureaucratic organizations on policy provides societal interests the opportunity to influence the legislature through influencing the bureaucracy (Yackee 2006). Further, organizations in the public bureaucracy may be more willing to accept the involvement of interest groups than are political leaders, given that their source of legitimacy is not as threatened, as is occasionally the case, with elected officials.[18] Indeed, those organizations within the bureaucracy often embody those social interests and may want to cooperate with interest groups to pursue policy goals.

Also, interest groups are crucial in implementing a variety of public programs so if they have a more legitimate status they are also more likely to be effective in that role. Just as the ideas of NPM have diffused widely and are making managerialism more common in a variety of settings, so too are ideas about using the private sector in implementing policies on behalf of the public sector (see Donahue and Zeckhauser 2012). This use of the private sector is justified in part simply by the need to save on the costs of administration, with the use of not-for-profit organizations being especially useful in this regard (Balboa 2018). The use of non-governmental organizations also may help legitimate the implementation of these programs in an era in which government is not highly regarded by much of the public. Even if government were in general more highly regarded, for some programs the familiarity of interest groups may make their involvement in the decisions important for legitimacy of the decisions.

This aspect of state–society relationships might have been thought to co-vary directly with the first variable describing these relationships (see pp. 26–30). That is, more state-centric, organic systems might be thought to

---

[18] The rational legal basis of bureaucratic authority may permit advice from expert sources, even when those sources also have an interest in the outcomes, while the electoral basis of legitimacy may feel more threatened by the existence of an alternative form of representation. But see Rokkan (1967).

exclude the potential influence of interest groups and to seek to preserve their own autonomy in the face of pressures from interest groups. However, that is not necessarily the case. It may also be that this organic conception of linkage between state and society will result in the acceptance of a more legitimate role of interest groups and with that a willingness to accept a diminished capacity of the state to exercise its own autonomy. Germany, for example, has been described as a "semi-sovereign state," in part because of the interest of social actors (Katzenstein 1987). Likewise, while we might expect government institutions (within state traditions based on a more or less formal contract between state and society) to encounter difficulties in maintaining their autonomy in the face of what might be considered excessive pressures from a society, that does not involve the state as the embodiment of a higher public calling.

The complicated relationship between state authority and the role of non-state actors will require careful consideration when discussing each of the traditions in the following chapters. These relationships are not simple and are at times paradoxical. The practice of governing reflects both political power and the ideas about the state that may be enshrined in political theory and in constitutions. Further, these relationships are not immutable and can continue to evolve as both the demands on the state for policies, the powers of social actors, and ideologies about popular participation in governance continue to change (see Pierre and Peters 2018).

Uniformity

One common value for public administration should be equality. Citizens should be treated fairly and equally according to their needs and their eligibility for services (Walsh and Stewart 1992). Especially in democratic regimes, the equal treatment of citizens is almost a defining element of good public administration. While equality is an important value, so are democracy and self-determination, and an alternative value is that citizens should have some opportunity to shape their own policy regimes. The opportunity to exercise that influence may lead to rather different policy choices for different parts of the country, if not for individual citizens. In addition, the willingness to accept differences in administration may permit greater efficiency, given that the policies as implemented will reflect differing conditions and preferences and hence may not encounter as much opposition as might policies perceived to be more alien and Draconian.

As well as reflecting values of and about citizens, the definition of a desired level of uniformity in policy and administration also says something about the nature of the state itself. Governments may attempt to enforce uniformity of services and policy over their territory, believing that this is a means of building a cohesive and integrated political system. Conversely, other constitutional arrangements may permit or encourage greater diversity in administrative systems, not only as a means of making experimentation with public policy possible, but also as a means of controlling potentially dictatorial central governments (Jacobs 1967). That enhanced local autonomy is clearly one aspect of the logic of federalism, and some nominally unitary states, for example Scandinavia, also encourage greater opportunities for variation in policy and administration.

Uniformity also was a strategy for state-building. In the case of France this was clear in the attempt of Napoleon, and to some extent the monarchs before him, to create a unified nation from a set of feudal structures that had varying degrees of allegiance to the previous monarchy.[19] As in Napoleon's famous statement, it was necessary to make Frenchmen, having first made France. This top-down strategy of state-building assumed that reducing differences among regions removed one focus for political mobilization and was the best way to generate commitment to the state. Of course, state-builders in federal states have assumed quite the opposite, and have attempted to create loyalty through recognizing difference, while at the same time providing for the public goods and services that are more appropriately provided in a more uniform and centralized manner. That federalizing strategy may not always be successful, however, as continuing pressures from governments in autonomies (especially Catalonia) in Spain have indicated.

The creation of uniformity, or at least the attempts to create uniformity, can be pursued through the law, but also can be pursued through a number of administrative structures and procedures. One of the most important of these structures is the use of prefects and similar officials as a means of imposing central policy control (Tanguy 2013). Although the assumption underlying this institution is that power will flow down from the top of government, the careers of prefects may depend upon the satisfaction of the locality they "serve," and that satisfaction may in turn depend upon the ability of the locality to get what it wants from the center (Gremion 1976).

The perceived need for uniformity was manifested in the colonial adventures of European powers, as well as in administration at home. We can, for example,

---

[19] See, for example, Hazaresingh (2005).

contrast the British tradition of indirect rule in India and much of its African empire with the French and Spanish tradition of direct rule, uniformity, and incorporation (see Lange et al. 2006). Britain ruled many of its former colonies using only a few hundred people, by tending to co-opt indigenous power structures to impose their control over the territory. In India, for example, a significant portion of the subcontinent was ruled through the indigenous royalty rather than through more direct means (Lange 2009); for most of the colonial period, more direct aspects of rule were channeled through the East India Company, rather than government officials per se.

In contrast, the French, Belgian, and Portuguese style of colonialism in Africa and Asia, and Spanish rule in Latin America, was to utilize administrators from the colonial homeland to rule. There was less utilization of the institutions and legal frameworks available within the indigenous society and more imposition of the policies of the colonial power through personnel coming from the imperial homeland. This style of colonial administration was more expensive than indirect rule, but may have been no more effective in instilling the political and administrative values desired by the colonizers. It did, however, in the short-run at least, create greater policy and administrative uniformity within the colony.

The need for uniformity is often associated with centralization and a unitary form of government but the two variables need not co-vary. Different forms of federalism or quasi-federalism may produce different levels of variation in policy and administration. The more coordinated federalism of Germany or Austria produces much greater uniformity than does federalism in Canada or in Belgium (Fenna and Hueglin 2010). And the quasi-federal governing system of the European Union demands substantial uniformity in some policy areas while retaining significant differences in many others (Radaelli 2002).

The experience of Italy and Germany in building their nations at approximately the same time in history demonstrates the alternative logics of dealing with centralization and uniformity (Ziblatt 2006). Italy, more influenced by following the more Napoleonic tradition of centralization (but see Legay 2009; Dreyfus 2013), chose to build a highly centralized state utilizing instruments such as prefects associated with the Napoleonic tradition as a means of ensuring uniformity (Fried 1963; Zariski 1983). Germany, on the other hand, opted for a federal solution even though the differences among its regions were seemingly less significant than those within Italy. Thus, the quest for uniformity and the capacity to actually produce uniformity may not be as closely related as might be thought.

Although uniformity is usually associated with unitary regimes, there are means through which federal administrative systems can create more uniformity than might be expected. For example, in Germany the civil service law and the civil service career are virtually the same at all levels of government. Even in many unitary political systems subnational governments will have their own personnel systems and movement from one level to another is unusual. With a more unified administrative career structure the processes of administration, if not necessarily the substance, will be more uniform.

Accountability

The final dimension that we will use to differentiate administrative traditions is the manner in which accountability is enforced within the public sector. This dimension of administrative traditions is in many ways related to the earlier dimension of law versus management, given that legal mechanisms are a central feature of accountability regimens within several of the traditions. There is also some element of the politics and administration dimension in this component of traditions, given that accountability may be in some systems a more political exercise for controlling bureaucracy than it is purely administrative. Although there are those similarities to other dimensions of administration, there is also something distinctive in the manner in which accountability is pursued within various traditions.

Accountability is one of the central, if not the central, variables in the analysis of public administration (Day and Klein 1987; Bovens 2007). Many of the complaints articulated concerning the power of bureaucracies center on the perception that these institutions are unelected, unaccountable, and have powers that many average citizens currently believe are unfettered (see, e.g., Brunet 1998; but see also Goodsell 2014). Likewise, corruption and abuse of administrative discretion for personal gain has been cited as central to problems of legitimacy and trust in societies (Johnston 2014). Citizens have more proximate connection with the bureaucracy than they do with most other institutions in the political system, and therefore they are more likely to be aware of malfeasance by bureaucrats than they might of elected politicians, leaving aside well-publicized cases such as those of Donald Trump and Italian Prime Minister Berlusconi. These day-to-day contacts are sometimes dismissed as "petty corruption," but for citizens the daily aggravation of bribery is often extremely real.

Powers are delegated to bureaucracies in all political systems, and consequently accountability mechanisms are needed to constrain and monitor the exercise of that discretion. The popular perception of almost absolute bureaucratic power is held despite the continuing and increasing efforts by political leaders to demand that public servants be more accountable, individually and collectively, for their actions. One reaction to the perceived problems in the public bureaucracy can be identified in attempts to reform the public sector. For example, some NPM reforms implemented over the past several decades have been directed at creating new mechanisms for accountability (Pollitt and Bouckaert 2017; Christensen and Laegreid 1998). Even rather modest reforms such as Citizens' Charters are intended in part to hold the individual civil servant accountable for his or her actions, and performance management has been a major attempt to enhance performance (Bouckaert and Halligan 2008). At the same time, other aspects of those NPM reforms appear to have reduced accountability and have necessitated further attempts at improving controls over bureaucracy (Peters 2001a).[20]

The institutional designer must also be aware that although accountability is a virtue, there may be limits on its utility as well (Gersen and Stephenson 2014). Excessive personal accountability will make civil servants unwilling to act and will promote "buck-passing" within government. Too much transparency in decision-making will make politicians and administrators less willing to make, or even advocate, difficult decisions that may be politically unpopular (see Erkkilä 2012). Thus, any administrative system must balance the virtues of accountability with the need for efficient and timely decision-making.

Although accountability is a central concern for all administrative systems, the manner in which it is enforced, and even its meaning, will differ across traditions. For example, in some versions of accountability the conception is largely political, with the principal agents for enforcing controls over the bureaucracy being political actors, especially the legislature (Strøm 2000). In other traditions, accountability is primarily an internal activity, and especially a function performed by legal actors within the executive branch itself. Again, however, there is more than just these structural factors to differentiate among the approaches to accountability. There are also fundamentally different ideas about the role of the mass public in enforcing accountability, and with that different ideas about the openness of government.

---

[20] The manner in which they have coped with pressures for reform will be one of the dimensions of comparison among the traditions. See Chapter 6.

Another dimension of variation of accountability is whether it is enforced *ex ante* or *ex post*. In most instances accountability is enforced *ex post*. The administrator makes decisions, or spends money, or issues a permit, and then other actors assess the legality and propriety of that action. This model of accountability permits the actor substantial latitude for action and avoids some of the infamous red tape (Bozeman 2000) that slows actions in bureaucracies. That said, only focusing on actions after the fact may permit substantial financial losses or incorrect decisions to occur, some of which may be impossible to recoup later.

The alternative format for accountability is to require prior approval of administrative actions, usually from some legal or quasi-legal organization. For example, in the Napoleonic model the Conseil d'etat or its equivalent (Terneyre and de Béchillon 2007) must approve administrative actions in advance of their implementation. This oversight can slow action within the bureaucracy substantially but it can also ensure that the activities of governments, especially secondary legislation,[21] conform to legal standards. This does not mean, of course, that the actions will be effective or efficient, but they will be legal.

As well as being anticipatory, this mechanism for accountability is also highly legalistic. Some of the same preliminary considerations of secondary legislation emanating from the bureaucracy can be done through more political and participatory mechanisms. For example, the "notice and comment" procedures in American administrative law permit several rounds of involvement of the public (usually businesses and interest groups rather than ordinary citizens) prior to their being formally enacted (Kerwin and Furlong 2017; see also Page 2001). In the Anglo-American tradition this prior overview is not required for ordinary administrative actions but is for making secondary legislation. But even that prior review of the legislation does not prevent legal challenges to the legislation after the fact, for either procedural or substantive reasons.

Summary

The seven dimensions of administrative traditions outlined above are useful in demonstrating the differences among contemporary public bureaucracies.

---

[21] By secondary legislation I mean the rules and regulations issued by the bureaucracy, used to implement or elaborate the primary legislation coming from the legislature. Legislatures increasingly write broad legislation, empowering the bureaucracy to fill in the details (Huber and Shipan 2006).

We could add other dimensions, but these enable me to differentiate among various forms of public bureaucracy in a relatively parsimonious manner. Further, each of these seven dimensions has some historical roots and, although modified over time (see Sager et al. 2012), each does link to the roots of these models of public administration. The real test of the variables and their general idea of traditions will come when they are applied to real administrative systems.

Individual countries within these traditions may still vary considerably along the individual dimensions—Australian federalism tends to create greater uniformity than does Canadian federalism—but they are still impacted by their traditions. Just as genes may express themselves differently for individuals, so too does the DNA that underlies administrative systems interpreted differently in different political systems, reflecting other aspects of the political setting as well as the specific challenges that history provides for those administrative systems.

The Four Traditions... and More

Using the above variables, and perhaps also some knowledge of historical developments and even some intuition, we can identify four fundamental administrative traditions among Western industrial democracies. The four traditions we will discuss are the Anglo-American, Germanic, Napoleonic, and Scandinavian. These traditions have been identified in other studies of the public sector in Europe. For example, Newman and Thornley (1996) identified the same traditions operating in urban planning in Europe, although based more on legal frameworks and the structure of local government than on public administration.

This book will focus initially on those traditions dominant in Western Europe, as well as countries such as those in North America and the Antipodes that are directly derivative of the European traditions. Even with this more limited selection of cases, however, there is substantial variance in the dimensions outlined above. Attempting to include a broader array of traditions and cases would not only exceed my own knowledge base but also bring in more extreme variations on the variables that would make comparison that much more difficult.

The other question which arises concerning the selection of these four traditions is to what extent individual cases are being forced into these categories. By definition each administrative system is *sui generis* and should be considered individually. The attempt to identify families or traditions, however, is an attempt to find a compromise between the assumption that all systems are distinctive, and an approach that might say that all bureaucracies are essentially the same. This halfway house permits us to understand some of the individual differences as linked by history and intellectual traditions, and to compare across traditions as well as look at some of the variation within each.

We should make several other points about the nature of the administrative traditions. The first is that, following from the above, there are marked internal variations within each tradition. This variation is perhaps especially evident for the Anglo-American tradition (see Halligan 2004), with the United States in particular developing its own distinctive approach to governing, albeit clearly within this general tradition of administration (Skowronek 1982). For all the traditions, however, there are also important differences that develop around the common core of ideas and practices. Therefore, for each tradition I will discuss one "defining case," e.g., France for the Napoleonic tradition (Wünder 1995), and then one or more "derivative cases" (Spain for this tradition; see Alba and Navarro 2011; Ramio and Salvador 2002). Even for the defining case, changes across time may have diluted some of the distinctiveness of the tradition. The fundamental values of these traditions become even more diluted when their former colonies are examined, and we can see the way in which French and British administration in particular have been interpreted within different cultural traditions that also had different needs for governing (see Braibanti 1966; Conklin et al. 2011). Even with those different interpretations, however, the influence of the colonial past does persist and in some ways becomes accentuated as the attempt is made to ensure that administration is being done properly.[22]

The ensuing discussion generally will locate countries within a particular tradition, but some European administrative systems also represent mixtures of the four basic traditions. The Netherlands, for example, combines some features of the Germanic model with some of the Napoleonic (see Martí-Henneberg 2005). The same mixture of influences exists in Belgium, although it is somewhat less clearly defined.[23] Further to the east and north within

---

[22] The Indian administration may be a good example here. First, the United Kingdom itself adopted some aspects of the pattern of administration designed for administering its colonies in Asia, and now the Indian Civil Service has become a rather extreme example of a formalized, rule-driven bureaucracy carrying on administration in a way that appears outmoded from the perspective of the contemporary United Kingdom (Bussell 2012).

[23] Canada and the United States are interesting cases, with one state or province in each having a Napoleonic background within the dominant influence of the Anglo-American administrative tradition.

Europe, Finnish administration has some (limited) remnants of the Russian tradition that dominated its government for the period 1809–1917, combined with a (now) dominant Scandinavian style of administration (Temmes 1998). That Nordic style was inherited in part from their earlier Swedish rulers, and has been reinforced by continuous contacts with their Scandinavian neighbors. For countries such as the Czech Republic, Slovakia, and Hungary there is also a mixture of recent Russian (Soviet) influences with the Germanic tradition derived from the former Austro-Hungarian Empire (Agh 2003; Meyer-Sahling 2009). If we were to extend the analysis further geographically, we might also identify Japan as having some aspects of the Germanic and Napoleonic administrative traditions adopted during the late nineteenth century, combined with the indigenous traditions and some Anglo-American influences coming as a result of the constitution largely imposed after World War II (see, e.g., Drechsler 2015).

I will also be cognizant that there may be different, and even contradictory, strands of thinking about public administration and governance within a single country. For example, the alternation in France between Jacobin and Girondist traditions has been occurring since the time of the Revolution and both remain embedded in contemporary politics (Hazareesingh 1994). The United States has been argued to have four distinct governance traditions— Hamiltonian, Madisonian, Jacksonian, and Wilsonian (Kettl 2000; Mead 2002). And the several countries within the United Kingdom have their own distinctive governance values and administrative traditions (Cairney and McGarvey 2013). Those differences may present governance problems so long as the general political climate is tolerant of the differences and does not seek to enforce uniformity (see above).

Finally, as implied above, there are significant pressures for convergence among these four traditions. It appears that most of these pressures are primarily in the direction of the public sector managerialism that has been typical of the Anglo-American tradition, even before the popularity of NPM in a larger range of administrative systems.[24] That having been said, however, some structural features of the Scandinavian administrative systems are being dispersed, and to some extent the strength of administrative law in the Germanic and Napoleonic traditions is being admired widely in systems that lack that as an instrument of accountability and control (Woodhouse 1997).

---

[24] In the United States and Canada there was an "old public management" beginning in the 1930s, meaning that although there is a managerialist tradition there was not the marked transformation experienced in many other countries (see Ayres 2014).

I will not examine convergence per se in this discussion, but rather will look at how these systems have coped with two pressures that might be thought to generate greater similarities; for many of the countries in which we are interested the European Union is also a source of pressures for convergence. The need to administer similar policies, and the development of standards about how those policies should be administered, are creating pressures for uniformity. The pressures have been even more pronounced for the accession countries in Central and Eastern Europe which have had to develop the ability to administer the *acquis communitaire* before being admitted to the Union (Fournier 1998; Meyer-Sahling 2009).

I will also be arguing that the seven dimensions of traditions can be applied to a wider range of cases. First, it is interesting to see to what extent the administrative traditions of former colonial powers survive in independent states in Africa and Asia. In particular, I will be interested in how British and French traditions have survived in the countries of Africa, and how the American influence survives in the Philippines. A somewhat similar question arises for the European Union, with the question being to what extent the administrative style of the European Commission reflects those of member states. And finally I will apply, albeit all too briefly, these seven dimensions of administrative traditions to a wide range of additional cases.

Plan of the Book

I have already mentioned that the argument of the book is that four fundamental traditions have shaped administration in the industrialized democracies, as well as the countries that have been influenced heavily by the European, North American, and Antipodean countries.[25] I will devote one chapter to each of these traditions, characterizing them with the variables already discussed in this chapter. In each of these chapters the focus will be on the dominant example of the tradition, e.g., France for the Napoleonic tradition, as well as on some derivative cases. There will then be a chapter that pulls together those characterizations of the individual traditions into a more comparative analysis of traditions and points to the differences among them (as well as the similarities) and attempts to draw out the sources of variation

---

[25] The Antipodes are now to some extent involved in a second-order transfer of an administrative tradition. The ideas shaping administration in these countries came from the United Kingdom when these were colonies and are now being spread to other countries in the Asia-Pacific region, e.g., Papua New Guinea and the Solomon Islands (Connell 2005).

as well as the internal logics of the several traditions. I will also consider how these various traditions have been transferred to former colonies, and the extent to which those traditions persist even after long periods of independence.

As well as looking at the traditions as important objects of inquiry in themselves, I will also examine their consequences for public administration. In particular, I will examine the impact of these traditions of three major activities of public administration. The first of these is administrative reform. Public administration in almost all the industrialized democracies has been engaged in major reforms during the past several decades, and I will demonstrate the consequences of traditions for the choice of reforms and their success (see Loughlin and Peters 1997; Jann 2003). Most of these reform agendas have been driven by market ideas, and those ideas are less compatible for some systems than others. Alternatively, some reform agendas have emphasized enhancing participation of both citizens and lower echelon employees (Peters 2001b).

The capacity of administrative systems to adapt to European Union membership is a second locus in which traditions can impact the success and failure of administrative systems (see, e.g., Connaughton 2015). The administrative style of Europe is to some extent a mélange of the styles of the member states, especially the original six, and individual systems must find ways to adjust their practices at home to the style emanating from Brussels.[26] Much of the discussion of the interactions of Brussels and national administrations has been in terms of "Europeanization" (Knill 2001) but I will also be concerned with the "nationalization" of European administration. That is, to what extent there is a distinctive European style of administration as opposed to the mélange of styles that we assume exists (see Ban 2013).

The Europeanization question raises the further question of the ability of administrative systems to remain distinctive in a globalizing and interconnected world (Sager et al. 2012). The tendency toward isomorphism in state structures in general has been noted (e.g., Meyer et al. 1997) and there are certainly pressures toward greater homogenization of public bureaucracies. Some of these pressures come from the ideas of managerialism discussed above, and further international organizations place pressures on governments to become more alike. Those pressures are especially important for

---

[26] One example of this adaptation can be found in the patterns of coordination of national government interactions with the European Union (see Kassim et al. 2000).

less-developed countries facing pressures from donor organizations, but are relevant for even the most affluent regimes.

Administrative traditions will also influence the manner in which administrative systems employ their delegated powers to make rules, otherwise referred to as secondary legislation. As a major component of the policy process, all administrative systems are major sources of binding rules for their societies, but they make those rules in a variety of manners, each reflective of its traditions and laws. And administrative organizations also have varying degrees of latitude when they make those rules (Caranta and Gebrandy 2012). As mentioned above, there are marked contrasts in the degree of political participation and the degree of legalism involved in making these rules, and these differences clearly reflect underlying traditions of administration and governance.

The use of administrative traditions can be a powerful tool for understanding how administrative systems function and how they change. That said, researchers still need to understand how the underlying traditions are converted into actual behavior of individuals and systems. Therefore, this discussion of traditions can best be considered the beginning of a comparative analysis rather than as the completion of that research. We can begin with an understanding of some basic patterns of governing but these traditions are interpreted differently across nations and within nations. Perhaps most importantly the traditions are interpreted in ways to provide political advantages to some segments of society or government. Thus, we will need to look at the traditions *in action* as well as a set of templates for action.

3

The Napoleonic Tradition

As well as being a being a military leader of substantial renown, Napoleon Bonaparte was a state builder, and he and his colleagues created a new state system for France and imposed it in some form or another over a good part of Europe. This mode of organizing the state and its activities has served as the basis for governing not only in France but also in a good deal of Southern Europe. The systems of governance in Spain, Italy, Portugal, and Greece are all clearly derived from the basic Napoleonic mode (Ongaro 2009), and Belgium and to a lesser extent the Netherlands still have strong traces of this tradition. Even when the French system per se was not in place for a considerable number of years, its influence over state structure was still significant.

As has been true for the Anglo-American tradition, the Napoleonic tradition has also been diffused well beyond Western Europe. France was a major colonial power in Africa and in parts of Asia, and the model was carried along as a part of colonial experience. The tradition was perhaps even more strictly applied, given that French colonialism was more centralizing and attempted to create "little Frenchmen" as well as control the territory (Hargreaves 2005). The more assimilationist model in French colonialism meant that there was even closer adherence to the basic model of administration and governance than was true for the Anglo-American tradition. Even in some cases that were not directly a part of the French Empire, this model was considered sufficiently successful to be copied, at least in part, by countries such as Greece (Lalenis 2003), Uruguay, and Argentina.[1] Further, as countries in Central and Eastern Europe have emerged from their domination by the Soviet Union the French model of the state, albeit substantially modernized, has had substantial appeal.

The imperial, and before that monarchical, roots of this system of administration remain rather evident. The drive toward uniformity and centralized control that were key elements of the tradition, for example, have been

---

[1] The Latin American countries had been influenced by their former colonial masters from Spain, but the French model was adopted directly, and in some cases completely, after independence. That model remains largely intact today, despite influences from the Anglo-American tradition and more recently from New Public Management. See Ramos (2019).

Administrative Traditions: Understanding the Roots of Contemporary Administrative Behavior. B. Guy Peters, Oxford University Press (2021). © B. Guy Peters. DOI: 10.1093/oso/9780198297253.003.0003

weakened substantially by the early twenty-first century, but they are still stronger than in most contemporary administrative systems. That being said, the administrative system has also been able to free itself from the political control that characterized it for at least the first 100 years of its existence, and to establish a greater degree of administrative autonomy. The weaknesses of political governments during the Third and Fourth Republics (Diamant 1968) placed a good deal of governing responsibility in the hands of the bureaucracy, and that helped to ensure the development of a more autonomous administrative system. The structures put in place by the Napoleonic system (e.g., the *grands corps*) formed a basis for a public bureaucracy that could function with autonomy and which could, in the end, provide functional elites for both public and private sectors.

The Napoleonic label should not lead one to think that these administrative systems remain as they were in the early nineteenth century. Nor should that label make us forget that there are some elements of the tradition that precede Napoleon. Like all political and administrative systems, those in this tradition have reformed numerous times and are in many ways different from their early roots (Dreyfus 2013). But at the same time some fundamental elements of the administrative systems persist after several empires and now five republics. My task in discussing this tradition, like all the others, is to demonstrate the influence that the DNA of the model continues to have, while at the same time accepting that these are modern systems with many features are not related to their initial formation.

Elements of the Napoleonic Model

The system of public administration that emerged was to some degree based on the centralized control of the *Ancien Régime* in France. The regime existing before the Revolution had sought to impose monarchical authority through a variety of administrative officials and procedures. Perhaps most important of those elements for the subsequent development of the Napoleonic model was the *intendant*, the territorial representatives of government dispersed throughout the country.[2] This official provided a means of monitoring the state of affairs throughout the territory, collecting taxes, and preventing the development of alternative power centers within the regime (see Kiser 1987).

---

[2] Spain used a very similar system for the governance of their colonies in South America (Fisher 1928).

The Napoleonic state added to these inherited control structures a set of structures that were designed to add capacity for economic development and legalism to the pre-existing system. The French state had been involved under the monarchical system in a variety of economic activities, and the need to be able to fight wars across Europe as well as maintain some level of domestic consumption required developmental activity. Further, the commitment of the Revolution to science and rationalism helped to underpin the role of engineering and technical education in the political system. This placing of the state at the center of the economic system, as well as a governing system, differed markedly from the separate development assumed in the Anglo-American systems (see Chapter 6; see also Culpepper 2008).

Unlike most other imperial regimes this tradition developed rather early a strong legal foundation for its actions, albeit a legal framework that functioned from the center and tended largely to serve the central state. At the same time that the administrative state was being created the legal state was also being created, with the Code being central to institutionalizing the rule of law within the system. Law was then central for governance as well as for creating the conditions for economic development—a position that has been recreated as international donor organizations now stress rule of law in their development programs.

Analyzing the Characteristics

The Napoleonic model of the state and its administration was designed to solve the problem of imposing control over a large geographical area, while simultaneously fighting a major war. The same problem was faced earlier, for example in Sweden during the Thirty Years War (see Stilles 1992), but the answer found here was markedly different from that of Gustavus Adolphus, or at least what emerged from that early state model. Part of that difference is a function of the scientific and developmental strands of thinking within the Napoleonic state that were not evident in the earlier Swedish case (but see Loriaux 1999).

State and Society I: The Conception of the State

The preamble to the constitution of the Fifth Republic in France describes the state as "indivisible," and also "sovereign." Those words are a clear statement of the étatiste conception of the state and politics that has been the dominant strand of thinking in French politics, and to some extent it also is present in other systems with a Napoleonic heritage. The state is very much a human creation, but once created there has been little of the contractarian conception of government central to the Anglo-American, and especially American, conception of the state.[3] The numerous changes in the French constitution over the course of several centuries since the First Republic have been carried out within the context of a strong and essentially continuous state.[4] Even the Vichy Regime during World War II maintained much of the same formal structure and legal procedure of the preceding regime, albeit administering laws shaped by cooperation with the Nazi occupiers of the other half of the country.

Although the state is sovereign in this conception of governing, it is a somewhat benevolent superiority rather than strict imposition of rule from the center. Indeed, some of the reason for the power of the state is to be able to ensure human rights and *service public*. The strength also represents a felt need for a significant part of this time period to combat centrifugal pressures within society. Initially, those centrifugal pressures were regional, but later more individual and cultural factors dominated. Tilly's (1986) notion of the "contentious French" is indicative of the difficulties that a government may face in attempting to govern, and hence the need to construct a powerful and at times autocratic state.

While the general conception of the state in France is that of a powerful unifying force overcoming potential social division, there are still alternative conceptions. Since the time of the Revolution these alternatives have been discussed as Jacobin vs. Girondist traditions (Mastor 2018). The former conception advocated a highly centralized state to address the need for unity and control within the country. The latter advocated a more decentralized form of democracy, with ideas of federalism and Montesquieu's separation of power forming part of their conception of the state.

Clearly the Jacobin tradition won out during the Revolution and the empire, and has been the dominant means of conceptualizing the state in France (but see Rosanvallon 2004). Despite periods of almost extreme democracy, or with democratic institutions that made strong government difficult (e.g., the Fourth Republic), the conception of a strong and autonomous state has remained central to governing. Indeed, this conception has been perhaps

---

[3] But see Baczko (1987).
[4] J. E. S. Hayward (1983) wrote that the French constitution has been periodical literature, but the state has persisted. That said, the constitution of the Fifth Republic has lasted for over sixty years.

more important in periods of divisive politics because of the capacity of the central state to continue functioning in the face of apparent blockage in political and social institutions. That state may be opposed, as with the "*gilets jaunes*" and the strikes against pension reforms in 2018 and 2019, but it continues to govern.

One of the important barriers to the creation of neo-liberalism and a less decisive state within Napoleonic states is the conception of the state as a provider of *services publiques*, and as a guarantor of rights. These rights include those of the employees of the public sector not to be treated as ordinary employees or fast-food workers but as the representatives of that state which protects all citizens (Beck 2001). Therefore, the monetary motivations usually associated with managerialism in the public sector may not be as applicable as they have been in other state traditions (Chanlat 2003). That does not mean that there will be a strong service orientation (see below) but it does mean that they do have a relatively high status in society.

Law Versus Management

One fundamental characteristic of public administration in the Napoleonic tradition of public administration is the reliance on public law to define the task of the administrator. In the Napoleonic state the administrator is perhaps first and foremost a legal official, in contrast to the managerial orientation of the Anglo-American tradition. The job of the administrator, very much like that of a German civil servant, is to apply the law to individual cases. The commitment to law is a means of placing the collective interests of society, and the state, above any more petty interests that may attempt to use the state for their own purposes.

This emphasis on the law in the role of the public administrator is related in part to the codification of law—what Rosanvallon (2004: 81) calls the "*L'ardeur codificatrice*." While common law is emergent and evolves through the actions of public officials which are later determined to be legal or illegal, code law attempts to define all actions as legal or illegal, and then apply that distinction to cases. While the absence of ambiguity in code law may be vastly overstated, the practice may proceed as if it were indeed true. Given the emphasis on the code, public administrators need to be sure *ex ante* that any actions are indeed legal.

The legalism of French administration, and other countries in this tradition, can be seen rather clearly in the role of the *Conseil d'État*, and analogous organizations in other Napoleonic systems. This organization, one of the *grands corps*, is to monitor the legality of administrative actions, and to approve or disapprove the actions of public servants. Unlike administrative courts, however, this approval must be sought *ex ante*, rather than having the legality of the actions assessed *ex post*. The need for prior approval runs counter to the managerialist approaches of governing in many other systems, especially after the rise of New Public Management (NPM) and its mantra of "let the managers manage."[5]

One major exception to the above generalization is that for graduates of technical *grands écoles* who become members of the technical *grands corps*. While these officials are civil servants they are also highly trained engineers, responsible initially for building roads, managing mines, and developing industry in the service of a developmental state. Although the state in France may now be somewhat less central to economic development than it was historically, these graduates of the *grands écoles* remain crucial actors in the economy.[6]

Of course, with the spread of managerialist ideas throughout the industrialized democracies the strictly legalistic conceptualization of the role of the civil servant is no longer completely viable. Several French prime ministers have instituted some administrative reforms not dissimilar to those found in the other industrial democracies, although substantially more modest and far from wholly successful (Bezes 2009). The one major reform that has been implemented with at least some continuing success has been decentralization, providing greater control over power to lower levels of government, as well as deconcentration within the state itself (De Montricher 1991).

That being said, however, this reform does little to alter the legalistic nature of public administration. Likewise, legalism has remained a dominant mode of administrative practice in other Napoleonic systems (see Alba and Navarro 2011). Given the importance of managerialism in public administration, there does appear to be at least some lip service paid to making public administration more managerial and less legalistic. But that can also be argued to be a form of legitimation for civil servants who want to appear "modern" but who may simply persist in their well-worn paths (Alcaras et al. 2016).

---

[5] The phrase is actually somewhat older than usually assumed, having appeared in a Royal Commission report in Canada in the 1950s.

[6] This is especially true when they move from the public to the private sector and become key actors in private firms (see below).

Finally, as well as being lawyers, or managers, or technical professionals, civil servants in the Napoleonic tradition are also servants of the state. Public servants therefore are expected to uphold some common interest—as represented by the state—and not to be tied closely to any social or economic interests. The primacy of the law facilitates maintaining that rather aloof status to society, but may also be a source of discontent among citizens, as manifested in populist resistance such as the *gilets jaunes* and protests against pension reforms in 2019.

Uniformity

The one characteristic of the Napoleonic state that appears to differentiate it most clearly from the other three administrative models examined in this volume is the emphasis on uniformity in policy and governance.[7] This perceived need for uniformity appears to arise from two ideas about governing. The first is the need for control within the territory of the state that to some extent goes back to the *Ancien Régime*. While federal or other more decentralized forms of governing do indeed govern, the degree of control being exercised from the center is necessarily more limited than in a unitary state such as France.

The other source of a desire for uniformity is the value of equality. While more decentralized systems of governing value the capacity of citizens to make choices more highly than they do equality, the Napoleonic state has tended to reduce levels of choice and to produce one common standard of *service publique* across society (Chevallier 2003); that standard of service is generally rather high but it is uniform and ordinary citizens have few choices in the type of education or health care they are able to consume. The equality of public service is also linked to the legal nature of the state, with those services contained in law as well as in administrative practices (Esplugas-Labatut 2018).

The development of the Napoleonic state included the development of a number of features designed to ensure that uniformity. One is the emphasis on law that has already been mentioned. Although civil servants in any society, even authoritarian regimes, will be able to exercise some discretion, the level of discretion offered to "street level bureaucrats" in these systems appears

---

[7] There are numerous anecdotes concerning the emphasis on uniformity in French administration. For example, that the minister of education would know what line of Latin was being translated all over the country by looking at his or her watch. Largely apocryphal, no doubt, but still relevant.

lower than in most other democratic regimes (but see Dubois 2012). And, as already noted, the role of the *Conseil d'État* in reviewing administrative action also reduces the capacity for independent action by public servants.

The second instrument utilized to ensure uniformity is the role of the *préfet* as an agent of the central government—specifically the Ministry of the Interior—in controlling administration throughout the countries under French influence). The traditional conception of the *préfet*, which in many ways persists (Oberdorff and Fromont 1995), was one of ensuring uniformity and compliance with the law in each *departement*, with *sous-préfets* responsible for smaller parts of those areas. While the various versions of the prefectoral system in Napoleonic France varied and the individual involved may have had different levels of power (see Fried 1963; Loughlin 2001), they were powerful administrators exercising substantial levels of control over political and administrative officials in their areas.

The centralization of policy areas that are in most other countries under the control of subnational governments is also important for creating uniformity. Control over education is perhaps the most obvious of the policy areas that is centrally organized. School teachers are employees of the Ministry of Education in Paris, not of local governments or school districts. Likewise, most policing is national rather than local. The central government thus penetrates the total territory of the state more deeply than most other governments, and can use its civil service as a means of creating greater uniformity.[8]

Having now painted a rather severe picture of central control by French bureaucracy, it is necessary to soften the image somewhat and examine how the system has operated in practice, as well as how it has been changing. First, the degree of uniformity assumed in the traditional model of the Napoleonic regime has not perhaps been achieved. For example, the powerful *préfet* was never quite so divorced from local politics and the local community as assumed. The *préfet* had to manage a career, and one way of undermining that career was to have complaints from local notables in the region. Thus, the *préfet* and the local mayors and other officials were engaged in mutual cooptation (Gremion 1976; Thoenig 2005).

Second, there are other features of the political system, especially in France, that tend to undermine centralized control over the regions. One of the more important of these has been the *cumul des mandats* (Knapp 1983), meaning

---

[8] For an assessment of the role of uniformity in dealing with the COVID-19 crisis, see Henstridge (2020).

that local politicians also simultaneously hold national offices. This arrangement allowed local influence and concerns to be injected into national politics and counteracts to some extent the administrative centralization of government. Although reformed once in the 1980s by the Socialist government and now largely eliminated by subsequent reforms, this pattern of representation persists in providing some decentralization in the system (Qazbir 2015).

Third, there have been a number of significant structural state reforms in France over the past several decades. Beginning in the 1970s and moving much further with the Socialist governments in the 1980s, there have been a number of moves to grant greater powers to regions and localities. These have included transferring greater policymaking power and financial resources to local governments (see Schmidt 1990). These changes also meant removing some of the direct powers of the *préfets* over local policy—*la tutelle* or guardianship of governance at the local level.

Although dramatic, these legal changes still left the French government more centralized than most other democratic governments. Local governments can now make more decisions on their own, but the *préfet* remains an *ex post* check on the legality of actions. Likewise, although the field services of some ministries were deconcentrated, the *préfet* also retained powers to supervise these services in the name of the state. And finally, some important functions, notably in the area of economic development, were still controlled largely from the center, even after reforms in planning (Booth 2009). As localities had few sources of local revenue, there was little they could do on their own in this area.

If we move to other examples of the Napoleonic model the degree of decentralization has been even more pronounced. The clearest example of that sort of change is in Spain which was once perhaps even more centralized than France but has now granted substantial power to the *autonomias*. Grants of power have been asymmetric, with some regions such as Catalonia and the Basque country being given the same sorts of powers that might be granted in a federal system, albeit with the assumption of shared sovereignty (Colomer 1998). Other regions have been granted fewer powers, but still have some financial and policy autonomy.

Although the change was somewhat more gradual than in Spain, the greatest exception to the principle of uniformity in countries heavily influenced by the Napoleonic tradition can be found in Belgium. The presence of a very strong linguistic cleavage in Belgium produced first a consociational solution for governing and then led to a rather extreme version of federalism. The current federal format leaves few policies under the control of central government and delegates policy to the three regions and to the linguistic communities (Swenden and Jans 2016). As demonstrated in the bargaining over the trade deal between the European Union and Canada, the powers of the Belgian regions extend even to international politics, unusual in even a federal government (McKenna 2017).

The ethnic foundations of decentralized government in Spain have some analogues in France and Italy, albeit not nearly so strong. Despite the centralizing tendencies of the French government over centuries, parts of the country such as Brittany and Alsace have their own regional identities that have produced some limited political pressures for greater powers. The *mezzogiorno* in Italy has had some special treatment for decades, and the quasi-federalization of governing in Italy has now given other regions, especially the North, some greater powers (Roux 2008), but there are few calls for independence as in Spain.

In sum, there is a sense of uniformity that has been part of the Napoleonic tradition, but like many traditional elements in all systems this is under pressure. In the case of uniformity, the pressures have arisen primarily from political forces attempting to create both more democracy at the local level and more capacity for regional and ethnic groups within societies to have increased capacity to shape their own policies. These pressures tend to be universal, but are perhaps particularly apparent in regimes that have had the long pattern of centralization and attempts to promote uniformity.

State and Society II: The Relationships of Administration with Social Actors

As might be expected given the emphasis of the Napoleonic tradition on law and central control by the state, there is not as strong a tradition of involvement of social actors in policymaking as found in other traditions, especially the Scandinavian tradition. The Jacobin strand of thinking in French government emphasized the republican principle of unity of the people, meaning that any associations existing between the state and the public undermined the unity of the society. During the French Revolution the Loi Le Chapelier (1791) was passed to outlaw associations of workers and strikes.

This aversion to groups returned to French politics a number of times during the various regimes that have followed the revolutionary period. The suspicion of the effects of associations has continued, and has included almost all types of organizations. In addition to the attempts of the public sector itself to limit membership in, and activities of, social actors there are elements in the culture that also limit the power of associations within French society, as well as in many other countries working within the Napoleonic tradition.

While some of this apparent aversion to group membership in Southern European countries has become something of a cultural stereotype,[9] there is also some truth in it. For example, if we compare the levels of group membership in countries in the four administrative traditions under discussion, then we can see that those in the Napoleonic tradition are lower than in the others, especially the Scandinavian (Table 3.1). The same pattern emerges when examining the level of membership in trade unions (Table 3.2). The popular image of widespread and disruptive strike activity in these countries is not mirrored in membership in these organizations.[10]

Table 3.1   Proportion of respondents belonging to one or more groups (2016)

Sweden	81
Finland	80
Denmark	79
Austria	64
The Netherlands	62
Belgium	54
Ireland	54
Germany	53
France	48
United Kingdom	46
Spain	45
Slovenia	37
Czech Republic	35
Italy	33
Portugal	33
Greece	31
Slovakia	26
Poland	25
Lithuania	16

Source: Eurobarometer (2016) (accessed December 23, 2019).

---

[9] See, for example, Edward Banfield (1967) and Robert Putnam's (1994) work on social capital in Italy.
[10] Those two pictures are, of course, not incompatible. While unions and other organizations, e.g., farmers' organizations, may be small they can still be militant and active. As noted above, Tilly (1986), among others, has emphasized the contentious nature of society in France and following from that the difficulties in forming effective social organizations.

Table 3.2 Trade union density (2018)

Sweden	65.6
Denmark	66.5
Finland	60.3
Norway	49.3
Italy	34.4
Austria	26.3
United Kingdom	23.4
Ireland	24.5
Germany	16.5
Netherlands	16.4
Spain	13.6
France	8.8

Source: OECD (https://stats.oecd.org/Index.aspx?
DataSetCode=TUD) (accessed December 23, 2019).

For purposes of administration and governance the presence or absence of high levels of group memberships is less important as a sociological fact than as a measure of a government's capacity to involve groups in government. If interest groups are legitimate actors in the governance process, as is true for corporatist or corporate pluralist systems in Northern Europe, then they can assist in governing both through providing information and advice on the input side of the policy process and implementing programs on the output side of government. This pattern of governing can reduce burdens on state actors and perhaps produce policies that are more acceptable to the population.

While the corporatist model has its virtues, it may not conform very readily to the Napoleonic model of an indivisible state acting in the public interest, rather than in the interest of the organized segments of society. Rather than representing the authority of the state and the law, in a corporatist regime public servants may become mere bargainers with interest groups, and would have to some extent cede some of that authority to non-state actors. While the reality is that in many cases (e.g., the *préfets*) bargaining is taking place and there is mutual cooperation between public and private actors (Duran 2000), much of the political and constitutional theory does not support those relationships.

There has been a long and spirited academic discussion on the extent of corporatism in France (Segrestin 1984; Keeler 1997). Corporatism in conventional tripartite bargaining appears less visible in France, but there are other mechanisms for linking state and society that can be as important in shaping policy and administration. For example, there are a large number of consultative bodies for a range of policy areas—especially in social policy—that permit non-state actors substantial influence (Jobert and Muller 1987). As is true for all other countries, the degree of influence of social actors may vary significantly by policy area so making any blanket judgment about linkages of state and society is difficult if not impossible. In some instances the state continues to act autonomously while other domains are "colonized" by industries and professions.

In addition to differences among policy areas, the decentralization that has been occurring in France has opened up more opportunities for interest group influence and meso-corporatism (Streeck and Kenworthy 2005). Again, this has varied by policy domain, with social policies as well as environmental policies being more influenced by social actors than most others (Filleule 2003). Attempting to assess the level of influence of social actors on French administration therefore requires specifying the level of government to be considered, as well as the policy area. The closer one gets to the localities and the more one moves away from the "defining functions of the State" (Rose 1976a) the more corporatist the French administrative system appears.

The other examples of Napoleonic regimes have been less resistant to corporatist models of governance than has France. Indeed, the Fascist government in Italy was an almost classic example of the corporatist state, albeit in a non-democratic form (Pinto 2014). Likewise, the Falangist regime in Spain produced a model of state corporatism that guided many aspects of economic policy. In the contemporary period the term "social pacts" has been used to describe the relationships between state and society in the countries of Southern Europe, but these pacts have some elements of corporatism. They certainly involve close linkages between the state and social actors, especially labor, and bargaining over many aspects of economic policy.

This discussion of corporatism, or the lack thereof, in countries in the Napoleonic model is perhaps interesting as an exercise in comparative politics (see Molina and Rhodes 2002), but for the purposes of understanding public administration, it points to important differences among these countries in the extent to which governments and their bureaucracies have been willing to cede some authority to non-state actors. Those arrangements between state and society in turn influence public policies and also shape the manner in which government interacts with society. While we know that even in extremely *étatiste* systems the bureaucracy does have to interact, and even bargain, with social actors, the extent of these interactions and their legitimacy will influence the behavior of public administrators.

The Career of the Public Administrator

Max Weber argued that one of the defining characteristics of a bureaucracy, at least as an Ideal Type, is that the career of the bureaucrat is a full-time job and is separate from other careers. The assumption in this model of the bureaucracy is that a public administrator joins the public service early in his or her working life and will remain in public service until retirement. However, like any element in an Ideal Type, this standard may never be attained in reality, and public employment is generally much less clearly differentiated from the rest of the labor market than is assumed in this model.

The model of employment for the Napoleonic tradition conforms to the model of permanent employment, or at least a permanent career, in some ways but in others it does not. Especially in France the state invests heavily in the selection and training of its own employees and attempts to shape their capacities to fulfill public functions in a certain manner. In the Fourth and Fifth Republics the upper echelons of state administration have been trained at the École *nationale d'Administration* (ENA). This school provides training in law, management, accounting and all the other skills that a high-flying civil servant will require (Meininger 2000).

The best-performing graduates of ENA then go into the *grands corps*.[11] These structures within the public service have something of a life of their own and influence the careers of their members. These structures also provide a network within government that enables a good deal of coordination among public programs without having to resort to more formal mechanisms.[12] Almost any significant organization in the French government will have a member of the *Inspection générale des finances*, one of the *grands corps*, and that individual can help facilitate any difficulties with budget or spending issues.

The education provided for public servants in France produces generalists rather than specialists. While many public servants at the lower echelons of the public sector may have specialized careers, those at the top are broadly trained and have fungible skills that can be used in most positions in government. The major exception to that generalization would be civil servants who are trained in the technical *grands écoles* and serve in the technical *grands*

---

[11] Those who perform less well will go into the lesser corps, or become part of the general administrative structure.

[12] That said, there are still a number of formal mechanisms for coordination, attempting to ensure the coherence and legality of public services. See Hayward and Wright (2002) and Marin (2016).

corps. The Napoleonic model of governance was created for a developmental state, and the engineering corps[13] were crucial for that developmental role. These schools and their graduates remain central to the economic life of the country, although the development role of the French state may have waned.

Although the French state invests a good deal of time and money in the training of their higher level public servants, these officials often do not spend their entire careers within the public sector. The practice of *pantouflage*, or civil servants moving from the public sector to the private sector rather early in their careers, is widely practiced (see Rouban 2010; France and Vauchez 2017) Many members of the *grands corps* leave their positions in government to take up lucrative positions in firms in the private sector. However, they remain members of the corps and retain the network of affiliations with organizations and individuals within the public sector.

Career structures for civil servants in the other states with a Napoleonic tradition are not as distinct or as separated as those in the French public bureaucracy. For example, while Spain has had corps structures for much of its higher civil service, there are more corps and the corps tend to be defined by policy domains rather than being general elites for the entire public sector (Parrado 2000). Italy also has a number of corps within their civil service, including both specialized functional services (e.g., forestry), as well as the equivalent of the French *grands corps*, but again these corps do not have autonomy from the remainder of the administrative apparatus as do those in France (Lewansky 2000).

Politics and Administration

As well as the potential conflict between law and management in the role of the public administrator, there is also a potential conflict between the role as a neutral civil servant and the servant of the public at large, and the role as the servant of the government of the day. All administrative systems have some level of politicization of their public bureaucracies, simply because political leaders want to be sure that those administrators who are responsible for implementing their policies, and who are responsible for giving them policy advice, are committed to the goals of the government. The question then becomes what level of politicization of the public employees is acceptable, and

---

[13] *Corps des mines, Corps des ponts et chaussées*, etc.

what are the consequences of the politicization (Peters and Pierre 2004a; Neuhold et al. 2013).

In the best of all worlds, at least from a bureaucrat's perspective, there might be very little politicization in public employment. The Weberian model of the public servant is someone who works according to the law and takes into account neither the political preferences of his or her leaders, nor the political affiliations of those being served. But can such a model actually exist in governments which are inherently political and which also want their civil servants to be responsive to the policy preferences of those holding office? And in a semi-presidential system such as France (Bourmaud 2001) the civil servant may not even always be clear over which government he or she is actually serving.[14]

The civil servant in the Napoleonic state exists in a tension between his or her expertise and impartiality, and the demands of functioning in governments that are inherently political. In addition to the movement into, and mostly out of, government among the higher civil service, individual civil servants may move into a variety of political positions. At the extreme, many members of parliament, ministers, and presidents of the Republic have been graduates of ENA, or other *grands écoles*, and have moved from the administration into political careers (Genieys and Hassenteufel 2012). In addition to the higher levels of politics, many civil servants will accept positions in the ministerial *cabinets* of ministers, or in other positions appointed by a political official.

The usual concern about the linkages, or lack thereof, between politics and administration, is the politicization of the bureaucracy. In France, and in some other European countries, there is also a concern about the bureaucratization of politics. A very large percentage of the political class in France, and to a lesser extent the other countries in the Napoleonic tradition (see Cotta and Tavares de Alameda 2007), has been trained as civil servants. While the integration of the two sets of actors may make for more harmonious governing than in many political systems, it can also separate the state apparatus more from society than might be desirable in a democracy.

---

[14] There have been three periods of *cohabitation* during the Fifth Republic in which the president and the prime minister were from different political parties. While in at least two of the three cases this potential conflict was handled with minimal difficulty, there is always the possibility of conflict and gridlock.

Accountability

All democratic political systems utilize a range of instruments to enforce accountability over the public bureaucracy. The fundamental goal of ensuring that the unelected segments of government have political or legal constraints imposed upon them is inherent in democratic governance, and involves a wide range of political and legal actors. That said, the various traditions that we are discussing in this book do emphasize different mechanisms of accountability, and rely on some more heavily than on others.

For France and for other administrative systems operating within the Napoleonic tradition, law is the pre-eminent mechanism for control. As already noted, administration is considered to be a legal activity, rather than managerial, despite the increasing amounts of instruction at ENA about management. The codification of law, and in this case especially administrative law, attempts to provide answers for every question that the administrator may face in his or her job. And, although this is certainly changing, efficiency is less important as a measure of performance than is legality.

As already noted, the legality of accountability is manifested in the use of *ex ante* controls over the bureaucracy. All administrative traditions use law as one mechanism for control, but that tends to be exercised largely *ex post*. The administrator generally can act first and then his or her actions are tested in court, rather than the opposite situation.[15] This emphasis on prior approval in the Napoleonic tradition is designed to prevent any illegal, or extra-legal, activity but can also place something of a mortmain on the activities of administrators attempting to pursue policy goals.

Even with demands for prior approval, there are still a number of *ex post* reviews of administrative action. There are a series of administrative courts to assess the legality of administrative action, and the regular court system may also deal with administrative matters if there is a substantive judicial as opposed to administrative question involved (Guichard et al. 2011). This is analogous to the capacity of citizens in the United States being able to appeal administrative actions into the federal court system if there is a substantive constitutional question involved. The appeal into the regular courts is significantly more infrequent in France, however, because of the maxim that "to

---

[15] A major exception would be common law writs such as *quo warranto* and *injunction* that either ask an administrative official to justify an action, or forbid an action. These have been common mechanisms used to slow implementation of controversial legislation, e.g., some environmental legislation, in the United States.

judge administration is to administer," meaning that administrative matters should be left to administrators and their courts (Louvaris 2019). The enforcement of accountability for financial actions also has a strong legal dimension. Again, while any country would want to check on the probity and legality of public expenditures, in the Napoleonic model this checking is done through the *Cours des comptes*—the Court of Audit. While in most political systems financial accountability is conducted through an audit office of some sort that is responsible to the legislature, the term here is "Court." And this is more than just a linguistic difference. Rather, the emphasis is on legality and the court is more or less autonomous from the legislature and the executive.

The legalism in accounting represents a marked contrast to contemporary practice in public accounting organizations that focus heavily on performance in addition to the formal accounting function (Ahonen 2015). Countries functioning with the Napoleonic model have moved to some degree toward performance accounting, and the Cours des comptes itself has introduced some degree of performance measurement into their practices (Fizot 2007). But the notion that the accounting organizations are indeed courts does tend to perpetuate a legalistic conception of their role and more a formal sense of financial accountability.

A second characteristic means of enforcing accountability within the Napoleonic model of administration is the use of inspectorates. The most prominent of these, the Inspection générale des finances was mentioned above but there are a number of other organizations within government charged with inspecting the actions of other organizations and reporting on malfeasance. There are, for example, inspectorates for education and for prisons. The notion of inspectorates also extends to enforcement of labor law where the entities being supervised are firms rather than public organizations (Viet 1994). Although the model of inspectorates has been copied widely in contemporary administration (see Hood et al. 1999) it remains central to the Napoleonic model for public accountability.

Third, public accountability in the Napoleonic model is personal as well as organizational. There is a greater sense of personal liability of public adminis-trators in these cases than is true for the other models of administration (on Spain, see Diez-Picazo 2013). This approach to accountability means that the individual public servant may have to make restitution for certain errors in the application of the law, and is liable for civil suits for "*fautes personnelle.*" That liability, in turn, may mean that the civil servant is reluctant to make autonomous decisions, and that reluctance will contribute to the familiar bureaucratic pathologies of red tape and "passing the buck."

Modernization of the Napoleonic Model

Throughout the above discussion there were a number of references made to changes occurring in the Napoleonic model of administration. The danger of developing a model of a tradition such as the one discussed here is that it becomes a stereotype and is placed behind glass in some administrative museum. That is not the intention of the development of any of these traditions. The fundamental point of using these Ideal Types is that even with decades and centuries of different sorts of pressure for change, some elements of the underlying models persist and remain useful for understanding how the systems function.

A second aspect of the argument is that these basic models of administration will interpret pressures for change in their own ways and to some extent "indigenize" the reforms (see, e.g., Torres 2004). The ideas of NPM and other common patterns of reform are important stimuli for change, but these ideas tend to provoke responses that depend upon the inherited patterns of administration within a country. This is true even for countries within the same general tradition, as the differences between the United Kingdom and New Zealand, on one hand, and the United States and Canada, on the other, demonstrate (Peters 2000).

Even with all the pressures for change, it is clear that the Napoleonic model has adapted less than either the Anglo-American or the Scandinavian versions of administration. For example, the managerialism at the heart of NPM, and therefore much of the administrative change over the past thirty years, is antithetical to many of the ideas of the Napoleonic style of administration. The emphasis on law and central control of administration simply does not fit well with the emphasis on managerial autonomy and more decentralized public organizations within the NPM approach to public administration.

That being said, Philippe Bezes and Salvador Parrado (2013) have argued that the reforms in the Napoleonic states—especially France and Spain—have followed a common temporal order. The first set of reforms (described above, pp. 61–3) involved decentralization and empowering territories within the state to make more of their own decisions. This was perhaps especially evident in the creation of the *autonomias* in Spain, and the creation of a quasi-federal system in Italy (Palermo and Wilson 2014), but has also been apparent in France (Schmidt 1990; Le Lidec 2005; Kada 2012).

A second major sets of changes in France has been associated with the *Loi organique relative aux lois de finances* (LOLF; see Barilori and Bouvier 2007). Just as was noted above in relation to the Cours des comptes, this law began to introduce management by performance into French administration. As well as imposing performance indicators on organizations, there has been some movement toward performance-related pay for individual public servants. This movement to individualize rewards, and management more generally, has represented a major move away from uniformity within the public sector (see above) and has not been received well by many elements within the public service (Forest 2008).

As has been true for many other cases, the economic crisis of the early twenty-first century slowed processes of reform in France and the other Napoleonic states, and to some extent more traditional patterns became more evident. While the LOLF did introduce performance management into the French administrative system (for a similar pattern in other European countries, see Di Maschio and Natalini 2013), the presence of economic pressures may have been more powerful. For example, in 2012 the French government launched an effort to modernize the state, meaning in part to downsize it and to stress greater efficiency (Le Gales and Vizinat 2014).

Summary and Conclusion

Referring to the administrative tradition shaping governance in France, Spain, Italy, and Portugal, among other places, as Napoleonic, is to pay homage to the role of Napoleon in creating the beginnings of the modern French state. But some aspects of this state tradition are rooted even deeper in the history of the state, and some aspects of the Napoleonic model have evolved beyond recognition. All that said, there has been a clear template for governance that was laid down in the eighteenth and early nineteenth centuries, and which persists. And although many of the roots for contemporary administration were planted then, they continue to grow and evolve.

Thus, unlike the other administrative traditions discussed here, there was a clear founding point and a set of documents that codified the tradition. Codification and the legal foundation for action have been important for this approach to administration. Also, this administrative tradition is perhaps more cohesive than are several of the others. Even when it has been transported beyond France, the rules governing public administration have tended to be institutionalized through law as well as practice.

That said, this tradition is not immutable and it has responded to many of the same pressures experienced by other administrative systems. But those responses have been less dramatic than those found in the Anglo-American or even the Scandinavian cases. And the responses have been to some extent muted by maintaining commitments to ingrained methods of doing public business. Similarly, change in other states within the Napoleonic tradition has been less dramatic than in those in the other traditions. The legalism of this tradition, and the integration of politics and administration, appears to have been successful in maintaining much of its identity in the face of numerous pressures for change.

4

The Germanic Tradition

When one thinks about public bureaucracy Max Weber naturally comes to mind—especially for Germans and other Europeans. As an intellectual model for organizing the public sector, Weber's bureaucracy continues to have a significant influence on scholars (Page 1992; Ahonen and Palonen 1999), and is also an important standard against which to compare real-world administrative systems. And that model remains more directly relevant for understanding public administration in Germany and other countries in this tradition than for others. But that said, although perhaps less reformed than in many countries, the German "bureaucracy" has reformed and is very different from the formal bureaucratic model often used as a stereotype of the German administrative system.

The Weberian legacy is present, but perhaps not as pervasive as generally assumed (see Jann 2003), and there have been responses to changing administrative ideas and reforms in Germany as elsewhere (Bogumil and Jann 2009). Although less accepting of the model than the other traditions discussed in this volume, New Public Management (NPM) and changing ideas about public administration have also affected Germany (Kuhlmann 2010). The responses to NPM have been more evident at the level of the *Land* and local governments, but even the federal government has adopted some NPM-style reforms (Schütz 2012).

Despite the change, there has also been a persistence of patterns of public administration over decades. Even with numerous regime changes over the past century or more, many elements of the civil service system have persisted, and some elements of the law and patterns of practice have persisted even longer (see Jacobs 1967; Hattenhauer 1993). And, although there was a tremendous amount of reconstruction of public administration required in the eastern *Länder* after reunification, there were some common foundations within administrative law that facilitated the process (see Seibel 2010).[1]

---

[1] The implementation of that administrative law may have been perverted during the time of the German Democratic Republic, but there was at least a common written legal framework for administrative action in place in the East.

Administrative Traditions: Understanding the Roots of Contemporary Administrative Behavior. B. Guy Peters, Oxford University Press (2021). © B. Guy Peters. DOI: 10.1093/oso/9780198297253.003.0004

Analyzing the Germanic tradition therefore will require comparing a well-known stereotype with a more subtle reality. This need to balance a simple stereotype with reality will be true for the complex relationships between state and society, as well as for even more complex patterns of thought about public administration. While the practice of public administration in Germany, and other countries within this tradition such as Austria, is influenced by the formal legal foundations of the tradition, there are other factors at work within these systems also. And the more contemporary aspects of administration theory, such as NPM—usually referred to as the *Neues Steuerungsmodell* in Germany—are in part being interpreted through the lens of the underlying values and routines contained in the administrative tradition (Naschold and Bogumil 2013).[2]

As well as other political and socioeconomic changes, public administration in all countries has been affected by ideas, and especially the ideas of NPM. The countries in the German tradition, however, have been less influenced by those ideas than most, especially at the central government level. In Germany the *Länder* and especially local governments have adopted some of the procedures and structures associated with NPM and the *Neues Steuerungsmodell*, but the *Bund* level has remained relatively unaffected. When examining this tradition, therefore, one of the most important factors is understanding how governments have wanted and been able to resist powerful global pressures (but see Chapter 3 on the Napoleonic tradition).

The State Tradition

The nature of public administration within the German state, and again others influenced by the fundamental model, is also heavily influenced by the nature of the state considered more broadly. The German state is at once a metaphysical, moral entity and a set of structures closely related to society and now is a fundamentally democratic entity. Major state theorists such as Hegel (see Weil 1998) developed the concept of the state as a counter to the centrifugal tendencies existing within the geographical area that is now Germany, consisting of numerous small states with little coordination or direction. In these narratives on the state it was society that required

---

[2] There are important differences between the *Neues Steuerungsmodell* and NPM, as will be discussed below. But there are also similarities and NPM certainly influenced thinking in German administration about the reforms implemented.

constraint, rather than the state as in the Anglo-Saxon narrative (see Chapter 6). Further, for Hegel the executive, including the public bureaucracy is the central link between state and society and the means of exercising control over particularistic interests within society which could undermine the welfare of society as a whole (Shaw 1992).

Although I began the discussion of the German state above with Weber, there was an even earlier tradition that offered a model of administration and public finance. Cameralism (Lindenfeld 1997) functioned as a model of governing in the eighteenth and early nineteenth centuries in Prussia and other areas of what would become Germany. Cameralism emphasized administrative efficiency as a means of building and maintaining a strong state. Interestingly, given the later dominance of legal training for the public bureaucracy, Cameralism was more focused on economics and philosophy as the foundations for administration. Given that emphasis on efficiency, the cameralist approach to public administration may be more aligned with NPM than is the legalistic approach, which became the dominant element of the German approach to public administration.

Despite the historical emphasis on a strong state, in more contemporary times Peter Katzenstein (1987) famously argued that Germany was a "semi-sovereign state." The absolute sovereignty that some might expect for the state had been eroded, he argued, by both the importance of interest group representation—a corporatist model that is even more prominent in Austria (Talos and Kittel 1999)—and by the constraints of law and the constitution. In addition, the federal nature of Germany further weakens central governance capacity. The movement away from any conception of absolute sovereignty in Germany and Austria has been accelerated even further by the increasing powers of the European Union,[3] despite Germany's high level of influence within the EU.

Ii is not only the federal nature of the German state tradition, and the importance of corporatism, that produces fragmentation and potentially some incoherence within the state structure, and especially the structure of the political executive. There are three fundamental principles for managing policymaking within the cabinet that to some extent provide competing sources of power. The political system of Germany has at times been described as a *Kanzlerdemokratie* (Chancellor Democracy) based on the power of the

---

[3] Although not a member of the European Union, Switzerland, with something of a Germanic tradition in governing, coordinates its policies closely with those of the EU (Church 2007).

Federal Chancellor, and the Chancellor is indeed responsible for the conduct of government in general; but the Chancellor does not govern alone.

This *Kanzlerprinzip* is important for policymaking and for governance in general, but is only one of the three competing principles involving executive governance. Individual ministries in the German government have substantial individual powers within their own domains—the *Ressortprinzip*. Ministers can within some limits make policy within the area of their ministry. One of the major limitations on the power of individual ministers is when the exercise of one minister's powers conflicts with the exercise of his or her powers by another minister. When such conflict among ministers occurs, a third principle—*Kabinettprinzip*—comes into play and conflicts must be worked out within the cabinet (see Müller-Rommel 1994). That cabinet principle may be more significant when there is grand coalition including both the Christian democratic Union (CDU)/Christian Social Union (CSU) and the Social Democratic Party (SPD), as was the case from 1966 to 1969, 2005 to 2009, and from 2013 until this writing. Although these coalitions have governed successfully (Schmidt 2002; Bussmeyer 2019), the differences in political and policy values among the partners has forced some issues upward to determination by the cabinet.

These contemporary developments of the state in Germany themselves represent something of a historical legacy of coping with a decentralized and seemingly incoherent governance structure. Individual parts of the various principalities and states were ruled, and continued to be ruled into the twentieth century, in a patrimonial fashion. Even the Prussian state (Clark 2006: 427ff.) was decentralized and required a strong bureaucracy to provide sufficient direction from the top, and to represent the Hegelian conception of the moral and integrative state. The legalism and formality of administration emerged even before Weber developed these capacities and provided a theoretical structure for administration that might otherwise have been excessively tied to the monarch and the amateurs of the court.[4]

An additional element that must be added to the German state tradition is the welfare state. Beginning with Bismarck in the late nineteenth century, Germany had a significant commitment to social programs, albeit one that preserved some of the social differentiation associated with patrimonialism and corporatism (Esping-Andersen 1990). Rather than being the autonomous

---

[4] Not forgetting, however, those administrators have their education and training in Cameralism. Therefore they brought with them an economic perspective on governing as much as or more so than a legal one.

and aloof institution of the Hegelian conception, the state became a major service provider and legitimated its existence in part through those social services as well as through its constitutional and legal, and even moral, status. The Austrian welfare state is perhaps even more corporatist and more entrenched than the German, and dominates state actions even more so than in Germany (Unger and Heitzmann 2003).

The commitment to the welfare state, and to a service state more generally, produced the need to move toward a reformed and smaller *schlanker Staat* in the 1980s and 1990s. As already noted at the federal level, Germany accepted relatively few NPM reforms but it did go through a major period of downsizing state commitments and privatization. Creating this "slimmer" state has been a challenge given the links of state and society, and democratic demands for high levels of service in the social market economy. The period of austerity in the first decade of the twenty-first century and subsequent years, has helped the system to become slimmer, but continuing policy commitments have made that movement difficult for governments.

The somewhat fragmented state is confronted with social actors, such as the unions, that are relatively unified and which tend to resist changes in the social and economic policies that benefit them (Schiller 2016). The creation of the social market economy in Germany and the continuation of corporatist bargaining in Austria (and to some extent Switzerland) made the state a partner in managing the economy and labor market policies, but the state could rarely dominate decision-making—again it functioned in a semi-sovereign manner.

All these pressures on the state, and the underlying ideas of the state, have produced a set of contemporary conceptions of the state and public administration (Jann 2003; see Table 4.1). Each of these has some validity and has its political supporters, and to some extent each is operational within contemporary governance. Although not presented explicitly, some aspects of the classic conception of the state remain contenders for influence over thinking about how governance should unfold within the German political system, but it is sung largely *sotto voce* amidst the more contemporary conceptions. These are different conceptions, not necessarily competitive but perhaps better seen as complementary visions that may be activated in different situations to cope with particular challenges to governance.

It is also important to consider the manner in which the German state was able to maintain many of the underlying patterns of governance and administration during the reunification process beginning around 1989. Although extremely expensive for the taxpayer and perhaps threatening to

Table 4.1 State traditions in Germany

Type	Characteristics
Classical and authoritarian tradition	Strong state to control particularistic preferences in society
	Role oft law
	Search for the public interest
	Limited accountability
Democratic tradition	State more connected to society
	Pluralism
	Public interest emerges from democratic political process, not from bureaucrats
Liberal tradition	Social market economy
	Greater personal liberty
	State and society not separate but differentiated
	Skepticism of the powers of the state
Marxist and socialist tradition	Need for a strong state but current state largely reflects interests of capitalism
	Return to a less pluralist conception of the public interest

Source: Adapted from Jann (2003).

some former adversaries, reunification reinforced the state tradition in Germany, albeit with some new legacies coming from the period of Communist rule in the eastern *Länder* (Wegrich 2006). But even with that added component to the mixture, the complex strands of thinking about the state have persisted and produced effective governance.

These alternative conceptions of the state also have their distinctive influence on the manner in which public administration is organized and practiced. One obvious impact of the alternative conceptions is on the degree of participation of public and social actors in administration. While the Swiss variation on the German model provides numerous opportunities for direct public participation (Kriesi and Treschel 2008) the other versions (as well as Switzerland) allow substantial participation by interest groups and other social actors. And the federal nature of these governments provides more venues for public participation than would be present in most unitary regimes.

One final point to be made is central to the links of the state tradition to the public bureaucracy. Although the German bureaucracy, as well as others within this tradition, has a strong commitment to legality and probity, they are also important players in policy. The influence of the bureaucracy is accentuated by two factors. One is the fragmentation of the executive mentioned above, with individual ministers having substantial policymaking capacity. The other is that fragmentation of the political nature of the higher level civil service may give them greater influence over policy than in other settings. I will now proceed to examine the linkages between politics and the civil service within this tradition.

Politics and Administration

The Weberian model of administration, generally taken as representing the founding principles of German public administration,[5] argues for the independence of public administrators from direct political control. While the legal framework of administrative action is to be established through political institutions, the implementation of the law is an administrative action to be done in accordance with the law. The adherence to law is reinforced by hierarchical control within the organization. The resultant pattern of administration appears to provide the individual public servant relatively little latitude for decision-making.

The Weberian model was not directly linked to democratic politics and government, and the underlying approach was designed to produce rational, legal governance and, indirectly at least, to provide citizens some rights vis-à-vis the state. If there were rules and those rules were knowable for citizens, then they would have some capacity to understand when the law was violated and expect to be treated fairly and appropriately. Thus, while the bureaucracy is often seen as an instrument used by state powers to oppress, or at least control, citizens it is also a means through which citizens may actually be empowered (Peters 2010b).

This idea of separating politics and administration is not as clear in contemporary German administration as in this more abstract model. While law is still a dominant feature of administration (see below) there is also some greater connection between politics and administration than might be expected from the legalistic foundations of German public administration. This is not to say that German administration is overtly political, but only to say that there are ways in which these two elements of governance influence one another—often subtly—and the separation model so familiar to students of public administration is not quite so applicable here.

Public administration in most countries is becoming more politicized and less shaped by merit principles (Peters and Pierre 2004b; Neuhold et al. 2013). The German public administration is at once highly meritocratic and also

---

[5] As often is the case, this generalization requires some qualifications. See, e.g., Seibel (2010).

political, having found at least one way of combining those two attributes in a single system. First, the vast majority of public employees in Germany are not hired as civil servants per se, but are hired under ordinary labor law. This means that although they are public employees they may have fewer constraints than a civil servant per se.

Second, senior civil servants, the *Beamten*, who are hired under a separate civil service law, are still permitted to be more political than would be true in Anglo-American countries. Indeed, at the upper levels of the civil service these public servants are expected to be political, and to have an affiliation of some sort (Veit and Scholz 2016). This means that when there is a CDU government, for example, the vast majority of the *Staastssekretaer* and other high-ranking officials within the government will be members of that party. If the next government is Social Democratic (SPD) then the CDU public servants will be replaced with SPD civil servants. These officials have all met the same merit criteria and those who leave office retain their status as *Beamten* even if not employed in the government of the day.

As I will be pointing out in more detail, Austria presents a somewhat different perspective on politicization than does Germany. The importance of the "social partnership" and "*Proporzdemokratie*" in Austrian politics and society (Lehmbruch 2003; Adams 2008) means that political considerations do become more important in administration than would be true in Germany or many other European democracies. Positions in the bureaucracy, and in other state institutions, have been allocated by party, to ensure that the major groups—Social Democrats and the Austrian People's Party (conservatives)—were treated equally. However, with the decline of the major parties, the deinstitutionalization of the party system more generally, and the rise of populist and green parties, this political division of offices is less significant.

The consociational dimension of politics in Switzerland (Bochsler and Bousbah 2015) provides another dimension to be considered in making appointments in government. Although by no means as institutionalized as the pattern of allocating positions in the public sector in Austria, the need to consider social and economic divisions in this *Konkurrenz* political system also influences the selection of public officials. This pattern of representativeness within public administration is important for maintaining stability within the political system, and perhaps more importantly is just seen as the "appropriate" way of governing.

Administration and Service

In modern governments in the consolidated democracy, a significant part of the role of public administration is providing services to citizens. This has, to some extent, always been true but the service provider role has become more significant, and has perhaps supplanted the Weberian administrative role. And is the increasing importance of service also apparent to Germany with its Weberian and legalistic foundations? The service role for public administration may be concentrated in the *Land* and local governments, but the federal bureaucracy may be able to retain more separation from the public.

As noted several times, the reforms associated with NPM have not been highly popular or successful in Germany, but other patterns of administrative reform, and governance reform more generally, have been accepted. For example, the concept of *Bürgernähe*, or closeness to citizens has been used to guide some changes in German governance, and public administration (Zypries 2001). These reforms have been closer to participatory reforms in numerous other countries occurring at approximately the same time as NPM (Peters 2010b).

If we assume that bureaucrats, and especially street-level bureaucrats, have discretion, then they can to some extent deviate from the formal rules that are meant to govern their behavior and the policies they implement. This is perhaps less likely within the German tradition, given the strength of legalism within the system. That legalism in the administrative system may produce a style of behavior among street-level bureaucrats that Zacka (2017; see also Jewell 2007) has described as "indifference."

The limited evidence available on public service motivation of bureaucrats in Germany and the other countries operating within this tradition points to a somewhat different conception of this motivation from that found in other countries, but at the same time a strong commitment to public service (Vandenabeele et al. 2006). Indeed, the argument is made that the German public service has had a longer commitment to implementation and delivery than others such as the United Kingdom's civil service, which has been more concerned with policymaking. The traditional separation of politics and bureaucracy in Germany (as least at this stage of the policy process) has produced an implementation "machine."

State and Society II

The brief mention of consociationalism and *Proporzdemokratie* raises another of the fundamental questions about public administration and its linkage to society in the Germanic countries. While, on the one hand, the Hegelian conception of the autonomy of the state has been important in thinking about administration, at a more practical level there have been, and continue to be, close linkages between social actors and governing. This linkage goes back at least to the Hanseatic League of cities around the Baltic which were largely governed by their merchant guilds.

This linkage of state and society later developed into corporatist linkages that permitted social actors from a variety of segments of society to influence governing directly. These linkages involved bargaining over economic issues such as employment policy and taxes, as well as some forms of political representation. For example, corporate representation persisted in the Bavarian *Landsrat* until the institution was abolished several decades ago. Ebbinghaus (2010) has argued that there are at least four ways through which the German state continues to "share public space (Crouch 1986) with social actors: (1) institutionalized consultation; (2) tripartite bargaining over economic policy issues; (3) delegation to public and semi-public agencies; and (4) self-regulation through collective bargaining.

The corporatist linkages between state and social actors are more visible in Austria than in the other countries within this tradition, although there has been some weakening, or at least modification, of those ties (Talos and Kittel 1999). This has been due in part to economic changes which have led to the reluctance of some unions and businesses to participate in central bargaining. Likewise, the increased political fragmentation of the country has made the agreement between the two major parties less viable.

Similarly, the strong pattern of corporatist bargaining in Switzerland, especially for social policy, has been weakening (Häusermann et al. 2004). Among a number of factors producing the change here are increased resource constraints coming at least in part from an aging population, a decline in the homogeneity of the population, and with that changing pattern of policy demands, and a general increase in politicization of policymaking (see Sciarini et al. 2015). It has also been argued that Europeanization is responsible for these changes, although the evidence is somewhat weak, and politicization appears more significant (see Afonso and Papadopoulos 2013).

For the public bureaucracy in these countries, the decline of corporatist patterns of intermediation with society may have several important consequences. One is that governing may be, and by some accounts is, more politicized. While some important aspects of policy would have been decided by social actors along with government, now political parties may become even more central to the policy process (Häusermann et al. 2013). This is one aspect of a general increase of political party involvement in policy, reflecting among other factors the "permanent austerity" (Pierson 2001) that now faces welfare states and the rise of populist politics in Germany and many other consolidated democracies.

In addition, policymaking with declining corporatist bargaining may develop some means of overcoming more fragmented and segmented policymaking that threatens contemporary governments (Pochet and Fajertag 2000). As social pacts have come to replace the historical pattern of corporatist bargaining there are more somewhat direct linkages between social policy decisions and economic policy. These pacts have not been able to overcome austerity in government since at least 2008, but they can provide some means of mitigating the effects. The pacts may provide some power to the bureaucracies that are in direct contact with the partners in these collaborative processes.

Structural Separation of Politics and Administration

There is less overt separation of politics and administration in German government than in the Scandinavian or Anglo-American systems. Although there are some more or less autonomous administrative agencies, "agency fever" has not infected administration in the Germanic systems as much as others (Bach 2014). That said, the pattern of decentralization in Germany does create some possible sources of political influence over policy, rather than attempting to limit the influences as intended by the agency model.

In the Scandinavian model, with small, policymaking ministries, the work of implementation is done by agencies governed by their own boards and run by professional administrators. Germany also has small policymaking ministries at the federal level, with most of the work of implementation performed by the *Länder* governments. While these implementers may not be under the control of federal ministries, they introduce another type of political influence into implementation. If the *Land* government is of the same political complexion as the *Bund* government then there should be little deviation from the policies of the center. On the other hand, if the *Land* government is of a different political stripe than the center, then different political considerations may be interjected into implementation procedures.

It is important to note, however, that the principal political concern in assigning implementation powers to the *Länder* in the federal constitution were not partisan. The principal concern at the end of World War II was to ensure that the central government could not gain hegemonic control over policy, and over the *Länder*, as it had during the Third Reich. While this has not been an issue in the *Bundesrepublik*, there is less autonomy in this form of implementation than there is in the Scandinavian model, which has implementation organizations with their own governing boards and a legal principle guaranteeing their independence.

Even with the policymaking powers lodged at the federal level, and a career system that is to some extent unified between the central and *Land* governments, there are still problems of vertical coordination (Adam et al. 2019). In addition to the potential for partisan differences that may exist between the levels of government, there are also cultural differences that may affect the implementation of programs, especially for Catholic Bavaria. And given that implementation almost inevitably involves making policy, different interpretations of federal policy in different *Länder* may indeed lessen the desired level of uniformity and coordination.

Personnel Appointments and Politicization

The manner in which individual civil servants are selected and retained represents another dimension of possible political control over the bureaucracy. While most scholars, as well as major international donor organizations, have stressed the importance of a merit system in hiring and firing public employees, there are still some virtues in having public officials who are politically responsive, as well as competent in the performance of their tasks. Germany represents an interesting attempt to balance these two virtues in the management of public personnel. Rather than separating the professional and the political, the model here is to integrate the two virtues in single individuals.

The senior civil service—the *Beamten*—are appointed on merit principles and their careers are largely defined by their capacity to perform the job of a civil servant. However, as they begin to reach the top of the pyramid in their department or other organization it becomes advantageous to adopt a political affiliation. Most of the *Staastssekretaer* (state secretaries—the highest civil service position in a ministry) will have a party card. So when, as at this writing, the CDU is in power, these top administrative officials will generally be affiliated with the party or perhaps, if in a coalition, with the coalition party.[6]

In addition to the (generally successful) attempt to blend professional and political competences, this model is important in that it retains the talented individuals when their party is not in power. When there is a change in governments the senior civil servants who have been occupying power in a ministry take "temporary retirement." They remain civil servants and receive their salaries but simply do not occupy the types of positions they had held, and can wait for the return to power of their favored party. This is an expensive way to manage talent for government, having to maintain several teams of qualified individuals, but it may give the German civil service the best of both worlds.

The Austrian pattern of proportional appointment to positions by party represented a distinctive use of political appointments in government. The ministries in government have been divided among the parties, and bureaucrats are as well. While in most cases political appointments are used to ensure control over the bureaucracy in many ways the proportional systems was designed to *prevent* control by any one party. Each organization in government would contain appointees from both parties, or more generally qualified individuals with political affiliations in both parties, and hence making and implementing policy would involve some degree of bargaining among the political factions, and some level of consensus building over policy.[7]

The proportional pattern of ministries has been more complicated because for some time the ministries were the bailiwicks of particular departments. For example, in most coalition governments, the Minister of Finance has been a minister from the Austrian People's Party (ÖVP). SPD (socialist) civil servants working in this ministry therefore may consider it a less friendly environment than a ministry such as Social Affairs, which has been dominated by their party. Thus, even with proportionality, the impact of different political civil servants may not be equal in all settings.

Perhaps the most important factor in both these countries is that the political affiliations of the civil servants are known, whether at the top in

---

[6] For much of its time in office the CDU/CSU have been in coalition with the Liberals (Free Democrats), and at times, as at the present writing, have been in "Grand Coalitions" with the SPD.
[7] This, therefore, is a clear example of the consensus model of governing discussed by Arend Lijphart (2012).

Germany, or deeper into the system as in Austria. Rather than being an impediment to good governance, as is often assumed in the literature on politicization and patronage (Bersch et al. 2017), these allegiances appear to be important for governance, and also to some extent for a sense of political fairness within the systems. For Germany, however, this also depends upon having the resources to support two or more teams of senior public servants.[8]

Uniformity

Given the legal norms central to public administration in Germany and other Germanic cases, one might expect a strong emphasis on uniformity of service provision for all citizens. That is, and is not, the case. As well as have strong legal norms, there is also a tradition of federalism with the constituent units of the German state maintaining some autonomy to make and interpret law. Various forms of confederations or federations governed what is now Germany from the time of the Holy Roman Empire until the present, with the principal exception of the Third Reich (Gunlicks 2003). The federal option made political union more feasible by recognizing differences and providing some autonomy.

The pattern of federalism in contemporary Germany has been described as "coordinated" or "cooperative," meaning that while there are independent governments in the *Länder*, there are also mechanisms for coordinating policy across all sixteen *Länder* (Fleischer 2011). Thus, on a dimension of the degree of uniformity among federal states, Germany would be much nearer the uniform end (along with Australia), while Belgium, Canada, and the United States would have significantly greater differences in policymaking among the constituent units of the federation (Hueglin and Fenna 2016).

The discussion above of the separation of policy and administration noted that in Germany much of public policy is made at the central government level, while those policies are implemented at the *Land* level.[9] The *Länder* also can legislate in most policy areas, albeit with some capacity of the federal government to coordinate those policies and assure compatibility with central government law. But that said, there are areas such as education and culture where the *Länder* have substantial powers and do make laws that diverge

---

[8] In the United States there are also two teams of political executives, but the one out of office earns its living from private sources rather than from the public sector (see Dahlström and Holmgren 2019).

[9] The *Bund* does implement some policies on its own, such as defense and foreign affairs, and some aspects of economic policy.

from one another; e.g., the role of the Roman Catholic Church in education and child care in Bavaria (Turner 2011).

Again, somewhat paradoxically, the German system permits substantial levels of autonomy for the *Länder* while at the same time constraining that autonomy in a variety of ways, primarily through financial and legal controls. First, the *Länder* have less financial independence than do states in the United States or provinces in Canada. The formula by which money is allocated to the *Länder* is negotiated every few years and between those times the money simply comes to subnational governments based on the agreed procedures and in the agreed amounts. The *Länder* have very little own source revenue (Table 3.2) and therefore do not have the capacity to deviate much from the pattern of policy expected of them. Indeed, the German *Länder* have substantially less financial independence than do local governments in unitary systems such as Sweden and Japan.

The expectations about policy come through law. As already noted, much of the lawmaking and policy direction in Germany comes from central government (and also from Brussels). The *Länder* may be able to make some relatively minor changes through regulations and also to choose how to implement, but their discretion is limited. While one of the standard justifica-tions for federalism is to permit innovation and difference (Saam and Kerber 2013), those attributes are much less important in German federalism. The coordinated style of federalism emphasizes the political more than the

Table 4.2 Own Source Revenues

Switzerland	53.0
Canada	51.8
Sweden	42.8
Japan	37.5
United States	35.6
Denmark	32.2
Norway	21.4
Australia	19.1
France	18.4
Italy	11.2
Germany	7.2
Portugal	3.3
United Kingdom	5.0
Greece	0.3

Note: Percentage of revenues of sub-national governments from their own sources. These data are somewhat dated but the relative levels are largely unchanged.

Source: Stegarescu (2005).

administrative dimension of federalism. This federalism was originally designed to constrain the powers of the central government, as well as to permit more representation at the *Land* level.

The other two countries central to this tradition—Austria and Switzerland—are at opposing ends of the dimension of uniformity in federalism. Switzerland is a confederation rather than a federal system, so that the cantons tend to have somewhat greater powers than in the other countries, or indeed in federal countries in general (Linder and Vatter 2001). On the other hand, Austria has become increasingly centralized, in part because the social conditions within the country are perceived to be more uniform than in other federal regimes (Erk 2004). But these are all federal systems with greater formal acceptance of administrative and policy diversity.

Accountability and Control

Enforcing accountability is a crucial question for any administrative system, and any administrative tradition. The common complaint about bureaucracies being autonomous and divorced from society leads to assumptions that they are abusing their positions and failing to respond adequately either to citizens or to their nominal political "masters." The stereotypical conception of German bureaucracy might appear to be especially prone to producing abuse, given its high social status and its apparent autonomy. But the reality of accountability may be very different, and German bureaucracy is bound in a web of control as much as or more powerful than any administrative system. The creation of a number of checks on the power of the bureaucracy in Germany and Austria may be in part a reaction to history, and the complicity of many civil servants with the Third Reich (Strobel and Veit forthcoming).

The Weberian model of bureaucracy involved control of action within government through law, and also through the training of individual bureaucrats. The public administrator was, and largely still is, a legal actor whose task is to understand, interpret, and apply the law. Thus, to some extent control over behavior is meant to be internalized through the acceptance of the law—civil servants are responsible as much as they are accountable. Further, the *Rechtsstaat* tradition has not assumed that the civil servant should be particularly responsive to citizens or to social actors. The law represents the normative structure that will protect the rights of those social actors.

To encourage greater responsiveness, and to ensure legal responsibility on the part of public servants, there is an extensive system of administrative courts, both general and specialized in areas such as the labor market, social policy, and fiscal affairs. Citizens have a right to access these courts when they have complaints against government actions. This legal system can handle most administrative matters but those which involve more basic rights under the constitution can be appealed into the regular court system. And there may also be possibilities of using the European courts to address complaints about administrative actions.

In addition to the traditional legal foundation of responsibility and accountability, the public bureaucracy in the Germanic administrative tradition is accountable to ministers and to parliament, as is true in other democratic regimes. And unlike parliaments in most other parliamentary systems (but see the Scandinavian tradition, pp. 121–2) the *Bundestag* in Germany is well organized to exercise oversight of the bureaucracy (Saalfeld 1998). The committee system in the parliament mirrors the structure of government, so that there is some specialized consideration of the actions of the ministries and the bureaucracy. In addition, the Petitions Committee considers all petitions submitted by citizens with complaints against the government.[10] While these rarely produce any significant action by parliament, it is an important communication mechanism for understanding possible excesses and failings by the bureaucracy.

In addition to the formal committee structure, the *Bundestag*, as well as the legislatures of the *Länder*, have a large number of individuals with a background in the civil service as members. Given the experience of these parliamentarians and the relatively low information costs they must bear, they often become active in oversight activities (Braendle and Sturtzer 2013). In particular, these parliamentarians are more likely to engage in the interpellation process, which allows party groups and individual members of parliament to ask for detailed written answers from government to questions submitted to it (Wonka and Göbel 2016). In some instances, the written answers may produce a debate in parliament.

In addition to legalistic and parliamentary forms of accountability, German public administration has borrowed the ombudsman institution from Scandinavian countries and to some extent elaborated it. In addition to the general ombudsman for complaints about the administration, there are more specialized officers functioning in the manner of an ombudsman. For example, there is commissioner to protect the rights of soldiers, and another

---

[10] The Basic Law of the Federal Republic gives all citizens the right to send written petitions to the *Bundestag*.

for public transportation. And both the federal government and some of the *Länder* have officials protecting the rights of prisoners (Carl 2013).

In summary, although the German bureaucracy is generally perceived as a powerful and relatively autonomous actor in governance, a number of factors limit that power. The most important of these is the presence of multiple veto-points within the German political and administrative system. The institution of the law and the constitution are a significant check, given especially that most German public servants are still trained as lawyers. The various principles governing action within the political executive may also at times constrain behavior, and require substantial coordination. The federal system, by giving the power of implementation to the *Länder* introduces another set of actors who may have some policy ideas of their own. And, finally, all of these actors are to some extent constrained through membership of the European Union.

Summary and Conclusions

Perhaps the most remarkable point emerging from this discussion of the administrative tradition in Germany, and the other countries influenced by this tradition, is the complexity of the tradition in contrast to the simple stereotype that is often presented. German history has had a number of severe discontinuities, but some elements of state and administrative traditions have persisted. But that historical tradition is being augmented and debated, and emerging patterns of governance have modernized the state without undermining many essential, and positive, features.

The German bureaucracy is powerful, as is the bureaucracy in all advanced democracies, but it is not the Leviathan that it is sometimes thought to be. The legal foundation of the administrative system provides one source of control, internalized through the legal training of most higher grade civil servants. Further, those legal foundations are enforced when necessary through administrative and regular courts. A number of other mechanisms have been developed that add alternative forms of control over the bureaucracy, both at the domestic level and at the European level.

As well as being constrained, the contemporary German bureaucracy represents a more complex administrative and state tradition than might be thought to be present. The Weberian tradition is indeed strong and, perhaps, dominant but it has been complemented with a democratic and a welfare state tradition. In the latter two aspects of the tradition the more aloof conception of the bureaucrat as legal arbiter must become more of a servant for the public. That shift has been occurring for public servants in all countries, but the shift within this tradition may be more pronounced. Further, pluralism within society has become yet another contributor to the semi-sovereign nature of the state.

In summary, the contemporary manifestations of the German administrative tradition are grounded in that tradition, but also demonstrate the effects of gradual reforms. Most of those reforms appear to represent democratic and welfare state alternatives to the Weberian tradition, rather than more managerialist reforms found in many other administrative systems. But at the local government level, concerned more with the delivery of tangible municipal services, managerial thinking has had some influence. Thus, as with all the traditions discussed in this book, there is a blending of the traditional elements of public administration with more recent ideas, with layers of ideas and practices defining the contemporary system.

5

The Scandinavian Tradition

The third major administrative tradition examined in this volume is Scandinavian. This tradition covers a smaller group of countries and a much smaller population than the other three, but it has a number of features that distinguish it from other European systems. This distinctiveness is manifested in the political dimension of governments as much as or more than in administrative patterns, but these political differences have important implications for the manner in which public administration is organized and functions.

This tradition applies primarily to four countries—Sweden, Denmark, Norway, and Iceland. Finland also has significant influences from this tradition, but its administration was also influenced by over a century of control by Russia (Temmes and Salminen 1994).[1] The history of these four countries has been closely intertwined for centuries, with Denmark and Sweden controlling all or portions of the other two, as well as Finland, at various times in their history. And some elements of the tradition may be dispersed throughout the Baltic region, which was once a "Swedish lake."[2] More recently, these countries have had a significant influence on government in the Baltic republics after they gained their independence from the former Soviet Union in 1991.

Although I will be treating this as a distinct administrative tradition, some aspects are similar to several of the other traditions. For example, the *Rechtsstaat* concept in the Germanic tradition, can be identified in these cases (especially Sweden). And the ready adoption of many ideas of New Public Management (NPM) is not dissimilar to some countries in the Anglo-American tradition. The acceptance of managerialism, and some aspects of its neo-liberal foundation, is particularly interesting in the heart of the welfare state. But even then, the underlying commitment to the welfare state and equality have

---

[1] Finland is not technically a Scandinavian country, but is included in the larger group of Nordic countries. Finland is, I would argue, a hybrid regime, although it is now much closer to the Scandinavian tradition than the Russian.

[2] When first visiting the University of Tartu in Estonia, for example, I was given an extensive lecture on the role of Gustavus Adolphus of Sweden in founding the university.

Administrative Traditions: Understanding the Roots of Contemporary Administrative Behavior. B. Guy Peters,
Oxford University Press (2021). © B. Guy Peters. DOI: 10.1093/oso/9780198297253.003.0005

mitigated some of the more extreme impacts of NPM on governance in the Scandinavian countries, and to some extent altered the meaning of NPM.

One of the most distinctive features of these countries is a long-term commitment to a welfare state that, in the terms of Esping-Andersen (1990), "de-commodifies" labor. In other words, there has been a commitment to provide some level of economic security for the entire population whether they are in work or not. That said, these systems also have capitalist roots, with many active labor market programs to keep people employed and in good jobs (Madsen 2006) rather than living on social benefits. While fiscal crises and the election of more conservative governments may have lessened the generosity of the welfare state (Andersen et al. 2017), it remains central to the Scandinavian model of governing and public administration.

The commitment to the welfare state also implies the need for maintaining a rather large and effective public bureaucracy. Broadly defined, the public sector in these countries employs on average roughly a 50 percent larger share of the total work force than do the public sectors of countries in the other traditions (see Derlien and Peters 2000). However, despite the central position of the public bureaucracy in the management of society and the economy, public service does not occupy a particularly privileged position in society. The egalitarian cultures (Bendixsen et al. 2018) of these countries minimize the creation of an elite that is set apart from the remainder of society, and the rewards for holding public office are very modest (Ahlbäck-Öberg 2012; Lægreid and Roness 2012) compared to those in many other affluent nations.

Globalization and Europeanization are additional major factors affecting public administration in the Scandinavian countries (Lægreid et al. 2004). All countries in Europe are impacted by these factors, but their relatively small size and the openness of their economies and societies make these factors particularly relevant for Scandinavia. As Jacobsson et al. (2016) argued for Sweden, given the extent to which these regimes are embedded in the international environment their governance decisions are influenced, albeit not determined, through the connections with the international environment. Norway is not a member of the European Union, but its public policies and internal governance are heavily influenced by its more informal connections with the EU.

The discussion of public administration in these countries, perhaps more than is true for the other traditions, will require understanding the broader pattern of governance within the countries. There is an extensive literature on "the Swedish Model" of governing (e.g., Palme 2015), but many of the features identified as peculiarly Swedish may also apply to the other Scandinavian countries. Shaping the role of the state, perhaps more than anything else in these four countries, is their strong commitment to the welfare state, as well as to a strong, trustworthy, and effective public sector.

At the heart of this Swedish, or Scandinavian, model of governing may be an apparent paradox—the co-existence of a strong state with commitment to extensive public participation and a strong civil society (Trägårdh, 2007). While this paradox may be more apparent than real, it does raise important questions about governance in these countries, and also identifies fundamental aspects of the state traditions. And those state traditions will, in turn, shape the nature of public administration and its role in governing. The fundamental question, then, is about governing when there is a strong society *and* a strong state (Migdal 1988). The question that follows is how does this model persist in the face of declining levels of participation in civil society, albeit a decline not felt as strongly in Scandinavia as in other societies, and declining trust in government?

State and Society I: State Autonomy

As already noted, the Scandinavian model of administration has some attributes in common with other types, but often represents some blending of the more clearly defined aspects of the others; that characteristic is true for the relationship between state and society. I have been defining that relationship to a great extent as a dichotomy between organic and contractarian models, but the Scandinavian system appears to have some elements of both. And, as with the Anglo-American model discussed in Chapter 6, there are also important differences among the national cases.

Among these cases the Swedish state comes closest to being an organic model. As Lindvall and Rothstein (2006; see also Kumlin and Rothstein 2003) point out, the conception of the strong state in Sweden was directly linked with the idea of a strong society. For Social Democratic leaders such as Tage Erlander (Ruin 1990) that were so central to the formation of the contemporary style of governing, these two elements were virtually the same, and both were essential for producing improved welfare for citizens, But in the other Scandinavian cases there were also strong societal linkages, and the existence of a "communitarian state" that supported the political state.

But if we begin with these models of the relationships between state and society as a foundation, there have been a number of political developments that have altered the original models. Tom Christensen (2003) has described four models of the state existing within Norwegian government. One is the strong, Weberian state that would correspond to some extent with the organic model. In this conception of the state the institutions of government are able to steer effectively and to do so largely on their own. Further, Lindvall and Rothstein (2006) argue that the strong state has for decades also been implied by a democratic logic, so that voters effectively select their policy choices when they vote.[3]

The second model Christensen refers to is the "institutional state," meaning here the more sociological institutionalism associated with James March and Johan P. Olsen (1989). In this version the state is a source of public values, and guides individual citizens through a logic of appropriateness, but to some extent citizens also shape the values of the state through a number of institutionalized mechanisms of political participation. This version of the state would also be similar to the organic model described in Chapter 1, with state and society closely linked by common values, and by continuing interactions defining and redefining those values.

The third version of the state that Christensen discusses is the corporate-pluralist state. Although other countries in Europe and Latin America have strong corporatist traditions, the involvement of interest groups as legitimate actors in the policy process is perhaps most developed in Scandinavia. As discussed in greater detail below, interest groups have legitimate participants in the policy process, with a number of opportunities to influence policymaking and implementation. As Stein Rokkan (1967) argued decades ago, these opportunities constitute a second pillar of democracy, and are legitimate influences on policymaking as elections. While the use of many corporate-pluralist techniques has been declining over the past several decades (Öberg et al. 2011; Pronin 2020), there are closer connections between state and society than in most other countries (see pp. 99–101 below).

The final model Christensen discusses is the "supermarket state." The logic here is that the state has lost most of its majesty and might and has become simply the provider of benefits to the public. The development of the welfare state and the array of other benefits to which citizens have become accustomed have made the state central to the social and economic lives of citizens, but at the same time they have made those lives somewhat more ordinary. In many

---

[3] Lindvall and Rothstein were speaking particularly of Sweden, but implied that much the same had been true for the other Scandinavian cases. This chapter was written in reaction to the power studies in Norway and Denmark in which at least the Norwegian study expressed substantial skepticism about the persistence of that democratic linkage to policy (Østerud et al. 2003).

ways, the supermarket version of the state is a contractarian model, albeit one based on taxation, expenditure, and services, whereas the notion of the contract for Locke and Hobbes was more about basic safety and the preservation of rights. The public pay their taxes and in turn expect to receive a host of benefits. If the state, or at least the government of the day, fails to provide those benefits then it can be argued that the contract has been violated (see Gilley 2009). This model of the state is to some extent the antithesis of the institutional state mentioned above, being based largely on a "logic of consequentiality."

Rather than being exclusive alternative visions of the state in the Scandinavian countries, and especially in Norway, Christensen is arguing that all of these four visions continue to have some validity simultaneously. The state in Scandinavia appears to be a complex overlay and mixture of the alternative conceptions of what a state should be and should do. Any one of these may be invoked at one time or another in order to cope with a particular policymaking problem, or to provide legitimacy for some action or another. They may also differ to some extent across the four countries, with Sweden appearing to come closest to the Weberian model, while the others may have more a contractarian perspective on the nature of the state.

Thus, the Scandinavian version of the state is perhaps more complex than others. The state is a source of authority that is to some extent autonomous from society, while at the same time deeply embedded in the society. It can be strong, but at the same time may share some of the semi-sovereign characteristics of the German state (see pp. 77–78) because of the close ties with interest groups, networks, and other social actors, and the power those groups have enjoyed in making decisions. However, as the politics of these countries becomes less dominated by social democratic parties and their close connections with those social actors—especially trade unions—then latitude for autonomous state action may have increased.

Law and Management

As already noted, Scandinavian governments have some of the features of the *Rechtsstaat* usually associated with Germany and other countries derived from the German model. In all these countries there is a strong legal foundation for state action.[4] That said, law and lawyers do not dominate public

---

[4] The opening of an ancient law in Norway was "*ad lögum skal land vårt byggnas*," or "with law will the land be built."

administration in the Scandinavian countries to the extent that they do in Germany, and management is perceived to be a central aspect of the role of the public servant. The openness of the labor market in the public sector (see below) also tends to de-emphasize legal qualifications for public servants.

One of the better indicators of the differences in the role of law in Scandinavian administration is the part that lawyers play in the administrative system. In Germany there is still largely a *Justiemonopol*, with the vast majority of civil servants being trained as lawyers. While there may be more lawyers in the Scandinavian systems than in others, such as Anglo-American bureaucracies, they are far from a majority. More civil servants are trained in public administration, political science, or perhaps in substantive policy areas such as social work or engineering, and an increasing number are also trained in management and the social sciences. For example, in Norway, the proportion of legally trained civil servants declined from 38 percent in 1976, to 22 percent in 2006, while social scientists increased from 4 percent to 24 percent (Christensen and Laegreid 2009).

Law was an important educational background among civil servants in the Scandinavian countries, but not the dominant background that is has been in the Germanic counties. There has been, however, a significant culture of the "administrator" that reflects traditional Weberian bureaucracy more than having a legal background per se (Bruun 2000). Top administrators in all four Scandinavian systems remain a distinctive group of public servants but have increasingly adopted a managerial focus for their careers, although they may have educational backgrounds in a variety of fields. That focus is perhaps especially evident for the top executives of the agencies that are charged with implementing government programs (Dahlström and Niklasson 2013).

Although there is a clear managerialist strand of thinking in the Scandinavian countries, that managerialism is constrained by the alternative tradition of involvement of workers in decision-making in organizations, both public and private. Public sector organizations are required to involve their employees in decisions, and this is more than a legal requirement; it is also part of the participatory and egalitarian culture of these countries. Thus, the strictly managerial bent of NPM may be softened somewhat with the alternative participatory style of reform in the public sector (see Peters 2000).

State and Society II: The Involvement of Social Actors

The description above of the state in Scandinavian countries has laid the foundation for this discussion of the relationship between state and society.

The integration of social actors into governance and the high level of interaction among them is perhaps the defining characteristic of the Scandinavian tradition. While the Germanic tradition also has strong elements of corporatism, especially in Austria (Karlhofer 2006), the corporate pluralism of the Scandinavian cases assigns perhaps an even stronger role to interest groups in making and implementing policy.

In his seminal paper on corporate pluralism, Stein Rokkan (1967) argued that the integration of interest groups into governance was a second pillar of democracy. That pillar was important because it allowed groups in society that were not controlling government at the time to have some influence and not be excluded from decision-making. The existence of this second pillar was important in these countries in particular because of the domination of government by social democratic parties for decades beginning in the 1930s. The involvement of a very wide range of actors—in contrast to the tripartite bargaining that characterizes more classical corporatism—permitted more conservative groups to influence policy.

As well as being one avenue of democracy, the involvement of social groups was also a means of improving the quality of public policy, and also of making the policies adopted more implementable. For example, the mechanism of commissions of inquiry (SOU) for major policy changes enabled the groups to present their views and to bargain over final policy proposals (see Hysing and Lundberg 2016) This bargaining among multiple actors also meant that there was less probability of opposition to the policy once it was adopted. It also enhanced the variety of information available to decision-makers and may further have improved the quality of policy decisions adopted.

Although central to governance in these countries, the strength of corporatism has waxed and waned over time. While the heyday of this model may have been in the 1950s and 1960s, the slowing of economic growth beginning with the oil shocks in the 1970s imposed greater scarcity on the public sector, even in these affluent countries. Scarcity, in turn, made providing the benefits associated with the "supermarket state" more of a zero-sum game among the participants in corporatist bargaining. Likewise, the influence of neo-liberal ideology (again, even in these social democratic regimes), has been associated with governments acting more on their own and without levels of consultation seen in the past (Rommetvedt et al. 2013). Those tendencies were reinforced during the economic crisis beginning in 2008.

Much of the discussion of corporate pluralism in Scandinavia focuses on policymaking, but interest groups are also directly involved with the implementation of policy. As the corporatist model has continued to evolve through the use of networks around policy areas (see Kristinsson 2016) there continues to be a definite role for groups in implementing policies, much as collaborative policy implementation has become more common in most consolidated democracies (Ansell and Gash 2008). These social actors are equally likely to be interest groups or a set of citizens who are affected by the policy in question (e.g., parental involvement in implementing education policy).

Politics and Administration

As noted in the other cases, there are two aspects of the separation, or integration, of politics and administration in public administration. The first is how the public bureaucracy and political institutions—ministries and perhaps the legislature—interact as policies are made and implemented (Askim et al. 2017). The second dimension captures the extent to which political considerations are involved in the selection and retention of public administrators. While all these countries have merit systems responsible for most appointments in the public sector, they—like all political systems—have some degree of appointment on political grounds.

Bureaucracy and Political Institutions

Perhaps paradoxically, an administrative tradition that tends to emphasize the integration of social actors into the governance process also attempts to keep some components within that governance process apart. The tradition of separating policymaking from policy implementation goes back several centuries, but has persisted over that time, and constitutes a central feature of administration in Sweden and to some extent the other Nordic countries (Pierre 2010). In addition, this model of separation served as one of the sources for the large-scale "agencification" of public administration under the tenets of NPM.[5]

The basic pattern of public administration in Sweden is based on agencies (*Styrelsen*) responsible for the implementation of policy, with small

---

[5] In particular, the British government of Margaret Thatcher thought they were copying the Swedish agency model when they created the "Next Steps" agencies, which subsequently became a model for the diffusion of this idea (see Verhoest et al. 2016). The copying was less than exact, leaving out the governance of the agencies through independent boards.

policymaking ministries. This pattern goes back to the 18th century, and was at the time a means of placing checks on the power of the monarch by creating boards responsible for administering public programs. While originally many members of the boards would have been the gentry, they have now become more professionalized and expert in the policy areas for which they are responsible.

Of course, this model, or any other model attempting to separate policy from administration, is less than fully successful. While the formal statements would have ministries linked to agencies primarily through policy directives and the budget (Tarschys 1975), the connections are in reality more pervasive. First, the budgetary linkage does provide a means of controlling policy. Further, the ministry may depend on the agencies under its supervision (Table 5.1) for information and advice about policy. And finally, implementation is often policymaking. Few pieces of legislation, in the Scandinavian countries or elsewhere, are so clear and so detailed that they do not require elaboration and secondary legislation during the process of implementation. While the two types of organizations in government may disagree about the extent to which the implementers should, and can, make policy, there is little doubt that it does occur.

The agency model is deeply enshrined in Swedish administration, but is somewhat less central to administration in the other Nordic countries. Although there is a significant number of agencies in the Norwegian government, some ministries in Norway, for example, have a more articulated administrative structure than in Sweden and may deliver some services. And in Denmark many organizations listed as agencies by ministries are institutions such as museums or libraries rather than organizations implementing ministry programs. Almost all Danish agencies report directly to a ministry, while in Sweden almost all report to a board and only indirectly to the ministries (Yesilkagit and Christensen 2006).

For all these countries, there have been pressures for decentralization of administration and public services, even in countries that by most standards

Table 5.1 Control of government, 1917–2019 (number of years)

	Denmark	Iceland	Norway	Sweden
Social Democrats, Labor*, other left	81	37	59	77
Other	21	65	43	25

Note: * Alone or in coalition.

are already decentralized. As well as using the agencies for this purpose they (and especially Norway and Denmark) have moved services down to the sub-national level. These administrative reforms (see Biela et al. 2013) have tended to make them function more like federal systems in which the states or provinces function to some extent as agencies might in the Swedish model. The obvious difference is that these local governments do have politics of their own and when the political preferences of the levels of government differ there can be coordination problems (see Adam et al. 2019).

Whether agencies are separated organizationally from ministries or not, there is still a sense of the separation of political work and administrative work within these governments—they were implementing some of the patterns of administration associated with NPM before that model became popular in the rest of the world. This tradition of separating these two activities of government does weaken the government's control over administration, but also creates more opportunities for local and agency autonomy; and that autonomy can be related to policy and management innovation.

We should also note that in addition to the capacity to remove political control over administration, the agency structure within Scandinavian governments also generates a high level of specialization of administrative action. The extension of the agency model to other countries around the world has created perceived needs for more institutions and procedures for coordination (Peters 2015), but these needs have rarely been met adequately. The inadequacies of coordination in turn have led to politicization of the bureaucracy as a means of restoring control, in Scandinavia and elsewhere.

Political Patronage and Politicization

The second dimension of the relationship between politics and administration addresses the selection and retention of civil servants. Governments in Scandinavia have a long history of being fair, open, and non-corrupt (Rothstein 2000, 2004). Unlike many other governments, even those in other parts of Europe, there have not been large-scale patronage appointments into public positions, and most public servants arrive in their positions through merit. But these systems may not be completely free of patronage and politicization and by some accounts the level of politicization of the public service is increasing.

It is important to note that because of the strong norms of merit appointment and neutrality in the civil service, politicization of the civil service in these countries may be somewhat more subtle than in other regimes, even Weberian Germany (see Bach and Veit 2017), but it is there in all these systems. For example, Dahlström and Holmgren (2019) find that there is a significant use of political criteria in the appointment of agency heads in Sweden. They argue that, in part because of the independence from political control of the agencies, appointment of the agency heads, which can be controlled by politicians, is important for management of the bureaucracy.

In Denmark, Christensen (2004) noted the changing tenure of top-level civil servants, and the increased movement out of those positions when governments, or individual ministers, changed. These changes were not necessarily driven by party political reasons, but were more driven by the policy priorities of the government and its ministers. Also, some of these changes appeared to be "anticipatory" (Peters 2014) as civil servants felt they would not be comfortable working with the incoming political leader. In addition, in some cases civil servants will not be dismissed from the ministry but simply shunted off to an often meaningless advisory position. The form of the merit system is followed, but perhaps not the substance.

Iceland is the one Scandinavian country in which significant levels of clientelism and patronage persist (Kristinsson 2012). Although professionalization of both politics and administration, and the privatization of many public enterprises, has weakened the capacity of politicians to distribute public jobs, there is still less of a constituency for an autonomous, professional bureaucracy in Iceland than in the other Nordic countries. The governance system is extremely decentralized, giving ministers a good deal of capacity to make appointments. This persistence of some level of patronage may also be a function of Iceland being a small country with a widely dispersed population.

What can explain apparent increases in the levels of politicization in the Scandinavian countries? One of the most important factors is that there are now turnovers in government to a greater extent than in much of the past. If a new government wants to make its mark with a policy decision, and is uncertain of the allegiances or policy views of a previous set of officials, it will be in their interest to change the officials if possible (for Norway, see Christensen et al. 2008); if there was a long continuation of dominance by a single party or coalition then the policy views might be thought to more predictable and stable.

The above explanation may be associated with some general decline in the consensual nature of politics in these regimes. The contrast that Lijphart (2012) makes between consensual and majoritarian regimes would probably still have the Scandinavian countries in the consensual category, having some broad agreements on the shape of public policies as well as the style of governing. But as the domination of the left-center parties has diminished, and new small parties with more distinct policy agendas gain a political foothold,[6] that underlying consensus is less capable of controlling policy.

A further alteration in level of politicization of the bureaucracy is perhaps associated with the decline of consensus, and the alternation of political parties in office. In Scandinavia there has been some of what has been described as the increased presidentialization of politics in almost all parliamentary regimes (Poguntke and Webb 2007; Bergman and Strøm 2011). Although increasing control of governments through the chief executive has a number of effects on governance, one is the increasing focus on control of public sector personnel and the role of "entourages" of that executive (Bioy et al. 2016; see also Askim et al. 2019). Those entourages, in turn, act to impose the policies of the prime minister and perhaps the whole cabinet on the rest of government (see Panizza et al. 2019).

Finally, the perceived, if not necessarily real, politicization of administration in the Scandinavian countries may be a function of some reforms associated with NPM. While the separation of policy and administration has been ingrained in these systems, the addition of employment through personal contracts has been an extra source of greater politicization (Binderkrantz and Christensen 2009. If individuals are hired into high-level administrative positions on the basis of personal contracts that are influenced by politicians, there is an obvious appearance of political influence. The individuals hired may be fully qualified, but they may still be perceived as "technopols" rather than technocrats (Panizza et al. 2019).

In summary, the tradition in the Scandinavian countries is to have a significant separation of politics and administration. This has been true structurally and it also has been true for the selection and retention of public employees. That said, a variety of factors may be generating pressures to weaken that commitment to separation, especially in the manner in which individuals are selected to work in the public sector. The administration in

---

[6] For example, several parties on the far right have had distinct anti-immigrant policies, and green parties have been advocating strong environmental policies, especially relative to climate change.

these governments remain less politicized than most other governments and has a strong commitment to trust-based forms of administration (Pierre and Peters 2017), but cannot completely resist the pressures toward politicization.

Career Structure

The career structure for members of the public administration in Scandinavian countries presents yet another paradox. As I have already discussed, there is a strong history of political neutrality for public employees, who tend to be referred to as civil servants. But the majority of public employees, especially in Sweden, would not be considered civil servants in many other contexts. The recruitment system for public employees is open and there is little distinction, except for positions such as judges and the diplomatic corps, in employment between the public and private sectors. Further, public employees are not centrally managed as a corporate resource.[7]

Employees in the public sector in Sweden are hired in much the same manner as in the private sector, albeit being subject to qualifications established in law, and also subject to a number of ethical and neutrality standards. Similarly, individuals within an organization are formally not given preference for promotion when a position becomes available. The other Scandinavian countries also do not have centralized personnel management systems and tenured civil servants, although the top positions in the Norwegian civil service are permanent officials. The Danish civil service has moved perhaps farthest away from traditional personnel management, with many officials not being on individual, limited-term contracts (Gregory and Christensen 2004).

Although the protections of civil service laws are important, more so in Norway and Denmark than in Sweden, there are also other protections for public employees. The public sector in all Scandinavian countries is very heavily unionized and the unions continue to provide substantial protection for the rights of employees. And, unlike some countries, union membership extends into the upper echelons of employees of the public sector. Further, ordinary labor law confers a number of rights on all employees that compensate for the absence of particular civil service regulations.

---

[7] The Swedish Agency for Government Employees (SAFE) does manage remuneration and some other aspects of human resource management.

There are three important points about the career of civil servants within Scandinavian countries. The first is that although these employees are not, for the most part, hired through a central process and may not have special laws applying to their status, they accept the values usually associated with the civil service. Indeed, levels of politicization and corruption are lower than in most other administrative systems. The strengths of these public values in the absence of formal laws are perhaps especially notable in Sweden, given the openness of recruitment into public service careers.

The second point worth emphasizing is the varying degrees of change from the underlying traditions of the civil service career among these countries. The public career in Sweden appears to have changed relatively little, having had the same open system of recruitment to civil service positions for decades. Likewise, personnel management remains as decentralized as in the past. The Danish system has changed the most, moving away from conventional personnel administration to individualized contracts, with some change in Norway, albeit not as much as in Denmark.

The third point is that the career structures of these administrative systems (especially in Sweden) have been conducive to some of the reforms associated with NPM. Not having a centralized career structure or centralized personnel management has made it much easier to introduce individual contracting for positions and performance-based management of public personnel. Further, the long history of probity among civil servants makes the potential for corruption within NPM-style administration less of a threat than it might be in other systems.

In summary, careers in Scandinavian public administration are distinctive. To some extent the capacity to have less structured patterns of personnel management within the public sector reflects the underlying trust and probity within these systems. The less-structured nature of the career systems can also facilitate adaptation to changing demands and changing ideas about governing. The historical legacies reflected in these career patterns are valuable, but may not be readily transferred to other administrative systems, even those in other consolidated democracies.

Uniformity

At first glance the Scandinavian countries should produce relatively uniform policy results for their citizens. These governments are all unitary regimes and they all have strong commitments to a range of welfare state benefits for all citizens. They are also all relatively small, at least in population, without significant internal social cleavages, albeit increasing diversity. But despite those factors all pressing toward greater uniformity, these countries do have differences in local government and in some ways are more decentralized than federal governments such as Germany or Austria. Paradoxically, this commitment to equality is paired with a commitment to decentralized government.

Several factors are associated with the relatively lower commitment to uniformity in the Scandinavian countries. One factor diminishing uniformity is the tradition of "communal liberty" (Walsh 1992). Even when there is a powerful state providing services, local government remains important in the lives of the population and these communes have a number of powers. The powers of these local governments in some ways exceed those of the *Länder* in Germany, for example. Perhaps most importantly the communes can levy their own taxes and as a consequence of having their own source revenues they have the autonomy to make real policy decisions on their own.

Having the resources to make their own policy choices, the communes in the Scandinavian countries (and especially Sweden and Norway) are given substantial delegated powers in the implementation of public policies, especially social policy (Seller and Lindström 2007). While there are certainly national guidelines for these policies, there are still opportunities for variations at the local level. Also, some policies concerning matters such as local economic development and the provision of local public services are delegated to a very large extent to local governments.

Variable implementation of health care policies represents another major source of differences, again within a national framework, and again especially in Sweden. The intermediate level of government, the *lan* (generally translated as county) provides most secondary and tertiary care in the health sector, and there is a history of competition among the counties in the provision of health care. Thus, while the standards and priorities for health care across the country may be the same, there are options for differences in the implementation of those standards (Anell 2005; Carlsson 2010).

Finally, education may be even more decentralized with the local schools, especially in Denmark, having a great deal of autonomy in how they operate (Sørensen 1998). Rather than being controlled directly even by local school boards, each school may be governed by committees of parents and teachers. This level of autonomy means that schools even within the same local government area may be run somewhat differently. There may be national standards that impose some uniformity on the curriculum, but much of the day-to-day operations of schools are controlled within the schools themselves.

In addition to the degree of autonomy granted to subnational governments in the Scandinavian countries, the Sami people are also given considerable rights of self-government and self-determination (Henriksen 2008). There are Sami parliaments in Sweden, Finland, and Norway, with the capacity to make rules governing their people, albeit within some constraints within national laws. The situation of the Sami is more complicated because, unlike North American native populations living on tribal lands, the Sami have the right to move themselves and their property across national boundaries at will.

All the above factors involved in the relatively low levels of uniformity in Scandinavian governments are related to some degree to strong commitments to the ideas of local democracy and participation. Even though policies at the national level are decided in an open and democratic manner, there is still a sense that local government is important for allowing citizens to influence many aspects of policy. Thus, rather than the notion of absolute equality imposed by a powerful state, as in the Napoleonic model, equality in these governments means having clear national standards but also some room for flexibility and adaptation.

Finally, it might be easy to make too strong a case for local autonomy and communal democracy in the Scandinavian countries. All three countries have national officials at county level who are analogous to the prefects in the Napoleonic tradition (Bjørna and Jenssen 2006). The powers of these officials do vary, with those in Denmark being the weakest, but in all cases there is some balancing act between the constitutional principle that local governments can do what they wish unless it is expressly forbidden (and they can afford it), and the need for uniformity in major policy domains such as economics and justice.

Service and Administration

We should expect a government and an administrative system responsible for delivering a large set of social, educational, and labor market services to have a strong orientation. This is largely true for the Scandinavian countries, perhaps especially at the local level where numerous consultative and participatory mechanisms are in place to help ensure proper and caring delivery of social services. But the general style of public administration in the Scandinavian countries at all levels is one of providing public service.

The movement of Scandinavian governments to a more marketized conception of service delivery has to some extent challenged the service ethos of governments. This market approach to social services has come into conflict with long-standing commitments to universal services, and with some of the political mechanisms available for accountability and control at the local level of government (Petersen and Hjelmar 2014). The assumption of the advocates of marketized services has been that treating citizens as "customers" might actually improve the quality of services provided, but that value tends to be overshadowed by drives for economy and efficiency.

Given the numerous observations about the structure of public administration and its commitment to public service, it is not surprising that survey evidence from Scandinavian governments points to a strong public service motivation. For example, Bullock et al.'s (2015) analysis of motivations among employees in thirty countries shows that the Scandinavian countries have by far the highest levels of service commitment, followed closely by Finland. Similarly, Houston (2011; see also Thunman and Persson 2015) found that the Scandinavian respondents among a smaller sample of nations were very high in public service motivation.

Accountability

Like all democratic countries, the Scandinavian countries have complex accountability structures that use a variety of methods to attempt to hold government, and especially the public bureaucracy, accountable for its actions. Although the particular mix of methods may vary, all governments use legal mechanisms, parliamentary mechanisms, and more public mechanisms as means for addressing problems of accountability. And, again in all democratic regimes, these forms of accountability depend at least in part on the role of the media in making information available to the enforcers of accountability.

Unlike some parliamentary democracies, the legislatures of the Scandinavian countries are well organized and staffed to exercise oversight of the government and its bureaucracy. In particular, they have legislative committees specialized by policy field that can exercise oversight of ministries (Mattson 2016) In addition, Norway, Sweden, and Iceland have powerful committees with general competence to oversee the operations of government. This capacity for parliamentary supervision is perhaps especially important given the deconcentrated structure of administration in the Scandinavian countries, with agencies operating largely independently from ministries.

Although there are important similarities with the other democratic regimes, there are several particular mechanisms and points of emphasis that distinguish the Scandinavian regimes. The institution of the ombudsman is now widely diffused globally, but this was originally a Swedish invention. While operating through parliament, the power of the ombudsman, and the relative ease of access for citizens, makes this mechanism potentially powerful in controlling the bureaucracy.[8] The ombudsman's office and its staff have the power to investigate any wrongdoing by the administration and to report those directly to parliament.

The ombudsman began as a singular office but has now proliferated into a number of specialized offices responsible for various aspects of public life— especially those affecting children.[9] As the number of ombudsman positions has increased, these institutions have become important for making rules to control both government as well as the private sector. In this process, they offer yet another avenue for the involvement of interest groups in the administrative process. For example, the Swedish Consumer Ombudsman works in conjunction with consumer advocates to mediate in complaints against businesses.

The historical openness of public administration and government in the Scandinavian countries also separates this tradition from others (Hall 2016). Beginning in the late eighteenth century, Sweden allowed public access to the majority of government documents, and that transparency has only increased. Although somewhat more restricted than in Sweden, governments in the other Scandinavian countries are also very open to the public and the press (Jørgensen 2014). The capacity for ordinary citizens and the media to find out easily what is happening in government obviously facilitates all the other instruments for accountability.

Of course, with the adoption of much of the NPM agenda, performance management has been added to the repertoire of control instruments over public administration (Hansen 2011). As noted previously, Scandinavian governments have not been averse to thinking about efficiency in the public sector, if for no other reason than the magnitude of public expenditure and public employment requires some attention to holding down costs. But the

---

[8] While this mechanism has been copied, at least in name, the copies often do not have the rights of access to parliament that the Scandinavian versions of the institution have, nor do citizens always have the right to bring their own cases (see Hongbo 2014).
[9] As noted above, the German ombudsman system is even more differentiated, having offices for (among others) prisoners and members of the armed forces.

advent of NPM has reinforced that commitment to providing efficient public services and also to finding market-based mechanisms for providing public services.

In summary, the Scandinavian administrative systems have strong formal mechanisms to enforce accountability, as well as a long history of openness and transparency. And they function within political cultures with high levels of trust and normative commitments to good governance (Rothstein 2000). While some administrative and political misconduct can be found in any system, no matter how well policed it may be, the Scandinavian systems have had extremely good records of probity and efficiency.

Administrative Reform in Scandinavia

The Scandinavian countries have been second only to the Anglo-American countries in their acceptance of the ideas of NPM, and their willingness to reform their public sectors for (presumably) greater efficiency and effectiveness (see Hansen 2011). For example, although the political and management cultures of these countries have a strong commitment to equality, performance management has become institutionalized in the public sector. The willingness of these essentially social democratic regimes to adopt what many consider to be neo-liberal reforms based on at least some market principles, appears paradoxical, and in many ways is. However, there are also some good reasons for these transformations.

The first reason is that some of the reforms were actually copied from the countries. This is most obvious with the use of agencies (see above) to implement public programs. This model was developed in Sweden in the late eighteenth century and was used to varying degrees in the other Nordic countries. It was then copied (at least in part) by the Thatcher government in the United Kingdom and from there spread throughout the world (Verhoest et al. 2016). Thus, just as we argued that the United States and Canada were not very involved in NPM because they had "old public management" so, too, there was little that Sweden at least had to do to accept this component of NPM.

The second reason for these countries adopting some of the ideas of NPM was that, having very large public sectors, they had a great deal to gain by improving the efficiency of service delivery. While the level of efficiency that can be produced by these reforms is questionable, given the nature of the services that government provides (see Schachter 2007), it makes sense for any government spending as much money as these governments do and delivering such a wide range of programs to seek ways of saving money. Cutting programs would be difficult, but delivering the programs more efficiently would not violate electoral commitments made to citizens.

Third, these reforms were more palatable than might be expected because some of them involve utilizing social actors, including market actors, to deliver public services—the NPM mantra of "steering not rowing." The corporate-pluralist nature of governing in Scandinavia again makes this dimension of administrative reform extremely compatible with these governments. The Nordic countries have been involving social actors for decades so the increased emphasis on delivering programs through non-governmental actors is not all that novel.

Finally, despite the fundamental social democratic nature of these countries, there have been some significant political changes over the past several decades. Although a social democratic party, alone or more often in coalition, has formed the government in these countries for most of the time since the 1920s (Table 5.2), there were breakthroughs for "bourgeois" parties beginning in the 1980s, and the last several decades have seen numerous governments of the political right. The reforms derived from NPM ideas tend to be more compatible with these governments than with social democratic governments.[10] But social democratic governments were not averse to greater efficiency in the public sector, given the great costs of the welfare state and growing resistance to taxation (Callaghan and Tunney 2001).

Further, there is some evidence that the social and cultural foundations of the Scandinavian model of governance have been weakening. The very fact of elections of center-right parties in governments in all three countries is indicative of some change. And, in addition to the mainstream parties of right, there have also been significant levels of voting for populist parties of

Table 5.2 Declining organizational participation

	Union membership (% of labor force)						
	1970	1980	1990	2000	2005	2010	2015
Denmark	60.3	78.0	78.6	73.6	71.9	69.2	68.6
Norway	56.8	57.9	58.5	54.1	54.7	53.6	52.5
Sweden	67.7	78.0	81.1	78.0	75.7	68.2	67.0

Source: OECD (2018).

---

[10] That said, the first major adopter of these reforms was the Labour government in New Zealand in the early 1980s.

the more extreme right (e.g., 17.5 percent for the Sweden Democrats in 2018). Nationalist, anti-immigrant politics are also to some extent related to neo-liberal economic and social policies that correspond to the general market orientation of NPM.

Conclusion

The administrative traditions within the Scandinavian countries present a number of contradictions and paradoxes, at least when compared with what would be the conventional wisdom in policy and administration. The conventional image of the Scandinavian state is as a strong service provider attempting to create equality across the country. These policy intentions might be thought to be connected to an *étatiste* style of governing that would depend heavily on a Weberian-style bureaucracy and relatively rigid style of administration. These stereotypes may be a good place to begin understanding the Scandinavian tradition, but they are not a very good place to end the process of understanding how governance works in these countries.

All the administrative traditions that I have been discussing in this book have internal complexities and have evolved over time, but the Scandinavian tradition appears to be perhaps the most complex and the one with the greatest internal contradictions. This is true for the mixture of policies as well as for the manner in which policies are administered. As one example, here are a set of nations that have been the classic examples of the welfare state but at the same time have active labor market policies designed to get people back to work rather than receiving unemployment benefits.

The examples of paradoxes and contradictions for the administration of policies are more numerous. For example, these countries have had long-standing commitments to equality for all citizens but yet have very decentralized forms of administration, and strong local governments, often resulting in regional differences and an apparent absence of equality. Likewise, policymaking is extremely inclusive and even despite some decline of the corporatist model still permits substantial influence by interest groups. At the same time, however, the separation of policymaking and implementation organizations within government appears to exclude some important actors from several aspects of these roles.

With all of these various paradoxes and contradictions, how can governance work and, especially, how can it work as effectively as it appears to in these countries? One of the answers is that some elements of the political culture are sufficiently pervasive to allow a number of paradoxes to exist without the system becoming dysfunctional. These elements include commitments to equality and "good governance." The other answer is that some of the paradoxes may be more apparent than real. But whatever may be true, the administrative tradition in Scandinavia is more complex than a simple story about social democracy and the welfare state might lead one to assume. As Bo Rothstein (2000, 2004), among others, has pointed out, governance in contemporary Sweden, and by extension the other Scandinavian countries, cannot be understood without understanding its past. That is, of course, the fundamental point behind looking at administrative traditions.

6

The Anglo-American Tradition

By nationality and by inclination I might have been expected to consider the Anglo-American tradition before the other three discussed in this volume. But in many ways this tradition is the least clear, and the most difficult to argue for a common foundation for administration in all the countries represented within the collection of countries usually assigned to this tradition. While certainly there are some common intellectual foundations and some common patterns of public administration, there are also some very fundamental differences. In some ways it is easier to argue that the American and the Westminster traditions of government diverge more than they converge. Despite the differences, however, there does appear to be sufficient commonality to consider this as one pattern of public administration, albeit one that requires numerous caveats and footnotes. Those caveats become more numerous when the tradition is considered within the members of the "Old Commonwealth" such as Canada and the Antipodes.

The Anglo-American Tradition

The shelves of academic libraries in both the United Kingdom and the United States are filled with dissertations and books written with the assumption that the British and American governments are somehow similar and therefore readily comparable. The assumption is that there is a common political tradition and style of governing that somehow overcomes the numerous other differences between the two systems. There are also a large number of academic studies comparing the United Kingdom with Canada or other Westminster systems (see Wilson 1994), or comparing those Westminster systems themselves, and even those may require some leaps of faith to assume a basic similarity (see Grube and Howard 2016).

Although they are sometimes presented as similar cases, in many ways the United States and the United Kingdom are most different systems.[1] The

[1] This is using the terminology of Teune and Przeworski (1970) concerning the logic of case selection in comparative analysis.

Administrative Traditions: Understanding the Roots of Contemporary Administrative Behavior. B. Guy Peters, Oxford University Press (2021). © B. Guy Peters. DOI: 10.1093/oso/9780198297253.003.0006

structural differences are clear. One spans a continent with a history of westward expansion and "Manifest Destiny" (Heider and Heider 2003), while the other is a small island with a history of expansion through colonization. One is federal and the other unitary, albeit experiencing a significant devolution of authority to the component units of the country (Bogdanor 2001). One is presidential and the other parliamentary. The question then becomes, are there sufficient similarities to justify an argument that there is an underlying state and administrative tradition that produces common behaviors in public administration, and in governance more generally?

The notion of a single Anglo-American political and administrative tradition may itself appear to be an over-extension of this concept, given the apparent diversity of the systems included in this category. It is rather conventional to discuss the existence of a Westminster tradition existing among the United Kingdom and parliamentary systems that have their institutional roots in the British Empire (Campbell and Wilson 1995; Rhodes et al. 2009). It is very easy to identify British roots in the administrative systems one encounters in Canada, Australia, and New Zealand, not to mention India, Pakistan, Trinidad, and a host of other former colonies (see Chapter 8). Many of the patterns persist after several decades of extensive administrative reforms, especially through New Public Management (NPM) reforms in the Antipodes (and the United Kingdom).[2]

The early departure of the United States from direct British influence, and its adoption of a presidential form of government, might make it appear to reside far outside the common heritage. Further, on some (but not all) of the dimensions of variation we will discuss in this chapter, the United States may lie at one end of the distribution of countries, while the United Kingdom resides at the other end. Likewise, Ireland left the British Empire under less than cordial terms but it has retained much of the Westminster pattern of governing, and administering policy. Despite those differences, we will argue that there is sufficient common ground in the administrative thought and practice in these systems (see Self 1973; Tayeb 1988) to argue that they do partake of a common heritage. Further, we will also be arguing that the administrative arrangements of these countries have substantially more in common than do other aspects of governance.

This greater similarity of administration than other aspects of governance may be explained in part through historical institutionalism. The concept of

---

[2] There has been some debate over the extent to which New Zealand and other Westminster systems reasserted the older Westminster system after NPM reforms (see Lodge and Gill 2011).

"path dependency" employed by historical institutionalists (e.g., Thelen and Steinmo 1992) to explain (or at least describe) the persistence of policy regimens across time can be used to describe the way in patterns present at the founding of a system persist despite fundamental political changes. Although that underlying path may be altered in part by layering or displacement (Mahoney and Thelen 2010a), some of the basic understandings and institutional patterns that existed at the time of formation of institutions may persist in the institutional DNA for administration. Gerard Roland (2004), for example, discussed the differences between "fast"-moving institutional changes in political institutions as opposed to the "slow" changes occurring in cultures and social patterns. We will be arguing that, despite differences, the slower-changing institutions of administration retain some important similarities.

The persistence of administrative patterns may also be explained by the relative invisibility of public administration when compared with other institutions of government. Very few political movements have been organized because of inefficient bureaucracies, or the failure of public administration to attain a Weberian ideal.[3] Citizens may complain about the bureaucracy but constitutional change rarely if ever arises from that grousing, Indeed, constitutions rarely mention public administration but their drafters appear to assume that these structures will emerge from necessity, and that those emergent institutions will conform to the usual expectations for administration in the particular society.

One of the best examples of this divergence of political structures and administrative structures can be seen in the countries of Latin America. After the Bolivarian revolutions, and the other revolts against Spanish and Portuguese rule, these countries adopted political systems that were heavily influenced by the American presidential system (Gargarella 2004). Their administrative systems, on the other hand, continue to be influenced by the colonial past of a highly legalistic and formal administrative system (see Chapter 8). The administrative systems also reflect a French influence, imported at the time of independence. That style of administration persists despite numerous reforms in government and in administration (Ramirez 2009), while political institutions have been altered significantly over the years.

In this chapter I will be discussing the two versions—British and American—of one tradition together, rather than building a major case and

---

[3] The one exception may be the populist movement in the twenty-first century that has focused in part on the "Deep State" and the linkage of the bureaucracy with other political system elites (see Bauer et al. forthcoming; Peters and Pierre 2019).

then discussing variations from it in a minor case. The manners in which public administration is practiced in these two systems are such that the differences may outweigh the similarities. Making the contrasts, and then looking for perhaps more subtle similarities, may be more appropriate for these two than the pattern followed in the other chapters.[4] Where relevant, I will also discuss the administrative systems of Westminster systems such as Canada, Australia, and New Zealand, and other systems with a Westminster heritage. There are, of course, many other governments that have been influenced by this model of administration through colonialism, but they will be discussed in Chapter 9.

State and Society I

The most fundamental dimension for comparison is the relationship assumed to exist between state and society in each of these countries. The most useful way of characterizing this relationship within the Anglo-American tradition is as "contractual," with there being some form of tacit, or even more explicit, bargain concerning the creation and maintenance of the mechanisms for governing. In such a conception of the state there is a social contract between government and its citizens, with the aggregation of citizens being the more significant and enduring entity. Indeed, the public may be conceptualized not so much as a collectivity—society—as it is as a collection of individuals who have natural rights. While prime minister of the United Kingdom, Margaret Thatcher may have voiced the most extreme version of this statement, arguing that "there is no such thing as society."[5]

In the Anglo-American tradition this conception of the relationship between state and society can be seen in the work of notable British political theorists such as John Locke (Dienstag 1996), and to a lesser extent Thomas Hobbes (Hampton 1986).[6] Although both of these theorists assume that the state arises from a contract between members of society and the government in order to facilitate some forms of collective action, Locke and Hobbes have

---

[4] The methodology implicit here is that of most different system designs in which one accepts the multiple differences but looks for similarities that exist despite the large differences among administrative systems.

[5] Interview in *Women's Own* magazine, October 31, 1987. While she was stressing the need for individual self-reliance vis-à-vis government, the point was that what we might call society is no more than individuals with rights and responsibilities.

[6] Jean-Jacques Rousseau was, of course, a significant contract philosopher in France, writing at roughly the same time as Locke and Hobbes.

rather different perspectives on the nature of individuals within that society. Hobbes's has a more pessimistic perspective related to a more authoritarian conception of the state that must be created. Locke's conception of society was more positive, assuming that limited government would be sufficient to maintain order and allow for individual development. This contractarian strand of thinking about state and society has persisted in political philosophy, being reflected in part in the work of John Rawls (see Freeman 2009) and David Gauthier (1986).

The influence of contract theory can be seen very clearly in the American Declaration of Independence and the Constitution of the United States.[7] Likewise, the Constitution of the Commonwealth of Virginia that Thomas Jefferson wrote at approximately the same time as the Declaration of Independence contained rather similar contractual language, arguing again that King George had violated the social contract between the citizens and his government. Perhaps most fundamentally, the people (individually and collectively) were argued to be the source of all powers for governing. The state was a much more fleeting entity than society, or even more importantly for Jefferson, the individual.

As we have already demonstrated in greater detail in previous chapters, the organic conceptions characteristic of Continental European systems political systems is in sharp contrast to this version of relationship between state and society (see pp. 26–30). In such an organic understanding of the relationship between state and society the two entities are inextricably bound together. In the Anglo-American conceptualization, and to some extent for all contractarian models of government, society tends to precede the state, and by implication is the superior party in the relationship. Again, the language of the Declaration of Independence, claiming the right of the people to eliminate any government that is inimical to their best interests, is a clear statement of the priority of society, or at least the priority of the individuals within that society.

The relationship between state and society has direct implications for the position of the public bureaucracy in governing. The most important implication is that in an organic conception of these relationships the civil servant becomes the embodiment of the state, and hence is more than an employee or

---

[7] For example, the phrase "…governments are instituted among men, deriving their just powers from the consent of the governed" is a clear statement of the contractual version of state and society relationships. Likewise, the preamble to the Constitution argues that "We the People do ordain and establish this Constitution," even though the state governments were in reality more direct participants in establishing the federal government than were the people.

even a "servant," although that is the term used in translation.[8] In this more organic conception of the role of the senior public employee,[9] holding a position of authority and public trust in government commands respect simply by being in the social position of a member of the state. In a contractarian state, the civil service is essentially an instrument with no higher moral authority, and hence can be readily reformed and manipulated by political actors (Knill 1999).

Although there are many common aspects to state–society relationships in the Anglo-American democracies, there are also some marked differences. As implied in the above discussion, the United States is probably the most clearly contractual of this set of democracies. This contractual stance is to some extent a function of the generally anti-state foundation of American government as well as the continuing pattern of resistance to *étatisme* of any sort (at least at the federal level). In the American conception of state and society the state appears very much an afterthought, although perhaps not so much as some scholars have argued.[10] As H. G. Wells argued in 1906 (quoted in Skowronek 1982), Americans fundamentally have no sense of the state. In administrative terms, members of the American civil service therefore have had little of the respect and status accorded to their counterparts in most other Anglo-American systems.

The American link between state and society was to some extent complicated by the informality of governance in the early days of the republic. While there was a small federal government in Philadelphia and then Washington (see White 1948) concerned mainly with defense, delivering mail, and tax collection,[11] most government activity was at the state and local level, and these governments were hardly differentiated from their societies. Governance through town meetings in New England, with little or no professional staff, meant that to some extent the local state and the society were the same. On the frontier, local governance was often even less formal, depending upon volunteer labor rather than public employees.

That said, even very early in life of the federal government there was an attempt to create a state, albeit one that was more dependent upon society

---

[8] The German term *Beamte* has the connotation of one who occupies a state position, has a high social status and has an almost judicial role in the making and implementation of public policy.

[9] It is important to focus here on the senior positions given that lower-echelon employees are hired often under ordinary labor law rather than under any particular statutes conferring particular status.

[10] Stillman (1996), for example, has argued that the United States was a "stateless society" in which government continues to have relatively little impact on social and economic development.

[11] In 1802, the US federal government employed only approximately 4,000 people.

and upon the constituent states than is true for most contemporary states. For example, the Northwest Ordinance of 1787 extended control of the new republic over the lands west of the Ohio River, establishing local governance, land rights, and a mechanism for admitting new states (see Duffy 1995). Later, the federal government used its vast land resources to promote both settlement of the West and the expansion of the railroads, as well as homesteading by new settlers. While by no means a developmental state when compared to the "Little Tigers" in Asia, or even with France, the American state did intervene in the economy and society to promote economic change.

The antithesis of this rather stateless perspective on governing in the United States is best characterized by the United Kingdom, and perhaps even more so by the Republic of Ireland. Although the term "state" figures rarely in British political parlance (Johnson 2000), the term "Crown" may well be a reasonable substitute. The Crown is taken to represent the enduring aspects of government, so that instead of acting for *raison d'état*, governments may be acting in the name of the Crown. Even with the reduction of the effective role of the monarchy, the notion of the Crown is a glue that can provide the means of justifying actions by the government of the day. The Irish Republic certainly abandoned the Crown when it achieved independence, but its republican form of government demonstrates a commitment to a more *étatiste* model of governing.[12]

The government of the United Kingdom may exist because of a contract, but in practice it is a strong state, much stronger than that of the United States at most times. In at least the Old Tory view of governing (Beer 1969), a strong state was necessary to preserve society, and to guarantee the rights of the individual. While American versions of individual rights are largely directed *against* the state, the British view has been more one of achieving rights, including economic rights, *through* the state. However, both views of governing are based on the separation of state and society, and the existence of some form of a contract to create governance.

Management and Law

Another fundamental dimension to consider when characterizing administrative traditions is the relative position of law and management in defining the role of the administrator. That is, does the education and training of an

---

[12] The emphasis on the state in Ireland may be explicable in part as a post-colonial state attempting to emphasize its own "stateness" after years of control by another power. See Keogh (2005).

administrator—especially a senior administrator—predispose him or her to think first about the legal character of an administrative issue, or to consider how to manage the organization to achieve specified policy ends? Likewise, does the public servant conceptualize the role of the administrator as one obeying and defending laws, or as making things happen? Of course, rather few public administrators would willfully violate the law, but the question is whether this is their primary consideration.[13]

In a broader comparative context, Anglo-American administrative systems can be characterized as emphasizing management rather than law in the performance of public tasks. This statement should not be taken to imply that illegality is favored, or even tolerated, but only that legal issues tend to be considered as a matter for legal experts rather than line managers. Thus, lawyers tend to be kept in separate bureaus within line departments and are called upon when needed for specific advice. Those line managers are interested primarily in designing programs and getting their programs implemented, taking legal advice as and when necessary.

If anything, this managerial dimension of public administration in Anglo-American countries has been strengthened during the past several decades as the ideas of managerialism and NPM have assumed paramount importance in most of this group. Indeed, it is not by accident that NPM has had its most visible successes in the Anglo-American democracies, notably New Zealand, Australia, and the United Kingdom. That said, the increased emphasis on management has tended to de-emphasize the policymaking role of senior civil servants in Westminster systems (see pp. 134–6).

Even if we accept that Anglo-American democracies have been the heartland of managerialism, there are also marked differences in the adoption of NPM within this set of countries. In particular, the two North American members of the group stand in marked contrast to the others in the extent to which they have accepted relatively little of the managerialist paradigm during the late twentieth century. The United States and Canada perhaps shifted away less from the more traditional style of governing (see Savoie 1994), but to the extent that change occurred there was a shift away from their managerial past.

That "traditional" style for North American governments was itself quite managerial when compared to the legalism of most Continental European systems, or most systems in Ibero-America, but had less of the emphasis on

---

[13] But sabotage of government programs can be an option available to civil servants who disagree with the government of the day (see Brehm and Gates 1997; Olsson 2016).

private sector techniques and market principles that characterizes most contemporary approaches to public management. The United States and Canada had less need for NPM because they had "old public management," going back to at least the Brownlow Committee in the United States (Newbold and Rosenbloom 2007) and Royal Commissions such as Glassco and Lambert in Canada (Hodgetts 2007). Various public administration reforms had already instilled some of the ideas of private sector management in the public sector long before NPM became popular.

The more traditional management style in these countries did have a strong managerial component, but emphasized control over inputs rather than outputs, and tended to stress (especially in Canada) the separation of a public service career from the private sector. That separation of the public and the private also emphasized the differences between public and private management, despite pressure from numerous reformers, and the very different nature of the tasks being undertaken in the two sectors. Rather than stressing a more activist form of management, this traditional style was more concerned with probity and accountability than with public entrepreneurship. Some reforms in Canada tended to reduce the separation of public and private careers, but again without as strong an emphasis on private sector techniques as in the United Kingdom and the Antipodes.

Of all the Anglo-American democracies the United States may have the greatest emphasis on legalism in public administration, although that is certainly rather minor when compared to, for example, Germany or France. This relative emphasis on legal principles in administration may reflect the general legalism of the culture, and the need of the public sector to defend itself from encroachment by private sector legal actors (Kagan 2001). The commitment to law appears, however, to run deeper. One obvious manifestation of that commitment is the Administrative Procedures Act of 1946, and the codification of the manner in which the public bureaucracy had to perform its tasks, especially in rule-making and rule adjudication (Freedman 1980; Mashaw 1985; Kerwin and Furlong 2019). None of the other Anglo-American systems has gone nearly so far in codifying administrative practice, or in the specification of the relationship of administrative powers to political power. The other systems have developed legal principles about these procedures (see Baldwin 1996; Page 2001; Bouchard and Carroll 2008), but have relatively little formal legislation that institutionalizes those procedures.

The emphasis on legal remedies in the United States, compared with the other Anglo-American democracies, can also be seen in labor–management relations. In the United Kingdom and the other Anglo democracies, most disputes over wages, working conditions, and so on within the public sector are managed by collective bargaining with often powerful public sector unions. In the United States some of these same issues at the federal level may be determined in the courts (see Bach and Givan 2011). At state and local levels, however, unions are strong and are engaged in collective bargaining with those governments.

The other dimension of legalism that is important in understanding the differences among these systems is the existence of a formalized constitution, especially when that constitution embodies federalism and/or a notion of the rights of citizens. Thus, on this dimension the United States and Canada have the most clearly legalist systems, with both of those principles enshrined in constitutional documents (Smithey 1996). On the other hand, two of the other systems, and especially the United Kingdom, are content to function with less elaborate constitutional structures and more limited conception of individual rights. This concept of rights is significant in defining the legalism of an administrative system, even if that legalism has somewhat different ramifications when compared to the codification of German or French systems. Specifically, although New Zealand does not have a formal constitution it has adopted an extensive bill of rights that has constitutional status, as well as several other basic laws.[14]

The Career Model

The standard model of the public servant, going back to Max Weber among other sources, is an individual who will spend their entire career within the public service. These public servants will be hired on the basis of merit determined through examinations or credentials, and their career will continue to be managed through those merit principles. The logic of this approach to the public service is to create a cadre of professionals who know how to make the machinery of government function and who will be motivated by public service values rather than economic gain.

Although this pattern of recruitment is now largely characteristic of the Anglo-American democracies, it was actually rather late in coming. Only in the nineteenth century did the United States and the United Kingdom begin to institutionalize a merit system for recruiting public servants, and the full

---

[14] The Treaty of Waitangi has served as a fundamental document since its signing in 1840 by the indigenous peoples.

adoption of this personnel system took even longer (Davis 2006). In some of the American states, a merit system was not fully institutionalized until the mid-twentieth century, and in some cities is still extremely weak. This aspect of administration was somewhat later in being institutionalized than were others, and as I will point out below is still contested in part.

Another dimension of the career model for public servants is the pattern of work assignments throughout their career. One generalist style would be to consider public servants a mobile resource within the public sector and to move them around within the system. This not only broadens the individual's horizons but also helps coordinate the public sector (Peters 2015). The alternative pattern is to hire specialists who are likely to remain within a single department, or even single agency, for their entire career. The logic here is to foster specialization and develop an organizational memory. The United States stands out in this group of countries for recruiting public servants with specialized skills and having career patterns that also tend to be specialized.

There are three major exceptions to this general pattern of careers. The most obvious is the United States, which has been unlike the other Anglo-American democracies in two important respects. The first is that some 4,000 or more positions at the top of the federal bureaucracy are filled by political appointees. In the other Anglo-American democracies, most of these positions would be filled by career public servants. The general quality of the appointees into these positions had been improving since World War II,[15] but the positions became more politicized during the administration of George W. Bush, and especially during that of Donald Trump (Drezner 2018).

The second major exception has come about because of the influence of NPM. As already mentioned, one of the tenets of NPM was that public and private management were essentially the same (but see Allison 1980), The argument from advocates went further, arguing for the opening up of government to managers from the private sector, for short- or even long-term positions. The assumption was that this would improve the quality of management within government, through competition for positions (if for no other reason). That assumption was largely untested, but what this change in the personnel system did do was to devalue the experience of career public servants.

The third major shift in these personnel systems—increased politicization—was facilitated by the opening of the career system. I will discuss this in

---

[15] The appointees may have been political, but they also were members of policy networks. While their party was not in office they would be working in think tanks, consulting firms, and universities, ready to come back into government (see, e.g., Durant 2016).

more detail in the following section of this chapter, but beginning at least in the Reagan/Thatcher/Mulroney period politicians became more skeptical of the civil service and wanted greater political influence over their advisors. This led to more political appointments at the top of the service, and the addition of increasing numbers of political and policy advisors outside the civil service (Savoie 1994; Eichbaum and Shaw 2008; Connaughton 2015). These political appointments especially diminished the policy role of senior public servants, and more generally reduced their influence over governance.

In short, the relatively recent development of the career civil servant in the Anglo-American countries continues to be threatened. The threats come in part from those who assume that the quality of personnel in government is not as high as in the private sector and want to enhance the management capacity of government, Additional threats come from those (sometimes the same people) who want to ensure political control over a potentially independent civil service (O'Leary 2013; Olsson 2016). However, despite those continuing threats, the idea of a merit-based career and apolitical civil service continues to be the standard expectation in Anglo-American democracies.

Politicians and Bureaucrats

Following from the discussion of administrative careers, another dimension defining the nature of an administrative tradition is the relationship between political and administrative roles. The most basic question here is the extent to which bureaucratic and political roles are incompatible, and whether the two sets of actors are competitors for power. The tradition in Anglo-American administration has been that those roles are indeed incompatible, with the political neutrality of the public service being a cardinal principle of traditional Westminster political systems. This dichotomy has meant that both the political and the administrative sides of governing have had some protection from meddling by the other. The civil service could claim that their decisions were not political and that there was excessive involvement in appointment and placement of civil servants. Likewise, politicians could demand that their prerogatives in making policy decisions should be respected and, although the civil service did have an influence, that they could claim responsibility/credit for policy design.

As already implied, the dichotomy between politics and administration has sometimes been more implied and theoretical than it has been genuine. Certainly, there was a professional civil service in all of these countries and there has been a well-developed merit system that controlled the majority of positions in government. That having been said, however, civil servants often have been political actors, whether their actions were to defend the perquisites and prerogatives of the civil service as an institution or to promote the interests of the particular organizations for which they worked. Further, civil servants have been a major source of policy advice for their political "masters," with the consequence that they have in many instances actually been able to control policy, rather than merely its implementers.

For much of recent history, the United States has had perhaps the least adherence to this aspect of the Anglo-American tradition. While there certainly has been a career civil service that covers the vast majority of federal employees, the upper-level management and policymaking positions in government have been filled by political appointment (see Hollibaugh 2015). On average, a president and his cabinet secretaries have had opportunities to fill several thousand positions in the federal bureaucracy, generally subject to confirmation by the Senate. The number of appointments in the United States available for political assignment has been increasing over the past several decades. First, the Senior Executive Service created under President Carter made some positions that had been careerist available for political appointment. Further, there has been a gradual accretion of the number of political posts, what Paul Light (1995) refers to as the "thickening" of government (see also Ingraham et al. 1995; Lewis 2007).

Most of the other Anglo-American systems also have become more open to political appointment since the 1980s, in part as a result of managerialism and in part as a result of conscious politicization of the civil service (Clifford and Wright 1997). First, adoption of managerialist conceptions of governing broke down dominance of the career civil service in these countries and opened many managerial positions to appointments that could be used for political advantage, although most participants would claim that merit principles were still the dominant consideration. Thus, managers might be hired to fill positions in newly created public sector agencies first because they were good managers and second because they were politically sympathetic to the government.[16] The opening of top managerial positions therefore has had the consequence of making the civil service a much less distinctive career in most Anglo-American political systems.

---

[16] It was argued, for example, that Mrs. Thatcher was less interested in political party affiliation than in whether the individual in question wanted to create more efficient, and smaller, government. This is what appeared to have been meant by those public servants being "one of us" (Hennessy 1989).

There also has been some more overt political use of positions in the public sector. One important example was the Mulroney government in Canada (Savoie 1994: 100–2), which created positions such as "chief of staff" within ministries and enabled ministers to set up political structures that to some extent mirrored the career structure of the civil service. More recently, the Blair government in Great Britain created many more positions of "special advisors" (SPADs) to ministers, and expanded the Prime Minister's Office and the Cabinet Office in order to be able to impose the will of political components of government over the ministerial system. These changes continued under subsequent Conservative governments. Further, appointments to quangos and other non-departmental bodies are increasingly filled by political appointees (Skelcher 1997; Vibert 2007). In Australia and New Zealand senior managerial positions in government are now considered by many commentators to be subject to manifestly political appointment, or at least subject to a great deal of overt political pressure (Craft 2015).

In summary, the political neutrality of the civil service in Anglo-American countries is now under a great deal of pressure. This pressure is to some extent a reaction to earlier reforms, and the loss of ministerial control over implementation of programs for which they are nominally responsible. It appears that, increasingly, political leaders in these systems fail to trust their public servants and seek ever increasing levels of control. Further, many recent governments in these countries have considered themselves as agents of change, with the associated need to have committed agents implementing those changes. Thus, the struggles required over decades to build the concept of "neutral competence" in the public service in Anglo-American democracies appear to have been forgotten and politicians are now willing to use their power to impose their own conception of good government. Further, once the civil service is politicized, subsequent governments are likely to think that it is necessary to introduce their own people in order to counteract the influence of the previous government.

That said, the civil service has not been totally quiescent, and has at times sought to reassert its independence. This pursuit of independence has been especially true in the United States when presidents whom the public bureaucracy have considered to have ideas contrary to the national interest, and their own interest, have engaged in a form of guerilla warfare with the president and his appointees. The most obvious example of this has been in the Trump administration, in departments such as the Environmental Protection Agency and the Bureau of Land Management (Kamisar 2017).

Uniformity

The tradition of Anglo-American democracies has been to permit a good deal of variation in law and administration within their territories. For example, in the United States and Canada the French inheritance of parts of the country results in marked differences in the content and style of governing in those regions. Likewise, the federal structure of Canada, Australia, and the United States means that there will be some marked differences in policy and administration, even without as great cultural differences as found in Quebec and Louisiana. This tradition of diversity, and substantial levels of autonomy for states and provinces, is in marked contrast to countries such as France that have attempted to create rather extreme levels of uniformity within their territories.[17] This diversity reflects in part the absence of the legalism that motivates much of administration in Continental European countries.

The three unitary regimes in this group of countries—the United Kingdom, Ireland, and New Zealand—have been less willing to permit variations in administration within their territories, although in the United Kingdom the legal systems in place in Scotland and Northern Ireland are substantially different from those found in England and Wales. Further, Northern Ireland has long had a separate civil service for implementing provincial-level policies, and with devolution the same autonomy will be characteristic of Scotland and (to a lesser extent) Wales. New Zealand and Ireland are more distinctive cases among these countries in maintaining a high level of uniformity across the country. Even there, however, the increasing autonomy granted to Maori bands to some extent undermines the uniformity in this system.

The United Kingdom is the most interesting of these cases in terms of the acceptance of policy and administrative diversity. On the one hand, as we have already pointed out, devolution has increased latitude for action for several regions of the United Kingdom. In addition, the creation of a large number of quangos and other quasi-public organizations has resulted also in increased diversity in the administration of policies in Britain (Hogwood et al. 2000). On the other hand, within England (and to some extent within the devolved administrations) there has been increasing centralization and control over the actions of local authorities. That centralization of control over local authorities began during the Thatcher government and has tended to increase since that time (see Copus et al. 2017).

---

[17] This tradition, too, is changing, with substantial decentralization in France (d'Arcy 1996), and even greater movement away from uniformity in Spain and Italy (Alba and Navarro 2011).

The case of the United Kingdom makes the role of public finance in promoting or permitting differences among components of the country more evident. In the United Kingdom local authorities receive the large majority of their income from grants from central government, and have little or no discretion over how they collect the small additional revenue that they do receive from their own sources. This control became very evident during conflict over the introduction of the "poll tax" during the Thatcher government (Butler et al. 1994). This latitude for subnational governments to make their own fiscal decisions is more evident in most of the Anglo-American democracies than in most other administrative traditions, with Scandinavian countries being the only other group of political systems approaching this level of financial autonomy.

The absence of uniformity in administration raises the question of the degree of inequality that can be permitted in these administrative systems while still maintaining adherence to basic democratic values. Even in those countries such as the United States and Canada that do have formal, written constitutional documents, those documents tend to focus as much on the limits on central governments in enforcing equality over the constituent units as they are about generating equality for individual citizens. The Fourteenth Amendment to the United States Constitution does guarantee "equal protection of the laws" to citizens, and the Charter of Rights and Freedoms in Canada has similar provisions, but these are additions to documents that tend to provide for geographical diversity as much as individual equality. Indeed, a major component of the logic of federalism is to permit and even promote differences among the components of the larger system (see Hueglin and Fenna 2016). That diversity is especially evident in the rights given to First Canadians and Native Americans to govern their own lands and peoples through their own laws and customs.

The popularity of NPM may accentuate any tendencies toward inequality in the Anglo-American democracies. First, if the market is to be an exemplar of good management and good public policy then accepting that idea is accepting a model based on inequality of outcomes—winners and losers—in how the public sector should function. Internal markets as a means of allocating resources in policy domains such as health care, and performance pay as a means of rewarding participants in government, may possibly enhance the performance of government (Jerome-Forget et al. 1995). Those same attributes also may enhance the inequality of outcomes for citizens in these countries—citizens, in fact, are often redefined as "consumers" of programs. Also, if the more participatory approach to reform is accepted, then differential capacities at participation are likely to produce differential outcomes for different social groups. The lack of strong commitments to legal equality in program delivery is one more manifestation of the absence of a strong conception of uniformity in the public sector in this set of countries.

State and Society II

One of the starkest differences between the Anglo-American administrative tradition and the other traditions reflects a different role for social actors in this tradition than in at least two of the others. Relationships between interest groups and the state in the Anglo-American tradition are usually defined as pluralist, as opposed to the corporatist arrangements in the Germanic and Scandinavian traditions. As already noted, these relationships in the Napoleonic tradition are somewhat ambiguous.

The pluralist approach to interest intermediation does not regard interest groups as legitimate representatives of segments of society, as is true in the corporatist model of interest intermediation. Rather, in the pluralist approach, interest groups are outsiders and must compete for access to government in order to influence policy. In this view the state, rather than being a party to negotiations with interests, is primarily an arena within which those interests compete for influence. Further, although neo-pluralists do recognize significant power imbalances, the assumption for most pluralist thinking is that any group can win in the political struggle, and that wins will tend to be short-lived.

The pluralist conception of the role of interest groups corresponds well to the contractual nature of the state in Anglo-American political thought. In this conception, the state is not bound by its ties to society but can behave more autonomously. This does not mean that society is not in the end the superior entity, but it does mean that until society chooses to act the state can be independent of society and social actors. But this does not necessarily imply that the state itself has a particular interest involved in negotiating with social interests, as would be true in corporatist conceptions of the state.

While within pluralism the state per se may not have interests when negotiating with interest groups, the public bureaucracy may. Pluralism implies that interest groups must compete for access to government, and that their power will be balanced over time. However, within single-policy domains there may be close relationships between particular interest groups and the bureaucratic agencies. Rather than engaging in open bargaining among interests, as in corporatism, there tends to be a more symbiotic relationship between interests and the agencies. The interest groups want access and policies that support them, and the agencies need political support for their budgets and their policy proposals.

While exclusive relationships between groups and agencies have been reduced somewhat with the growth of policy networks and epistemic communities (Goldsmith and Kettl 2009), these relationships remain closer and more exclusive than in most other consolidated democracies. And at least in the United States under the Trump administration there has been some tendency to make the relationships even more exclusive. Advisory groups for government agencies such as the Environmental Protection Agency and the Food and Drug Administration have excluded individuals and groups who do not agree with the administration's position (USGAO 2019).

Accountability

Finally, all political systems must have some means of holding their public bureaucracy accountable. While all democratic systems utilize a variety of mechanisms to enforce accountability, each also has particular favorite mechanisms for achieving that end. The choice of mechanisms is generally embedded in the administrative DNA of the system, and reflects not only administrative traditions but also broader constitutional and legal frameworks that shape governing and the relationships among institutions.

For the Anglo-American systems there has been a pronounced emphasis on the role of the legislature in enforcing accountability. On this dimension of the tradition, the Anglo and the American versions of this tradition are relatively similar. In the United Kingdom the principle of parliamentary sovereignty means that the cabinet and public administration are ultimately accountable to parliament for their actions. In the United States the presidentialist system produces dual control over the bureaucracy, with Congress competing with politicians in the executive to control public administration (Rosenbloom 2001).

But although the principle of parliamentary responsibility is enshrined in the unwritten British constitution, there have been changes in that model that have lessened the capacity of parliaments to hold the political executive accountable. In particular, the "presidentialization" of politics in all parliamentary regimes (see Poguntke and Webb 2007), including the United Kingdom, has tended to increase the autonomy of the executive relative to parliaments (but see Dowding 2013). Because of party loyalty and the capacity of party leaders to control the careers of politicians within a party, parliaments have become more like rubber stamps for the executive than sources of accountability. In the United Kingdom, however, debates over Brexit have led to the reassertion of legislative oversight (McConalogue 2020).

The second major change in the reliance on accountability to parliament has been the increasing judicialization of governing in these, and many other countries (Hirschl 2004). Within the Anglo-American cases the United States stands out as having the most developed, or over-developed, system of judicial review. But the other countries have increasingly been adding accountability through judicial action to their repertoire of controls over bureaucracy. The greatest shift has been in the United Kingdom, in large part through the role of the European Court of Justice and the European Court of Human Rights.[18] While there was always recourse to the judiciary for excessive administrative actions, or to prevent actions, the European dimension has added something approaching unconstitutionality concerning administrative actions. The adoption of the Charter of Rights and Freedoms in Canada also made major additions to the role of the judiciary in accountability. As already noted, the Administrative Procedures Act in the United States, and similar statutes in many states, have codified the legal foundation of administrative practice in order to reduce "arbitrary and capricious" actions on the part of public administrators.

NPM has added another dimension of accountability to the Anglo-American administrative systems—one based on performance (Halligan and Bouckaert 2007). The fundamental idea has been to establish indicators of performance—individual and organizational—and to use those to hold the bureaucracy accountable. These performance standards are argued to depoliticize the accountability process and to focus on the actual outputs of government for citizens. While used to some degree in almost all administrative systems, performance management systems have been especially important in the Anglo-American systems, perhaps given the emphasis on management rather than law in public administration.

Why Was Reform Possible?

Perhaps the most remarkable aspect of public administration within the Anglo-American countries is the extent to which these systems have been

---

[18] These two courts have also been involved in major increases in judicial review in the Republic of Ireland.

transformed during the past several decades. From a traditional administrative system founded on the familiar principles of hierarchy, political neutrality, and anonymity of public servants, the public service in most of these countries has been radically transformed. They have become increasingly market-oriented structures with substantially reduced separation from outside political forces (Hennessy 2005). Perhaps especially for the public services in New Zealand and the United Kingdom, the manner in which public adminis-tration was conducted in 2001 seemingly bears little resemblance to what had occurred previously (Walsh and Stewart 1992).

Does the above observation about change and reform negate the import-ance of administrative traditions for understanding public administration in these systems which we have been advocating throughout this volume? It might appear to do so, but I am arguing instead that the reform process, and especially its relative success in these countries when compared to reforms in other traditions such as those more characteristic of Continental Europe, can-not be understood without taking the traditions into account. The concept of tradition is especially important when we attempt to comprehend some of the differences that have occurred *within* this set of countries, with the two North American members of the group taking rather different approaches to reform-ing their administrative systems than have the others. In addition, the Irish state appears to have reformed rather less than any of the other members of this group, whether the reforms are considered as participation or market-driven (Hardiman and MacCarthaigh 2011). Even for the Anglo-American countries taken as a group, some aspects of the tradition help to make the seeming departures from historical patterns more comprehensible.

The most obvious point to be made about the role of traditions in under-standing the reforms is that the majority of the reforms adopted during the past several decades (Peters and Savoie 1998) stress management, and that is a very clear and central component of the Anglo-American administrative trad-ition. In earlier manifestations of public administration operating within this tradition, the perspective on management was to some extent overlaid by emphasis on other aspects of the tradition, for example political neutrality and anonymity (see Schaffer 1973). Still, the concept that public administrators are managers and are responsible for ensuring that programs are delivered is a central component of the Anglo-American tradition. NPM certainly empha-sizes that aspect of the role more strongly than would have the traditional model but it can be argued that this is more a question of degree than of type.

There is a second important approach for understanding that the rather radical reforms of public administration within the Anglo-American democracies do indeed conform to the fundamental ideas of the tradition. This argument is that public administrators are not themselves considered to be virtual components of the state in the way in which they might be within other traditions. The contrast is especially marked with the Germanic trad-ition, in which the role of civil servants has many of the trappings that might be more associated with judges in the Anglo-American tradition, and occupies a particular role within the social system. Certainly, a civil servant in the United Kingdom may be styled as a "servant of the Crown," but yet he or she is not considered a part of the Crown per se. They remain employees who have accepted a particular bargain as a condition of working within their chosen profession. Therefore, changing the status of the public service and individual public employees does not imply the fundamental reordering of political and legal relationships that might be implied in other types of systems.[19]

Following from the above point, we must remember the pragmatic and incremental nature of governing that pervades Anglo-American political sys-tems. In contrast to most Continental political and administrative systems, ideology plays a relatively minor role in Anglo-American politics, and per-haps even less in public administration.[20] This pragmatism is also reflected in the legal system associated with these regimes, with common law in Anglo-American systems being adaptive and evolutionary, in contrast to the greater rigidity of civil law systems (Damaska 1986). Thus, administrative reforms not only do not violate any fundamental conceptualization of the nature of the state system, but their outcomes can be made to fit readily into existing legal principles. As already noted, the somewhat greater legalism and consti-tutionalism in administration in the United States may make reform slightly more difficult, but that is only a relatively minor institutional difference to account for some rather marked differences.

The above having been said, there are some important internal differences among these countries in how acceptable certain types of reform have been. The most interesting case here is the United States, which might have been thought to be the most managerialist of all the regimes but which has adopted somewhat less of the managerialist agenda than most other countries operating within this tradition (Peters 2001b). There are two reasons for this; the first is

---

[19] On the changing nature of the bargain defining the relationship of employer and employee within the British "state" administration, see Hood and Lodge (2006).

[20] Although politicians such as Thatcher and Reagan are typified as "conviction" politicians, their convictions often appear solipsistic rather than ideological. There is a broad vein of neo-liberalism in all these systems but yet their particular policy stances and ideas tend to be more individualistic. On this fundamental difference between Continental and Anglo-American systems, see Sartori (1969).

that the United States (and Canada) has a populist, democratic tradition in governance (see p. 123) that stresses other approaches to administrative reform which depend more on participation by both employees and clients of programs. Some of the managerialist conceptions were adopted in the North American countries, but the emphasis has been on participation by employees and clients of public programs.

The second reason for thinking that the major market-oriented reforms associated with NPM may have had less relevance for the United States is that the prevailing managerial culture has been sufficiently strong that many of these managerialist ideas were already in place, or are simply taken for granted by public as well as private managers. The market-based ideas driving public management were perhaps less visible in the United States than they are now in the United Kingdom and the Antipodes, but they were certainly present—there was an "old public management" that went back at least to the Brownlow Committee under Franklin D. Roosevelt. The long history of commissions dealing with public management (Arnold 1986), and the domination of private sector management ideas in those commissions, produced a culture within government that was more compatible with the private sector than that encountered in most other countries.[21]

Summary and Conclusions

The Anglo-American democracies have developed a distinctive style of administering public policy. That administrative style is a consequence of a variety of social and political forces, having developed over centuries within several different political contexts. The legal and constitutional framework, generally stressing limited government and popular control over political elites, within which public administration is conducted is one several important factors that continues to shape public administration. This framework is associated with the generally contractual understanding of the state in these societies. In addition, the general culture of management and organizational structures in the society as a whole affect the way in which public management is conducted, and the understanding of the role of the civil servant in

---

[21] Most American businessmen would have a difficult time accepting this proposition, believing as they do that government is highly intrusive and out of touch with the needs of the private sector. They lack, of course, any comparative frame of understanding of their good fortune in dealing with the U.S. bureaucracy rather than many others.

governing is similar. These various factors work together to produce a pattern of public management.

Despite some common, and important, similarities in the style of administration among the Anglo-American countries there are also pervasive differences among these systems. One of the most marked contrasts is between the United States and the other regimes that have retained that particular version of parliamentary government usually described as the Westminster system. The presidentialism of the US affects the responsibility and accountability of the bureaucracy, as well as relationships among the major political institutions. In addition to the structural aspects of government, the participatory political culture of the United States is to some extent shared by Canada, a factor that has been important in shaping the reform strategies of these two systems. This emphasis on participation in the reforms—participation by citizens and by administrators—is in marked contrast to the more market-driven reforms encountered in the United Kingdom and the Antipodes.

Thus, understanding administration, and understanding changes in administration, in these or any other set of countries involves balancing the general with the particular. An understanding of the tradition within which any one administrative system is situated provides a major route through which to interpret the behavior of that system. The administrative systems discussed in the several chapters of this book point to numerous similarities in the structure and behavior of governments in these countries, as well as equally relevant differences among them. The concept of traditions used here helps us to understand both the general and the particular among this set of countries, just as similar concepts of traditions can be identified for other groups of countries in the West, and for Confucian regimes in Asia, and for a variety of other patterns of administrative systems. The Anglo-American tradition has been spread not only to these regimes but also to a number of former colonial systems. We can see here how strong the tradition can be, and how it can persist in the face of numerous changes and challenges.

7

The European Union as a Distinctive Tradition?

It appears rather foolish to begin talking about administrative traditions in a government that has been in existence for only just over sixty years. But the bureaucracy of the European Union poses a special challenge for understanding the ways in which administrative traditions function and change, and perhaps are terminated. The six decades of the various manifestation of the European project—EEC, EC, EU—have brought together politicians and administrators from the member states, ranging in number from six to twenty-eight from 1956 to the present. The individuals coming from the member states have brought with them ideas about government that have had to be merged into some more or less common patterns of governing.

The European Union, and specifically the European Commission, is perhaps the ultimate hybrid administrative system. The EU has brought together administrative officials, and therefore administrative traditions, from those twenty-eight member countries. Those countries contain examples of all of the four major European administrative traditions discussed in the preceding chapters, as well as representatives of the Eastern European and even Russian styles (see Chapter 8). Further, for several countries, there has been some influence, albeit perhaps minor, of the Islamic tradition, stemming from their one-time membership of the Ottoman Empire.

The presence of these multiple administrative patterns within the European Union presents at least three alternative outcomes. One possible outcome of the continuing development of the European Union is that the Commission will develop its own distinctive style of doing business. There are good reasons for assuming that such a distinctive style or tradition will emerge, but there are equally good reasons to assume that the style might be a somewhat unpalatable stew of the numerous patterns of administration coming from the member states, and of different internal subdivisions. One should expect the routinization and institutionalization of patterns of behavior within EU structures over time (Silberman 1993), but that institutionalization could be itself fragmented given the internal structures of this and other bureaucracies.

Administrative Traditions: Understanding the Roots of Contemporary Administrative Behavior. B. Guy Peters, Oxford University Press (2021). © B. Guy Peters. DOI: 10.1093/oso/9780198297253.003.0007

An alternative perspective would be that administrative practices within the EU are composed of an amalgam of the traditions of one or more of the constituent "families" of nations already discussed. This alternative, and indeed the first alternative of a distinctive style, are potentially impacted heavily by the changing fads and fashions in the practice of public administration and thus may not be stable over time. In particular, beginning in the late 1970s and continuing (at least to some extent) to the 2020s, New Public Management (NPM) (see Hood 1991; Christensen and Laegreid 2010) has been a continuing source of pressures for changing public administration within the EU and within the member nations (Ellinas and Suleiman 2008).

A third option is that there is no single European Commission style, but rather a variety of internal styles based primarily on the nature of the Directorates General (DGs) that compose the internal structure of the Commission. These would be the equivalent of ministries at the national level. They may develop internal administrative cultures or traditions based on the tasks being performed (Financial Affairs as compared to Health and Food Safety), or on the historical pattern of leadership from particular countries (e.g., the Scandinavian countries and environmental policies), or on the basis of linkages with civil society actors (and national governments).

It is impossible to sort out these alternative patterns without exhaustive in-depth interviews and observation, but at the same time there is a good deal of available evidence about the way in which the administration of the EU functions. This evidence can provide some initial answers. European political science and public administration scholars have been almost obsessed with the development of the EU—with good reason—and have invested a great deal of time and energy attempting to understand how these institutions function and how they shape the behavior of the "Eurocrats." This evidence is in part anecdotal but is also in part systematic, so we can understand these patterns with some degree of confidence.

The Structure of the European Commission

The European Commission is the administrative structure for the European Union. Other institutions within the EU have some administrators (e.g., the policy advice organization for the European Parliament and the General Secretariat for the Council; see Christiansen and Vanhoonacker 2008), but the bulk of public administration for the European Union is located in the Commission. Although organized in some ways as a conventional bureaucracy, it also has a number of distinctive characteristics that affect what the members of the organization do, and how they do it.

First, the Commissioners, the rough equivalent of ministers in a national government, are appointed on the suggestion of national governments, and approved by the European Parliament for a fixed period. And this level of the executive is representative in a sense, with each of the member states having at least one commissioner, although this does give disproportionate representation to smaller member states relative to their populations. There has tended to be some specialization among the countries, with, for example, the Northern European nations frequently having responsibility for the environment and social issues, and France and Spain have dominated agriculture.

Second, a very large proportion of the staff of the Commission is on secondment from national governments. Thus, rather than having its own staff, the Commission is heavily influenced by temporary employees who are presumably good Europeans while in Brussels (or at one of the various European agencies scattered around the Union) but also expect to return to their national bureaucracies. Because their career paths may be more determined by officials at the national level, these seconded officials can be reluctant to become too much the creatures of Brussels (Trondal et al. 2015). Further, the temporary nature of their involvement may make them less easily socialized into a common administrative culture.

Third, the Commission is rather small. Whereas most national bureaucracies—even for small countries—may number in the hundreds of thousands, the Commission employs roughly 33,000 people. This small size is in contrast to the image of a massive Brussels bureaucracy that dominates the governments of the member states. Many of these employers are translators—crucial in an organization that uses twenty-four working languages—so the number of professional employees is very small. Despite the multinational nature of the organization, therefore, the small size can facilitate internal discussion and coordination.

Fourth, unlike most bureaucracies, the European Commission actually does very little implementation. European regulations and directives are implemented largely through the national governments, with the Commission assuming a monitoring role rather than performing the implementation directly themselves. The Commission therefore can remain relatively small when compared to national public administrations (e.g., the Belgian national civil service numbers some 200,000 people[1]) and can remain a policy bureaucracy rather than a more comprehensive public bureaucracy.

Because policymaking is the principal task of the European Commission, some of the differences between it and the upper echelons of national bureaucracies may be reduced. The upper echelons of those national bureaucracies may be more similar than are the structures of public administration as a whole, given that the upper echelons in all systems tend to be more in touch with political leaders and to be more hybrid- and chameleon-like as they negotiate the two worlds of politics and administration. Further, this level of the administration may be experts more concerned with designing effective policy than with the political issues arising from the implementation of those policies.

Fifth, the Commission is divided into the equivalent of ministries called DGs that are responsible for particular policy domains. There are thirty-five of these entities along with service departments and quasi-autonomous European agencies. For a small organization, therefore, there is a good deal of fragmentation that counteracts the possibilities of easy coordination and coherence created by the small size. Like all governments coordination is a problem for the EU, although in this case it may be more a function of institutional design than in many other governments (see Kassim et al. 2000).

Several of the DGs have similar or overlapping policy mandates, creating the possibility or even probability of bureaucratic politics. Although national interests are supposed to be subsumed under the banner of the European project, the interests of various policy domains and their clients are a source of internal political wrangling (Peters 1987). And the individual commissioners—the equivalent of ministers—are more political and also more tied to their national governments. Some of the fragmentation of the Commission is a function of the need to give every member country a commissioner, so that the organization as a whole is perhaps even more divided than it might need to be.

Finally, the European Commission is connected to national government and social actors that have an influence over the policies that are adopted and then implemented. Again, the popular and simplistic image of the Commission is of a remote and powerful bureaucracy, but the procedures for making policy do permit, and often mandate, more involvement from outside the Commission (QuitKatt and Finke 2008; Durán 2018). While perhaps not

---

[1] And because of the rather extreme form of federalism, the national civil service of Belgium is relatively small on a per capita basis when compared to other European countries.

as closely linked to social actors as national bureaucracies, the European Commission is still a political actor that must deal with lobbying as well as with more formalized mechanisms for interest group participation.

These factors may combine to make the Commission less European than might be expected from the formal emphasis on eschewing nationality in favor of a European identity. That said, survey evidence does indicate that a significant majority of the members of the Commission do join that organization because of a commitment to Europe (Kassim et al. 2013: 55–7). However, much of that commitment appears to exist prior to joining the Commission rather than as a function of socialization after joining.

Images of the European Commission

Jarle Trondal (2010) provides another set of lenses for examining the European Commission, and the executive apparatus of the EU more generally. He argues that there are four alternative and potentially competitive images of the officials working for the Commission. These four images must be considered when attempting to understand how individual public servants in the Commission perform their tasks, and how the institution as a whole performs. These images are directed more specifically at the particularities of the Commission and the EU than other analyses of administrative culture and values. That said, these images can help illuminate the underlying culture of the Commission, and hence the way in which the underlying administrative traditions function.

The first two of these images—the supernational and the intergovernmental—focus on the attitudes of Commission employees toward the role of the European Union relative to the powers of the constituent national governments. These images are important for the commitment of European civil servants to the relative power of the Commission and other European institutions relative to the member nations of the Union. This normative commitment to the European project is an important, if variable, component of the working lives of members of the Commission (see Christensen et al. 2008). While largely independent of the national administrative cultures mentioned in previous chapters, differential commitments to supernationalism may be influenced by different levels of the commitments of the home nation to that value.

The third of the images presented by Trondal (2010) emphasizes the importance of membership in a particular DG or agency within the

Commission. The implicit argument here is that there are departmental cultures or operating routines that may dominate other allegiances or values.[2] Within the national administrative cultures described above, there may be strong internal cultures within individual organizations. These generally represent the nature of the policy domain they administer (Goodsell 2011), but may be more simply about the way in which they do business internally. Within the EU the departmental view, the member of the Commission can be seen defending and representing his/her own DG in the usual policy battles of governing (see Peters 1992; Rhinard and Boin 2009).

Other scholars have emphasized the importance of organizational involvement in shaping the behavior of officials in the European Union. Morten Egeberg (1996, 2004), for example, has emphasized the role of structure along with nationality in explaining the performance of this organization, and the structures—the DGs—within it. Despite some of its singular characteristics, the Commission is in most ways just one more public sector organization (or institution) and can be understood as such. It is a bureaucracy and in many ways its members will behave like other bureaucrats.

Finally, there is an image of the executive order that Trondal (2010) described as "epistemic." By this he is referring to the varying patterns of connections which members of the executive have with actors within society, and their role as gatherers and sorters of information. This perspective may be similar in some ways to the departmental view, but it also represents connections with interest groups within society and hence may be a more political, albeit not partisan, perspective on the role of administration.

Although perhaps not as clear within the EU as in national governments, public administration constitutes the major interface between state and society (see Zacka 2017), and these connections may define perspectives on policy, as well as the roles of administrators. Members of the Commission, or other European executives, deliver few public services on their own, but the national bureaucracies responsible for delivering them on behalf of the Union do have that contact and are seen as delivering European as well as national policies.

This epistemic lens developed by Trondal links with the literature on networks within the European Commission itself, and between the Commission and social actors.[3] There is a substantial literature on the role of networks in

---

[2] This perspective is analogous to the argument of institutionalists who propose that behavior within institutions is determined by "myths, symbols, routines..." that constitute a "logic of appropriateness" (see March and Olsen 1989).

[3] For a more general discussion of epistemic communities involved in policymaking.

the EU, pointing to the importance of these connections in making and implementing EU policies (e.g., Börzel 1997). These networks appear in the formulation of policy as well as in their implementation, and the use of seconded experts helps to bring those networks directly and legitimately into the proceedings of the Commission. Thus, like national bureaucracies, there are close connections between society and the bureaucratic organization that are useful for both policymaking and legitimation.

Interestingly, Trondal does not mention the professional, Weberian bureaucrat as one of his alternative visions for the Commission. This image may not be relevant for Commissioners who are the analogues of ministers in a national governments, or for their immediate staff, but that image is certainly relevant for the remainder of the organizations. Liesbet Hooge (1999), for example, contrasted Weberian and consociational styles among higher level Commission bureaucrats. She focused on the contrast between the bureaucracy as legal, technocratic policymaking organizations and the European Commission as a representative structure for the national members.

While that representative function appears to conflict with the pledge to eschew national sentiments while in Brussels, it must still be considered as one factor in defining the behavior of members of the Commission. The effects of nationality may not be overt, but there may still be more subtle differences based on cultures and traditions that affect both administration and policy choices. The very fact that all countries are entitled to a Commissioner does reflect the representative function of the Commission, as does the need to keep employment within the organization reasonably balanced by nationality (but see Christensen et al. 2008).

Untangling the Puzzle

The above discussion of the available literature provides three alternative ways to consider and analyze the administrative style of the European Commission. One is that it is *sui generis* and has developed an internal administrative culture that pervades it and its members, so that the Commission functions somewhat like the unitary actor of administrative legend—an animal rarely found in the real world of administrative and governance. Some studies of the Commission (e.g., Cini 1997; Schön-Quinlivan 2011) have tended to argue, even if implicitly, that this institution is indeed a rather well-integrated organization that has been able to create its own style of making and administering policy. That style may be dependent in part on the leadership at the time and hence may change over time, but the institution still marches to a single drummer, or at most to a very small number of drumbeats.

Although stressing the internal fragmentation of the Commission, Kassim et al. (2013: 77ff.) also stress its distinctive features as an administrative body. As well as its multinational nature and its extensive use of non-career officials, the Commission can be distinguished from other bureaucracies in several other ways. It has an ensemble of tasks, and a central role in the policy process that distinguishes it from bureaucracies in national governments. In addition, its pattern of handling cross-cutting issues is more reminiscent of the Soviet Union than of a contemporary European administrative system, given the need to move issues to the top of hierarchies before engaging in any significant attempts at coordination.

The second perspective is that the Commission is an amalgam of the various national traditions that comprise it, or even that it has become dominated by one tradition to the possible exclusion, or at least diminution, of others. For example, many observers coming from other traditions likened the Commission (at least in its early days) to French administration with its legalism and *ex ante* controls. Later, the creation of accountability institutions such as the Ombudsman may make it appear more like a Scandinavian system (Vogiatzis 2018). Making the argument on behalf of this version of the Commission would require identifying certain aspects of the structure of the Commission, and the behavior of its members, that had clear connections to the styles of national administrations. While that connection may be visible, demonstrating the etiology behind the appearance of those patterns is more difficult.

The third possible pattern is that the structure of the Commission produces a more highly differentiated and segmented organization. That fragmentation may occur first on the basis of the policy domains for which the various DGs are responsible. The fragmentation may also be a function of the national administrative styles of the Commissioners and the *cabinets* that serve those Commissioners (Egeberg and Heskestad 2010).[4] And finally, the Commission may be fragmented on the basis of linkages with actors and groups within the society. These linkages may reinforce the fragmentation produced through policy domains, but may also create their own divisions within the organization.

The internal fragmentation of the European Commission, and the politics over policy within the institution, remains an important perspective on

---

[4] The conventional wisdom at this time is that the *cabinets* have become less shaped by national patterns than in the past. See Kassim (2018).

administration within this system. The bureaucratic politics within the system (Peters 1992) appear to continue unabated, or perhaps even have increased. The agencification of the EU, following the pattern established by NPM, obviously exacerbates the internal divisions within the executive order of the European Union, and can create yet another source of internal bureaucratic politics (see Williams 2005).

Each of these three images of the European Commission can tell us something about the way in which the organization functions. Very much as Graham Allison did with the Cuban Missile Crisis (Allison and Zelikow 1999) using different lenses provides different, if perhaps contradictory perspectives on the subject at hand. Those contradictions are perhaps to be expected, given that we are dealing with a complex organization with multiple dimensions of variation within it (functional, national, political, etc.). And utilizing the multiple perspectives, even with contradictions, does enable the researcher to understand the organization being investigated and its decision-making processes.

What Do We Know about Administrative Traditions in the European Commission?

In this section of the chapter I will present some arguments for each of the contending conceptions of the nature of the European Commission bureaucracy. While I am primarily interested in the administrative legacies, and the styles brought into the Commission from the member states and their public bureaucracies, the other two perspectives should be considered carefully. The evidence available for this analysis is hardly the type that could be used to test any hypotheses in a conclusive manner, but even these "data" can provide some inklings about the complex internal workings of the institution and the relative strengths of the alternative visions of its performance.

It is important in this analysis of administrative cultures not to equate the importance of those cultures with the role of nationalism in European Union decision-making. There are numerous studies that question any significant role of nationality in the behavior of Commission officials (see, e.g., Gravier and Roth 2016) and the purpose of this analysis is not to say that the Commission is more or less controlled by national perspectives. Rather, the question is whether there are still administrative styles of individuals within the Commission, and of different understandings of the ways in which organizations in the public sector should and do function that shape behaviors.

Some of these elements of administrative culture may have little to do with the public sector per se, but are more conceptions of how management within organizations—any organization—should be conducted.[5] The question of nationalism in administration is reinforced by the large number of officials on secondment to the Commission from their national governments (see Suvarierol et al. 2013). As noted above, this secondment is a distinctive feature of the European Union administrative system, and can be conceptualized as a means of training national administrators in EU procedures and socializing them into EU values. But it can also be seen as putting cuckoos in the nest, given that these officials retain their primary career path within their national governments, and hence may not want to undermine the interests of their home country in any way.

The Distinctive Nature of the Commission

Some elements of the distinctive nature of the Commission were discussed above, notably its relatively small size, its composition of members coming from many national backgrounds, and its absence of significant implementation work as compared to a national bureaucracy. The role of secondments, already mentioned, is certainly one element of the distinctiveness of the Commission and its officials within the European Union, and in addition this provides a mechanism for the transmission of national styles of administration into the EU.

The dossier system for managing files within the Commission is one of the most distinctive features of the European Commission as an administrative system. Administrative action, whether concerned with policy formulation or with implementation, is delegated to an individual within a DG. S/he is then responsible for managing the dossier until some resolution is achieved. This administrative procedure is in marked contrast to practices in most administrative systems where the file would be moved up the hierarchy and the initiator would soon shed responsibility for managing it. This administrative pattern may impact especially the coordination of activities, given that the lower-level official is unlikely to be empowered to work with officials from other DGs.

---

[5] This observation is obviously related to the research of Hofstede, House, etc., mentioned in Chapter 1.

Legacies from the Member States

All the above having been said, the administrative style of the European Union does contain some elements of the traditions of the several member countries. For example, the administrative style within the Commission does appear more legalistic than managerial, perhaps reflecting the legalistic administrative styles of the founding members of the EU. Further, this legalism is perhaps to be expected for an organization whose function is primarily to make and monitor law rather than to manage programs itself. But beyond the tasks required of members of the Commission, the emphasis has been on compliance perhaps more than on designing programs that can be efficient and effective (Treib 2006; König and Madder 2014). Internally, even after attempts at reform such as those introduced by Neil Kinnock (see Ban 2013) inspired in part by NPM, the management of the Commission as an institution does not appear to be the principal concern of the central "management." This legalism appears to be a function of the dominance of Continental European countries at the founding, while more managerial Anglo-American and Scandinavian systems came later. The legalism may have been reinforced when countries from Southern Europe and Central and Eastern Europe were added in successive rounds of enlargement.

Given that the European Commission is not a government composed along partisan lines, as would be true of the executive in one of the member countries, one might expect the issue of politics and administration to be of little or no concern.[6] However, there is an increasing body of literature on the Commission that argues for the existence of role conflict for EU administrators between political and Weberian understandings of their function (see Bauer and Ege 2013). In this case the "political" sense of their role is both institutional, defending the Commission and the particular DG, and defending the European project against national interests. Further, within the institution itself, departmental politics is apparent among the DGs as they resolve policy conflicts.

There is also some evidence of conflict between the Commissioners, who are appointed in a more political manner, and the career service within the Commission. Wille (2013) has argued that relations between politicians and bureaucrats within the EU are becoming similar to those found in national governments. The commissioners have become less technocrats who would

---

[6] The *Spitzenkandidat* system may be making the selection of the president of the Commission more directly political.

work with career staff on policy and more political. Likewise, the bureaucrats are less mandarins cooperating with politicians at the apex of government and more managers and conventional bureaucrats. Thus, in Wille's terms, these relationships have become normalized and look increasingly like those of a nation state.

For those officials who occupy permanent positions in the Commission bureaucracy, a career is rather distinctive, although many will have had administrative careers in national governments prior to coming to the EU, and perhaps afterward. Spending some time in Brussels may become a necessary step in the career of someone who wants to reach the top of a national career structure, given the importance of EU policies for national governments. Further, the agencification of the EU may be affecting career patterns somewhat, certainly by making them more specialized and increasing the internal fragmentation of the administrative structures of the Union (Flinders 2004). The creation of so many specialized structures has also created more posts for seconded national experts recruited to provide the technical expertise that more generalist EU administrators may lack.

Also, there appears to be a significant concern with creating uniformity throughout the territory of the European Union, setting the EU administrative system more in the Napoleonic style. This is true even though the EU is a proto-federal state structure (Fabbrini 2010). The assumption since the inception of the Union has been that for the single market to function it is necessary to create uniform practices throughout the member states. That said, implementing such EU policies has meant that there will be variation, *de facto* if not *de jure*; adding the national governments to the implementation process may have been politically necessary, and has kept the Commission relatively small as a bureaucracy.

Finally, accountability has been something of a question within the European Union, albeit less perhaps for the officials operating within the administrative structures than for the commissioners themselves (Bovens 2007). While the Lisbon Treaty, as well as other changes to the system of responsibility of the Commission to the European Parliament, has improved accountability, it does remain somewhat problematic. Further, the system of delegation in the implementation process also raises major concerns about the accountability and transparency of many processes within the Commission (Peers and Costa 2012). Although there may be some controls in place for monitoring the effects of delegation, substantial autonomy remains for the Commission bureaucracy.

Fragmentation and Internal Differences

The third alternative pattern for understanding public administration within the European Commission would be defined by the existence of distinctive cultures and operating procedures within the individual DG and agencies, rather than any more general pattern of administration existing within the institution as a whole. This sort of fragmented pattern of administrative styles is familiar from national governments in which different ministries or departments may develop their own internal cultures and maintain those cultures even in the face of political change and pressures for homogenization.

The available literature points out that many of the DGs, and especially the agencies, do develop their own internal administrative styles or cultures. These cultures are based in part on the subject matter for which they are responsible—economic DGs are dominated by economic thinking, and so on. The cultures are also based in part on the "colonization" of various administrative organizations within the Commission by particular national groups who import their own styles of practice (Ellinas and Suleiman 2012). But those internal administrative styles can also be influenced by individual leaders (Ban 2013: 45–7), and hence change when the leadership of the organization changes.

While the above background features do definitely affect the internal cultures of organizational components of the Commission, including the agencies, there may also be more political reasons for fostering a distinctive pattern of commitment and beliefs within these organizations. Building an internal culture and a commitment to the programs of the organization can be used to promote the interests of the DG or the agency in the inevitable conflicts with other organizations over policies and budgets (Wayneberg 2017). Further, this internal "logic of appropriateness" (March and Olsen 1989) provides guidance for administrators when making policy and monitoring the implementation of policy by the member states.

Finally, I should point out that although this chapter has been concerned primarily with the effects of national patterns of administration on the Commission, the more common concern for European scholars has been the flow of influence in the opposite direction. That is, the creation of a "European Administrative Space" (Olsen 2003; Trondal and Peters 2013) has been a means for the Commission to influence policymaking across Europe more generally. As such, public administration has been an often underrated mechanism for European policy steering (Sbragia 2000) and for advancing European integration.

The extent of the Europeanization of national bureaucracies (Knill 2005) has been debated among scholars of European public administration. The question which arises concerning this influence of Europe on national government is again whether there is a common European administrative pattern that is being diffused, or whether Europeanization in reality means something different. One interpretation of Europeanization could be that the most important values to diffuse are those of a commitment to the European project, regardless of any particular interpretation of that project. This somewhat "softer" definition would imply that structural or procedural changes were not necessary but some changes in policy priorities might be.

Even if Europeanization does not mean the adoption of a common European pattern of administration, it may mean that the national patterns of administration are to some extent made less relevant. Simply the necessity of complying with European regulations, and to transpose regulations into national law, will require greater attention to policy and administrative patterns outside the particular nation state. The conception of European in this version of change can be somewhat amorphous and vague, but there is some influence on national administration nonetheless.

Conclusion

The European Commission is a unique administrative structure, but it is composed of individuals who come from a variety of administrative traditions and cultures. While all member countries and their civil servants have some common European administrative background, they still represent different approaches to administration and perhaps different levels of commitment to the European Union. The question that arises, then, is the extent to which a common administrative fabric can be woven from these disparate threads.

The national differences are important, as are the sources of those differences, but there are also differences that may arise because of variances in the subject matter being administered. Those differences are real but they may also reflect the bureaucratic politics that exists within any public (or private) bureaucracy. Each segment of a larger organization will attempt to defend its own turf, and will use the ideas associated with its policy domain to distinguish itself from others and to attempt to secure greater levels of resources.

Although the degree of commonality that exists within the European Commission bureaucracy, and the degree of Europeanization of national bureaucracies, are interesting research questions, they are also challenging. Identifying which structures and behaviors reflect a national pattern, and which ones reflect a distinctive Commission focus is difficult if not impossible. We have supplied some evidence above, but it must be considered inconclusive. The complex structures of the Commission and the multiple pressures on the occupants of roles within the Commission make any conclusive judgment about the role of traditions difficult, if not impossible, at least for now. More specialized survey instruments and more detailed analysis of decisions may be able to unravel more of the complexity surrounding this question, but for the time being we are left to ponder just how distinctive the EU bureaucracy really is.

8

Other Administrative Traditions

To this point, I have been focusing in this book on the principal administrative traditions among Western, democratic political systems. These traditions are, of course, important, and there is also a good deal of variance among them. But these four traditions are but a subset of all the patterns of administration that exist in public sectors around the world. Even if we assume that patterns of administration functioning in former colonies of these Western countries continue to manifest the administrative pattern from the former colonial power (see Chapter 9), I would still be ignoring a great deal of public administrative practice if I did not cast my net wider and consider long-standing patterns in Asia, the Islamic countries, Latin America, and Russia and Eastern Europe.

This attempt to consider a wider array of countries requires a number of prefatory comments to explain the logic of this analysis. The first is that administration in the former colonial dependencies of Western countries, whether in Asia or the Islamic world, may well be influenced by their former colonial power, but there will also be indigenous influences that reflect the values of the population, especially the more rural parts of the population. For example, traditional patterns of administration and the administration of justice may exist alongside the more Westernized versions, and there may be some tensions between the alternative conceptions of administration. This pattern exists in former colonized countries of Africa (Lund 2006; see also Chapter 9 in this volume), and can be seen in Islamic and some Asian regimes. And some of these traditional patterns may engage in what Fred Riggs (1964) called "doublespeak," using "modern" language at the same time as conveying more traditional values, and using modern (or at least Western) administration in parallel with more traditional discourses about governance.

A second point is that dealing with Asian bureaucracies will be extremely complex; not only is there the question of the influence of colonialism by Asian (Japan in Korea, Taiwan, and Manchuria), as well as non-Asian powers in the region, but the traditions that exist along with the colonial influences are quite varied (see Burns and Bowornwathana 2001; Cheung 2013). There is certainly a Confucian tradition that has been identified for China and for

Administrative Traditions: Understanding the Roots of Contemporary Administrative Behavior. B. Guy Peters,
Oxford University Press (2021). © B. Guy Peters. DOI: 10.1093/oso/9780198297253.003.0008

other countries in Northeast Asia (Drechsler 2018).[1] But then there are other traditions in Southeast Asian countries that are not as heavily influenced by Confucianism, as well as influences of Islamic administration in Indonesia, Pakistan, and Bangladesh (Zafarullah 2016). As is true for Europe, it is impossible, or at least not very helpful, to say there is a single Asian administrative tradition.

Thirdly, I am discussing Latin America and the Caribbean distinctly from the countries of Africa and to some extent Asia with a strong colonial legacy (see Chapter 9). While it would be difficult to deny that the countries of Latin America and the Caribbean have all been affected by Spanish, Portuguese, French, British and other forms of colonialism, it is also true that in most of these countries *direct* influences ended almost two centuries ago. The patterns that have become institutionalized in Latin American countries do certainly have some legacies of the past (Moreno 1969) but they also reflect a good deal of autonomous development, as well as autonomous borrowing of administrative patterns from the Napoleonic tradition (in several cases France was more influential as a model for administration after independence than was Spain; see, e.g., Mirow 2000). Government in these countries also reflects some influence from the United States, particularly in having presidential forms.

Fourth, Russia, along with Central and Eastern Europe (CEE), represents the confluence of several administrative patterns, and again these countries have a good deal of internal variation. The Russian administrative tradition was, and remains, hierarchical and legalistic, albeit also being open to substantial personal influence. The Russian tradition influenced many countries of the CEE area, but several of these (e.g., the Czech Republic, Hungary, Slovenia, and Slovakia) were also part of the Austro-Hungarian Empire with administration more akin to the German tradition (Hendrych 1993), while others, such as Poland and Romania,[2] had their own administrative patterns and traditions that were activated at times when these countries were not controlled by others. In particular, Romania has had and continues to experience significant influence from the Napoleonic tradition (Cretu 2014). All of these factors were made more complex by the period of communist domination (Vanagunas 1995). I have argued that several European countries can be

---

[1] The case of China is, of course, made all the more complex because of the influences of various forms of Communism, along with the Confucian background.
[2] Romanian administration has been influenced also to some extent by the Napoleonic tradition.

described as hybrids, and this is certainly a good way to describe many of the CEE countries.

Finally, all of these systems have been influenced, in some way or another, by changes in managerial ideologies and theories coming from Western countries. The presence of a tradition does not preclude learning and adaptation (but see Sager et al. 2018; see also this volume, pp. 199–201). In particular, New Public Management (NPM) has been to some extent imposed on these countries by donor organizations, although certainly some countries have pursued these practices more autonomously. Whether any adoption was autonomous or not, NPM has influenced governance in these countries, and indeed all countries. NPM was, however, particularly important for CEE countries because their independence from communist rule was during the heyday of NPM, and it was difficult at the time to separate any administrative reforms from attempts to impose managerialism (Nunberg et al. 1999).

With these numerous caveats in mind, I will proceed with a discussion of these administrative traditions that have developed independently of, or at least in parallel to, European and American influences. Attempting to cover all these traditions in one chapter means that inevitably the treatment will be significantly less detailed than the discussions of the four traditions in Europe, North America, and the Antipodes, but I think that broadening the discussion of traditions does demonstrate that there is substantial variation in the ways in which public administration is organized and functions. The often advanced notions of convergence appear even weaker once one leaves the Western world and considers the wide array of patterns of public administration that exist across the world.

These discussions of administrative traditions in these four sets of countries will demonstrate also that despite some differences these various patterns of administration do have some coherence empirically within each of the four sets. I will demonstrate that coherence in part through the description of the traditions, but will also point to some of the survey work that has been done on organizational culture to demonstrate that these are important points of connection among the countries within each of the groups. That internal coherence has been discussed in more detail in previous chapters, but it is clear that traditions do continue to matter and to define in part the "families of nations."

And finally, these cases demonstrate that the variables used to characterize the administrative traditions in the Western countries also have some utility in these other settings. I will not discuss each of the attributes of traditions for each of these groups, but will emphasize some that do distinguish the traditions. In some instances using these dimensions reveals paradoxical and perhaps unanticipated consequences within these administrative traditions. It is easy to assume that all components of an administrative tradition will reinforce each other, but the relationships within the models of administration are often more complex and the dynamics among the elements are at times paradoxical.

In addition, in the descriptive evidence concerning these traditions, I will utilize evidence drawn from Geert Hofstede's research on comparative organizational cultures. Most of the dimensions developed by Hofstede do not correspond directly to the dimensions that I have developed, having been constructed for somewhat different purposes. However, those dimensions do still help when trying to understand the dynamics of these administrative systems. They also help in understanding some of the paradoxes that emerge from the more descriptive discussions of administration in these systems.

Asia and the Confucian Tradition

Most of the literature on Asian administrative traditions has focused on the concept of a Confucian tradition (Drechsler 2018). In this literature the three dominant questions have been whether that tradition exists as an identifiable entity, and if so what the elements are of that tradition. Further, how far does the Confucian tradition extend? Does it include Japan (Painter 2010)? And South Korea (Kim 2001; Im and Cha 2013)? Or Vietnam (Painter 2003)? And further, is Confucian administration just a way of saying meritocratic, ethical, and accountable administration?

Several principles stand out in descriptions of the Confucian tradition of administration. The first is the emphasis on identifying the right personnel and meritocratic selection to positions in the civil service. Western civil services remained largely patrimonial for centuries after Chinese administration had institutionalized a system of testing for admission to the civil service.[3] The mandarins selected through this system tended to be the "best and brightest" and constituted an administrative elite at the apex of imperial government. The capacity to recruit an intellectual elite was in part possible because of the very high prestige of the civil service in imperial China.

---

[3] One cannot, however, discount the importance of kinship and personal ties in the bureaucracy emerging from this examination system. See Van Der Sprenkel (1964).

The second, important element of Confucian administration was its emphasis on values, and the character of the individuals selected for positions in this bureaucracy. To some extent, the examination system mentioned above contributed to that ethical form of administration, given that the traditional form of the examination was commentary on the philosophical works of Confucius. But beyond that, the emphasis placed on the role of the individual civil servant as a source of "good governance" required individuals of strong character to be mandarins (see Yang and van der Wal 2014).

A third important dimension of the Confucian tradition is an emphasis on performance. The reason for having a strict examination system and an emphasis on an individual's character is to ensure high levels of performance in office. Over time the Chinese Empire became more bureaucratic, and depended upon these officials for good a good part of its governance. Individual civil servants were given substantial powers with fewer accountability mechanisms than would be found in Western systems. As the US Marine Corps used to advertise, what they needed were a few good men.[4]

It is also important to note the paradoxes that exist within the Confucian system of public administration, in practice if not in theory. On the one hand, there is a strong emphasis on merit recruitment for the civil service, but at the same time there are persistent patrimonial links, at least after examinations have been passed. Likewise, there is a strong emphasis on values in administration, but at the same time there has been and continues to be, a high level of corruption within the Chinese civil service and other civil service systems that have Confucian roots (Lu 1999). These paradoxes reflect the difficulties found in every tradition in making normative standards of good administration work in practice.

Is Confucius Still Alive and Well?

We have yet to answer in any definitive manner whether Confucian styles of administration persist. As is true for many questions in the social sciences, this appears to be a matter of who is making the assessment. It is clear that the Confucian system per se in China has been overturned by the communist system, with its own set of particular concerns about the administration of policies (but see Fan 2011). But it is also clear that in other cases such as Taiwan some of these values do tend to persist more clearly (Ling and

---

[4] And at the time they were all men.

Shih 1998), and there have been extensive arguments about the degree of Confucian influence in South Korea as well.

Japan appears to be a case in which there is significantly less influence of the Confucian tradition. This relative lack of influence is in part a function of having an administrative tradition of its own, as well as the conscious borrowing of administrative patterns from Europe toward the end of the nineteenth century (but see Nishikawa 2007). At the time of the Ito Constitution there was a conscious attempt to borrow ideas from the best performing systems in Europe for policing and general administration, some of which became components of a general modernization and Westernization campaign of the government of the day.

Thus, again like other traditions, there are overlays of contemporary influences on underlying values, and arguing that the tradition continues to exist is difficult. Clearly the Confucian systems does survive to some degree in South Korea, Taiwan, and part of Southeast Asia but it is overlaid with more contemporary ideas about management and about government more generally. To the extent that democratic values have taken root in these countries, the hierarchical and meritocratic system of Confucian administration may be undermined. And to the extent that managerialism has become accepted, the ideas of performance may also be altered, although they will remain in place.

But we also need to remember that Confucianism is not the only strand of tradition within East Asian bureaucracies. Japan in particular borrowed from other administrative traditions during its development, notably from Germany (Martin 1995). In addition, the Japanese bureaucracy developed its own patterns that survived the transition to democracy at the end of World War II, and the economic and political development since then. In particular, the dominant role of bureaucracy in policymaking, and close connections between the bureaucracy and industry have been significant aspects of governance in Japan (Painter 2010). And the long involvement of the United States with South Korea has produced also some subtle influences of public administration there.

India and South Asia

Although much of the discussion of administrative traditions in Asia has been centered on the Confucian model, the administrative traditions in South Asia may be as strong and as distinctive. There was an empire that required administration in China, but the Mogul Empire in what is now India and

Pakistan also required administration, as did the Maratha Empire in the eighteenth century (Sen 1976). Indeed, administrative tasks may have been more demanding, given the multicultural nature of the latter, when contrasted to the relative homogeneity of China.

It is also important to remember that the experiences of the British East India Company, as well as the British government itself in India, had some influence over the development of public administration back in the United Kingdom. British public administration prior to the 1860s was not the model of merit recruitment and limited patronage that is has become.[5] In this case, influence on administrative practices went in both directions, and after being to some extent refined in the United Kingdom some practices of the East India Company, and then the British government per se, were returned to India (see Painter and Peters 2010b).

In addition to the ethnic fragmentation of the region, and to some extent reflecting it, the pattern of administration in the Mogul Empire (c.1555–1720) was much less direct than in the Confucian, centralized tradition. This empire was managed on more or less federal principles (implicitly) so that there was relatively little attempt to impose uniformity across the length and breadth of the sprawling political system. This pattern of decentralization was later reflected in the indirect rule of the British government in India. Clearly, this style of administration did not impose the aspirations for uniformity found in other Asian systems.

As well as not aspiring to uniformity the Mogul Empire also did not aspire to the type of meritocratic style of public administration associated with both Confucian administration and the British Raj (in the form of the British East India Company at least) that replaced it. The administrative system was patrimonial like most imperial systems of the time, and depended upon personal connections (Blake 2011). That said, the bureaucracy was expected to perform its tasks in a skillful and timely fashion, and was considered essential for binding together the extensive empire and creating some order.

Comparing Asian and European Traditions

I will now utilize some of the same dimensions of administrative traditions that we used for the European traditions. Space constraints prevent detailed

---

[5] In particular, the publication of the Northcote–Trevelyan report on the British public service reflected the experience of the Raj and the need to develop a merit-based, professional civil service.

discussions of each of the dimensions used above, so I will attempt to highlight the more important dimensions for comparison, and whether they demonstrative congruity or difference from the European cases. These important dimensions for comparison are presented in Table 8.1.

One of the clearest points for comparison is the emphasis on meritocratic recruitment in the Confucian tradition. As already noted, this aspect of public administration may be observed more in principle than in practice, but the idea is still deeply ingrained. All of the European administrative systems also have a commitment to merit principles for recruitment, but vary in the extent to which those merit values are complemented by political and patronage values. For the Asian systems, however, other values such as family and political connections may in some administrative systems overshadow those Confucian principles. That merit principle was not, however, central to other major administrative systems in Asia.

The question of management versus law is a second important dimension of administrative tradition. This conflict of values appears to have been less relevant in Asian systems than in others. Management, and especially hierarchical forms of management, are important in Asian bureaucracies, but again may be tempered by personal networks, and conducted within a legal framework. Further, the ideas of NPM have been diffused, especially to less-developed countries through the power of donor agencies, and have been adopted in many counties but certainly not all (Common 2004).

Principles of accountability represent another important point of comparison. The Korean tradition contained a very strong system for controlling the emperor, and for permitting complaints against government (Ahn 1980). In some ways, this appears to parallel the later creation of agencies in Sweden as a means of reducing the control of the king over policy, and of strengthening the citizenry against government. While that parallel may well be overdrawn, the fundamental point is that there is a tradition of accountability, including "withdrawing the mandate of heaven" for failing emperors.

And as well as being institutional, the Confucian tradition also emphasizes personal responsibility on the part of public servants. The public servant is expected to be an ethical actor who makes decisions much as a Weberian bureaucrat might be expected to act—*sine ira et studio*. Thus, accountability in this tradition involved not only institutions for control but perhaps more importantly values inculcated into the individual administrators so they would act appropriately. Again, away from the Confucian tradition, this personal responsibility has been less important than hierarchical and later legal controls.

Table 8.1 European and Asian administrative traditions

	Anglo-American	Napoleonic	German	Scandinavian	Asian*
State tradition	Contractual	Organic	Organic	Mixed	Organic
Law vs. management	Management	Law	Law	Management	Mixed
Administration and politics	Separate	Fused	Fused	Separate	Fused
Administration or service	Service	Administration	Administration	Service	Administration
State and society II	Pluralist	Mixed	Corporatist	Corporatist	Pluralist/illegitimate
Uniformity	Diverse	Uniform	Diverse	Diverse	Uniform
Accountability	Political	Legal	Legal	Mixed	Mixed

Note: * As noted, there is no single Asian tradition; this table emphasizes the Confucian tradition as developed in the text.

Islamic Public Administration

The Islamic tradition for governance and public administration is derived from a religious foundation, as well as the history of administration in extensive empires and individual states. In the twenty-first century, principles of Islamic administration influence are practiced in several dozen countries on three continents. As already noted, the influence of Islamic administration over national systems may be tempered by colonial experiences (e.g., the French in North Africa, the British in Egypt, Pakistan, and Malaysia, and the Dutch in Indonesia). But there does appear to be a clear set of principles that affects administration in these countries. The Islamic tradition may also be tempered by the historical experiences of the countries, such as empires that existed prior to the time of the spread of Islam (Farazmand 2002; Branine and Pollard 2010).

In considering the Islamic tradition of administration there should perhaps be some special consideration of the Ottoman Empire and its successor state of Turkey (Heper 1987, 2000). As was true for both China and India, the administrative tradition in this case was developed to manage a sprawling empire, and like India a sprawling multicultural empire. Although the effects of the Ottoman Empire may be seen most in Turkey and in areas of the Middle East, it is important not to forget that there remains some impact in the Balkans (Drechsler 2013a, 2013b), although that influence may increasingly be overcome by other European influences, especially with attempts at accession to the European Union.

When one begins to examine the principles of Islamic administration as articulated by several scholars (e.g., Hoque et al. 2013; Samier 2017), the emphasis on religious and humane values, rather than on management as control, becomes evident. For example, several of the principles of administration presented by Samier emphasize justice, fairness, and honesty as central for administration. Conversely, there is little about monitoring and controlling personnel, or organizing the appropriate structures for administration that are so central to European public administration. As was true for the Confucian tradition, there is greater emphasis on individual probity than on institutional controls. But this reliance on individual probity may reflect a form of legalism, with the law having a religious rather than public sector origin (Aliabadi 1998).

Another feature that emerges from an examination of Islamic public administration is that like the Scandinavian (and to a lesser extent the Germanic) tradition there is a significant reliance on non-state actors for the delivery of public services. For example, in contemporary social policy, there is some reliance on organizations such as *waqfs* to deliver services to the needy, guided by both religious and administrative principles (Saeidem 2018). The availability of these civil society organizations lessens administrative burdens on the public sector, while also perhaps enhancing the legitimacy of the state.

Although there is widespread use of non-state actors, that does not necessarily mean that there is a strong civil society that supports public participation and provides an alternative to the state. This absence of a strong civil society is perhaps especially apparent for countries that were heavily influenced by the Ottoman Empire (Heper 2000). As is often true for imperial systems, there is a hierarchical legacy which has not been conducive to the development of civil society. And to the extent that civil society organizations do exist, they are often coopted by the state, or even created by the state, and therefore serve more to legitimate the state than to express citizens' demands or grievances.

The involvement of non-public actors in administration may extend beyond not-for-profit organizations or their analogues to include family and clan influences over governing. Again, these influences may be more related to cultural patterns within individual countries (e.g., the importance of clans in Afghanistan; see Murtazashvili 2016) rather than more general patterns of Islamic governing. But this style of public, or not so public, administration does appear sufficiently common that it may be considered a significant part of the Asian tradition. Andersen (1987) points out that not only does the degree of involvement of social groups with the state vary across Islamic countries, but so, too, do the beneficiaries of that involvement. The beneficiaries may range from royal families and their allies to specific tribes and clans to technocrats. There may be an extensive level of patronage (at least by Western standards) in all these countries, but the nature of that patronage, and its impact on governance, will vary widely.

The involvement of members of various social and ethnic groups within some Islamic administrative systems may be seen as a mechanism for representative bureaucracy. The representativeness of these social groups may be concerned with language or more subtle ethnic differences than are generally discussed in the representative bureaucracy literature within the consolidated democracies. But within these societies the differences are important, and may help to legitimate the bureaucracy. That legitimation may be purchased, however, at the cost of some undermining of the universalism of administration, and even the probity of the administrative system (see Nagel and Peters 2018).

Patterns of governance and the involvement of social actors in governance processes in Islamic public administration should be placed in the context of a formal pattern of government and a career public service. Many of the Islamic countries are traditional monarchies or authoritarian regimes. Although these regime types may be consultative, that consultation will extend only so far (Hashmi 2002) and hierarchical control will dominate most policy decisions. At the same time, however, the presence of consultative methods does provide some checks on the hierarchy.

Comparing European and Islamic Administration

In terms of contemporary and continuing patterns of reform beginning in Western countries and then diffused around the world, Islamic administration appears to be contradictory to one and supportive of another.[6] First, Islamic administration is almost diametrically opposed to the market-based values of NPM that have become central to administration in many European systems. In addition to the emphasis on allocative efficiency contained within NPM, this approach, even more than other Western approaches, tends to deal with individuals in an individualistic manner, rather than as members of a community. That community orientation appears central to Islamic administration and governance, even if the definition of the community may at times be exclusive.

On the other hand, however, Islamic administration appears compatible with the participatory strand of thinking about administrative reform (Peters 2010a). Many of the principles of Islamic administration discussed by Samier (2017) and others involve providing members of the organization the right to be consulted and to have some influence over decisions. The principle of *shura*, for example, advises that individuals making decisions consult with those whose lives will be affected by the decisions. This is very similar to ideas of participatory management in organizations going back to scholars such as Argyris (1990), as well as to contemporary ideas about collaborative governance (Ansell and Gash 2008).

As was true for the Asian models of administration there appear to be several apparent paradoxes and contradictions in the Islamic tradition of

---

[6] Note that "European" also includes North America and the Antipodes. The basic question is how does Islamic administration compare with the four traditions developed in greater detail in Chapters 3–6?

administration. For example, the principle of participation in administration appears in rather stark contrast with the governance of the individual states which is often monarchical, or at least very hierarchical, and appears to permit little discussion (Hinnebusch 2006). Limited democracy in many Islamic states contrasts sharply with organizational principles that often stress consultation.

Some of these differences in administrative values and traditions can be seen in the empirical studies of organization culture such as those of Hofstede and GLOBE. For example, in Hofstede's analysis of organizations the managerial values of Islamic countries were aggregated to create a composite score (Table 8.2). When compared to other administrative values in other areas of the world, these scores are relatively high on the power distance and masculinity dimensions, and relatively low on the long-term orientation dimension.

From the available qualitative and descriptive evidence, the Islamic tradition of public administration is deeply influenced by religious values, as well as other cultural values. To the extent there is a "managerial style" it is consultative and does not emphasize control over others within an organization. This style of administration, leaving aside some of the imperial legacies that contribute to the tradition in places, is less hierarchical than others, and there does appear to be a stronger sense of service than is true for either the Asian or Russian traditions discussed in this book.

However, qualitative evidence from a number of sources conflicts with the data in Hofstede's cultural surveys. These surveys show attitudes that are hierarchical and not particularly consultative, emphasizing as they do decisive decision-making. There may, therefore, be a good deal of internal tension within public administration in these countries. Some values emphasize collaborative management while others emphasize control and hierarchy, making for potential conflict within public organizations. There are tensions in all administrative systems, but these appear more clearly identifiable than in many.

Latin America

Administrative ideas and practice in Latin America is the third administrative tradition to add to the European and North American traditions. As already noted, this tradition poses some particular challenges for interpretation. The first is that a strong colonial heritage established some of the foundation for continued state development in these systems. Leaving aside the several

Table 8.2 Dimensions of organizational culture

Country Groups	Power Distance	Individualism	Masculinity	Uncertainty Avoidance	Long-term Orientation	Indulgence
(1) Islamic states						
1.a Total	78.4	27.5	52.3	65.4	30.6	32.6
1.b MENA	80.5	32.1	52.5	71.25	19.9	30.0
	75.9	22.1	52.1	58.4	41.3	35.1
(2) Asian states						
2.a Total	75.0	29.6	50.6	55.9	47.0	36.4
2.b Islamic	81.4	26.9	52.4	65.6	33.5	36.5
2.c Non-Islamic	66.4	30.6	50.2	47.7	59.2	36.2
(3) Central and Eastern Europe	65.1	48.0	50.0	75.6	64.3	25.9
(4) Western Europe						
4.a Total	44.5	62.6	44.7	673	54.3	55.1
4.b Southern Europe	57.2	49.6	49.4	91.2	45.8	44.6
4.c Non-Southern Europe	39.9	67.3	43.1	58.7	57.3	58.9
(5) Latin America	71.0	22.1	47.8	81.0	20.9	72.4

Note: Scores for organizational culture by country groups.
Source: Hofstede Insights: https://www.hofstede-insights.com/product/compare-countries/.

smaller countries with British, French, and Dutch influences,[7] Spanish and Portuguese influences over Central and South America have been dominant. These colonial powers were expelled earlier than those in Africa and Asia but vestiges of their impact are still visible (Lange et al. 2006). For example, John J. Johnson (1964) has argued that the pattern of domination by conquistadores and other military rulers created a continuing pattern of governance characterized by personalism, pride, and violence that resonates even today. Similarly, Robert Tignor (1999) has argued that, unlike later versions of colonialism in Africa, district officers in Spanish colonialism gained their posts through personal ties, or by purchasing them. In the latter case, this inevitably led to attempts to recover the money spent (and more) and institutionalized patterns of corrupt governance that may well persist to this day.

Second, although not a colonial power per se, for these countries the United States also exerted significant impact on styles of governing, perhaps especially in Panama and Mexico (Crowther and Flores 1984). Positive ideas of democracy and gunboat diplomacy were used to attempt to enforce those ideas (albeit often propping up dictators in the pursuit of stability and economic gain) and created significant American influence, which was reinforced economically, again for good or ill, both directly, and through international organizations such as the World Bank and the International Monetary Fund.

A third point to consider is the instability that has afflicted many Latin American countries, so that there may be an overlay of styles even for more contemporary governing and administration styles. The most obvious example would be the role of the military in governing in a number of instances in many of the countries of Latin America. While the military may be the best organized element of the public sector, the other values it would bring into public administration would not be so positive. The pattern of "bureaucratic authoritarianism" identified by O'Donnell (1988) involved control of society through a military junta supported by the bureaucracy, along with the suppression of participation. As such it is in marked contrast to the more participatory styles of most European traditions, and with the often populist forms of governing in Latin America when there is no military control (Panizza and Miorelli 2009).

Even taking into account these various confounding factors for an argument that there is a Latin American administrative tradition, or at least style, there does appear to be some common traits that appear in administration in these countries. The first, and in some ways the most obvious, is the legalism

---

[7] And leaving aside also French Guiana which remains part of France.

of these administrative systems (see Ramos and Milanesi 2020). All bureaucracies must function within administrative law, but the detailed and seemingly convoluted nature of administrative law in Latin America imposes significant burdens on citizens and businesses. For example, World Bank measurements of the ease of doing business rank most Latin American countries relatively low when compared with European and many Asian countries—the highest ranking Latin American country (Mexico) is 52nd in this worldwide ranking.[8]

The difficulty in doing business with Latin American bureaucracies, both as a business and as an ordinary citizen, is indicative of an administrative style with a great deal of *ex ante* control, not dissimilar to the Napoleonic model (see pp. 58–9). That is, if a citizen wants to engage in any government activity, even something as simple as registering a birth (Duryea et al. 2006), there may be multiple steps and multiple signatures required. Failure to perform those bureaucratic tasks in the right order and in the correct manner may lead to an inability to receive the service without extensive court action.

Legalism within Latin American public administration is to some extent exacerbated by organizational proliferation and associated corporatist structures. For example, rather than having a single social security system in the country there are, in many countries, dozens based on occupation, or unions, or region.[9] Privatized options are now being added to this corporatist structure of service provision, responding to pressures for marketization. Rather than being competitive, which might improve efficiency and competition, in most instances this fragmentation merely contributes to administrative challenges and solidifies social structures (Mesa-Lago 2008).[10] In the late twentieth and early twenty-first centuries, organizational proliferation has increased in many areas beyond social policy, as Latin American countries have suffered from "agency fever" associated with NPM (Ramos et al. 2020).

The administrative cultures of Latin America also emphasize centralization and control from the center (Véliz 1980). This may reflect colonial heritage, but that legacy has been reinforced by unitary governments that want to exert control over their populations. However, the paradox that arises is that the apparent demand for uniformity is contradicted by the presence of numerous

---

[8] See http://www.doingbusiness.org/rankings.

[9] In fairness, the system of *Krankenkasse* (health insurance funds) in Germany is also fragmented, but not as significantly and they are regulated so that their basic benefits and management are very similar.

[10] Thus, the social policy arrangements in these countries are analogous to what Esping-Andersen (1990) called "corporatist" or "conservative" welfare states, based on the Bismarkian model.

differentiated structures within government, and the pattern of providing differential benefits to groups and individuals based on clientelism and *amiguismo*. Somewhat paradoxically, centralized Latin American states may produce less uniform benefits for citizens than federal states such as Germany or Austria.[11]

As has been true for my discussions of many of these administrative cultures, there are several significant internal contradictions in administrative cultures in Latin America. Most importantly, co-existing with the importance of legalism, as just noted, there is a strong administrative law tradition and the use of legal rules to define the possibility of public action. On the other hand, there is a great deal of particularism that goes along with the legalistic universalism. Patrimonialism, *clientelismo* (Stokes 2007) and a number of other concepts have been used to describe the use of discretion to favor some individuals over others, especially when based on familial and/or political ties of the public employees making decisions.

If we examine the organizational cultures of Latin America as measured by Hofstede (Table 8.2) some of the descriptive evidence concerning Latin American public administration appears supported. In particular, the very high score on the dimension of uncertainty avoidance can be related to legalism within the culture.[12] Further, the very high indulgence score may reflect the clientelistic nature of politics and governing in these countries, with administrators willing to provide selective benefits to their families and friends. This survey evidence appears to confirm the paradox within these administrative systems as identified through other accounts of administrative history and practice.

It is important to understand that not all Latin American public administrations are identical, despite having some common traditions. For example, Uruguay comes close to the *Rechtsstaat* model of administration associated with Continental Europe (Ramos et al. 2020), and others such as Chile may have some more managerial orientation (see Alberts et al. 2020). Still others, such as Argentina, may be more clientelistic and depend more on patronage and personal contacts. But these differences may be more of degree than of type, and there do appear to be some common elements in these administrative systems that reflect the legacies of the past.

---

[11] That said, one of the standard recommendations for reform in Latin America has been decentralization and the empowerment of local governments and citizens. See Falleti (2010).

[12] Importantly, this uncertainty avoidance is important for the bureaucrats themselves who have job security unless there is a legal violation. Following the letter of the law may be slow for clients but it does protect the civil servant.

Russia and Central and Eastern Europe

Finally, the administrative systems of Russia and Central and Eastern European countries represent something of a bridge between the European traditions already discussed and other patterns of public administration. While historically tied into Europe and engaged in European wars and European politics, Russia had its own distinctive patterns of governance (Kotchegura 1999). As already noted, other countries of Central and Eastern Europe had other linkages with European traditions, as well as other influences over their governance styles, including in some cases an Ottoman inheritance. These various historical legacies all deserve treatment on their own, but space limits the capacity to do that here.

In addition to the varied historical roots of public administration in these countries, there was one uniform influence on administration—the almost half-century of Communist rule. The literature, both during and after the Communist period, identifies a number of key features of this style of administration (see Ekiert and Hanson 2003). But even that influence was not as uniform as it sometimes appeared in the West, ranging from hard-line regimes in East Germany to more participatory styles in Yugoslavia (Simmie 1991) to personalistic regimes such as Romania under Ceaușescu (Fischer 1989).

Because of those varied experiences under communism, at least in part, there has been substantial differentiation of governance and public administration after independence. These differences have been manifested both in policy choices and in the styles of administration. Kitschelt (2003), among others, has argued that these differences in governance in the CEE countries may represent the underlying traditions, or legacies, of the past, as well as the specific policy choices made after gaining independence. He does, however, demand that these explanations also contain some mechanisms that can explain the differentiation, rather than just saying it represents the legacy of the past. I will discuss mechanisms of that sort more generally later (Chapter 10) but will also attempt to identify some of the social mechanisms at work here.

In addition to the (somewhat) uniform influence of the communist period on Central and Eastern European countries, the European Union and the accession process have been a common influence for many Central and European Union countries. Ten countries that had been republics within the Soviet Union or dominated by Communist governments of some sort, have become members of the European Union (see Olsen 2003). To gain admission these countries had to go through a detailed accession process that involved getting the administrative system, as well as political and economic systems, ready for the European Union. The standards created for the accession process, however, have decayed in a number of cases (Meyer-Sahling 2011; Mazur et al. 2018).

Nørgaard and Winding (2007) have provided an important examination of how administrative traditions in the Baltic republics which gained their freedom in 1991 are influencing public administration in contemporary governments. That said, these authors focused primarily on the effects of Soviet legacy without examining earlier influences on administration. Although the Soviet inheritance was uniform, underlying traditions within CEE countries, including the Baltics, were less so. For example, while Lithuania had been an independent and once powerful country for some time, Estonia had had only limited periods of independence in its history (Taagepera 1993).

Meyer-Sahling and Yesilkagit (2011) attempt to provide more complete explanations of how administrative traditions will have impacted the variations in regime types after independence. They differentiate, for example, between deeper historical legacies and seemingly less historically grounded administrative traditions. They also point to the varieties and inconsistences that may exist within administrative traditions, especially in cases such as CEE countries that have very complex patterns of layering of regime types (see Capano 2018). Finally, many administrative changes in CEE countries have not been autonomous but imposed, whether by Communist or EU regimes.

While much of the literature that has developed in attempting to understand types of administration after communism has focused on CEE countries, there is some sense that Russian public administration is not vastly different from that which had served the czars, or the Soviets. While almost certainly an overstatement, there does appear to be a deeply embedded pattern of administration that depends upon hierarchical controls that co-exist with reliance on personal networks, clientelism, and corruption. In particular, historically there has been a very weak service orientation in the Russian administrative system and that continues into the present (Kotchegura 1999).

The reassertion of legacies and underlying administrative traditions may actually be generating some increased diversity of administrative systems, rather than homogenization, with CEE countries. One can certainly see the political differentiation, as Hungary and Poland move down a more nationalist and populist path than do other nations such as the Baltic republics (Hajnal and Boda forthcoming). The political dimension of change is reflected in administrative systems, with significantly greater use of patronage in Hungary especially, although patronage has been increasing in most CEE countries.

Having spent some space addressing the complexities of administrative traditions in CEE countries, what do they contain, and can we identify a clear pattern across the region? The answer to the second question is clearly yes...and no. As with several of the other cases above, as well as the cases discussed in Chapter 9 on colonialism, there are rather clear historical legacies but they may be disguised or discussed in more contemporary language. And there may be informal mechanisms available to political and administrative leaders that complement the formal, and make it possible for the formal to work (see Helmke and Levitsky 2004).

In terms of the dimensions that I used to characterize administrative traditions in Western Europe and North America, these are clearly legalistic administrative cultures, to some extent similar to those in Latin America. Administrative law is more evident in the day-to-day workings of the bureaucracy than would be true for many Western European bureaucracies, and many public servants have their first education in law. There are, of course, some exceptions to that generalization as countries such as Estonia have adopted a more managerial approach (Randma-Liiv 2008) but the basic pattern is legalistic and often rigid. The style of governing is also very formal, as might be expected from the emphasis on law. Another factor that stands out in CEE countries is the absence of a strong public service orientation—they have the lowest scores, on average, among groups of countries in an international survey (Table 8.3).

In addition, public administration in CEE countries has become increasingly politicized, especially after accession to the European Union was completed, although some have argued that the process of backsliding began even prior to accession. Despite attempts—historical and contemporary—to reform and create meritocratic civil service systems, the level of patronage appointment in the public sector remains high. This is perhaps especially true for the Russian Federation (Gaman-Golutvina 2008), but is also true for some CEE countries (e.g., Hungary, Romania, and to a lesser extent Poland and Slovakia) that have been backsliding from the merit systems created at accession (Kopecký et al. 2012; Peters 2020). As well as the historical legacy, a politicized public service's current levels of patronage and loss of professionalism may reflect the volatility of party systems and rapid turnovers in government.[13]

---

[13] That said, Russia has had perhaps the most stable system for the past two decades, but the level of politicization is largely unchanged.

Table 8.3 Levels of professionalization of civil service systems in Central and Eastern Europe, and Western Europe

Central and Eastern European Countries	2012	2015
Latvia	4.3	3.2
Poland	3.8	3.2
Lithuania	4.1	3.3
Estonia	3.1	3.3
Slovenia	4.2	3.9
Czech Republic	4.1	4.0
Romania	4.4	4.1
Croatia	3.5	4.3
Bulgaria	4.5	4.3
Hungary	4.4	4.6
Slovakia	3.8	4.9
Average	4.0	3.9
Western and Southern European Countries	5.2	5.3

Source: Quality of Governance Institute, University of Gothenburg (https://www.qogdata.pol.gu.se/search/).

In addition to partisan patronage the weak accountability structures in many of these cases allow public officials to pursue the interests of favored social and economic groups in society as well as their own. A relatively weak sense of public interest, along with few constraints on behavior, allows public servants to distribute particularistic benefits such as public sector jobs to members of society. This pattern has been a part of the legacy inherited from autocratic regimes of the past, and tends to persist in contemporary administration, perhaps especially in Russia (Oleinik 2008). Some scholars, however, have argued that rather than being a function of the legacy, contemporary corruption is simply a product of scarce resources (Humphrey and Sneath 2017).

Again, somewhat inconsistently it appears, with the emphasis on formal authority levels of accountability and levels of individual discretion for individual public administrators are high (Solomon 2008). This level of delegation to public administrators may make sense, assuming that they are partisan or personal loyalists and therefore will follow what those political leaders would want done, but it still undermines any conventional notion of the rule of law in public administration. It creates what Margaret Cohn (2001) has called "fuzzy legality"; it has the appearance of great legality but in reality involves sweeping delegation to administrators with few controls.[14]

---

[14] Again, the ideas of Fred Riggs (1964) about the existence of two (or perhaps more) ways of doing the business of government within developing countries appear relevant. There is the appearance of legality but the practice of illegality. See also p. 183 in this volume.

Again, the evidence concerning dimensions of organizational culture drawn from Hofstede appears to support findings from other types of evidence. Central European countries rank highly on uncertainty avoidance, indicative of the formality and legalism within these systems. Likewise, they have the strongest long-term orientation of any of the groups of countries which perhaps reflects the years of planning during their communist years. But, again, not all these countries are identical—there does appear to be an interesting pattern that helps understand some other observed patterns of behavior within public administration.

Do These Traditions Make Any Difference?

These various administrative traditions do, I would argue, appear to make sense on historical and geographical bases, but when examined comparatively do they help to differentiate patterns of administration among the countries of the world? And do they have any impacts on the outcomes of administrative actions or on the relative success of public policy? Even if the traditions exist and there are manifest differences in underlying administrative styles across countries and across regions the overlays—NPM and/or neo-Weberian governance—may overwhelm the impact of the traditions and be the primary source of administrative behavior.

In addition to the influence of alternative traditions of public administration, there are numerous other factors that will also affect administrative behavior within the political system. For example, as well as having an administrative culture affecting the public sector, other broad cultural factors, including the perceived importance of the market relative to the state, may affect governing and the choices made by administrators. Further, shifts between democratic and authoritarian forms of governing will influence the autonomy of bureaucracy and the degree of political control being exercised.

Even with all the above caveats in mind there do appear to be demonstrable differences in administrative systems. And if we assume that most of the external pressures on these administrative systems are toward greater uniformity (see Pollitt 2015), then the presence of diversity and in some cases increasing diversity, requires consideration. That diversity may reflect the persistence of significant underlying differences with historical foundations. Some of these pressures for diversity may be socioeconomic, some political, but many may also be cultural and represent the persistence of traditions. The very fact that scholars of public administration continue to discuss Confucian public administration some two and a half centuries after the death of the philosopher speaks to the persistence of those cultural values.

Summary and Conclusions

The above has been an all too brief foray into attempting to understand administrative traditions outside Western Europe, North America, and the Antipodes and to relate those traditions to the models of traditions developed in the earlier chapters. Each of these four traditions would deserve a chapter, or several books, of its own and I do hope that someone will do that work. Likewise, for a number of countries discussed here we could ask some of the same questions we did about the former colonies of European countries in Africa, and attempt to assess the importance of colonialism.[15] But for the present book this chapter will have to suffice, and I do believe it raises some important points.

One of the points that stands out from the brief examinations of alternatives to the European traditions in public administration is the emphasis on legalism and formalism. This is not to say that European traditions do not have strong legal elements—the Germanic and Napoleonic traditions certainly do—but law appears dominant and often dysfunctional in several of these traditions. I say dysfunctional because of the costs that the multitudes of forms and clearances can impose on the public who depend on government for some basic services. Law should, of course, create predictability and equality but it is difficult to say where those positive attributes end and red tape begins (Bozeman 2000).

Another characteristic of these administrative systems has been the existence of paradox and contradiction within them. Paradoxical situations within public administration are hardly confined to these cases (see Hood and Peters 2004; Handy 2005), but the disjuncture between norms and practices do seem pronounced in some of these cases. This conflict of values may be, as Riggs (1964) argued, merely a function of the developmental processes through which these countries are passing. The traditions on which these administrative systems are founded may simply not be compatible with modern administrative practice, much less with the concepts of NPM.

---

[15] Also, among these countries, there was also colonialism, with Japan and China acting as colonial powers over, for example, Korea, Taiwan, and parts of Southeast Asia.

And finally, these traditions, perhaps more than the European ones developed in more detail in the preceding chapters, make any facile idea of convergence among administrative systems appear even more suspect. The paradoxes within the systems make it clear that despite external pressures—mimetic or coercive (Dimaggio and Powell 1991)—some aspects of historical traditions persist and may even be strengthening. The underlying administrative traditions do continue to influence behavior and do continue to guide administrative practice, just as they do in all the cases we have been discussing. The influences may be subtle and overlaid by others, but they are real.

9

Transferring Traditions

The Colonial Experience

When the European countries seized their colonies around the world, they took with them their forms of governing and their administrative traditions. The political formats for government in the colonies were largely irrelevant until those colonies began to gain their independence in the 1940s onward, but the forms of administration were extremely important. The colonial powers had to establish some form of control over their territories, and the military and the bureaucracy were obvious sources for imposing that control. Colonial governments also trained at least some of the local population to participate in those administrations, and attempted to inculcate some administrative values into local employees.[1]

Although faced with relatively common governance challenges the various European powers (as well as the United States in the Philippines and its other territories; see Go 2011) confronted the challenges differently, following their own administrative traditions at least in part. Some of the differences in the challenges were a function of various social and cultural patterns in the areas being colonized, for example the level of centralized control existing within the regions of the continent (Boone 2003). But the colonial administrators tended to think rather little about those differences. Most of the differences in patterns of administration therefore were a function of their different conceptions about the goals of colonization and the different ideas about proper public administration held by the colonizers.

The question here is to what extent the administrative patterns imposed, or at least in operation, during the colonial period have persisted after independence. To some extent Chapter 6 on the Anglo-American tradition has argued that the British pattern of administration has had a continuing influence on the United States more than two centuries after the end of colonialism. Of course, that case is different from eighteenth- and all

---

[1] In some cases, such as India, there was a sizeable local civil service, albeit supervised by individuals from the imperial power.

Administrative Traditions: Understanding the Roots of Contemporary Administrative Behavior. B. Guy Peters,
Oxford University Press (2021). © B. Guy Peters. DOI: 10.1093/oso/9780198297253.003.0009

nineteenth-century colonialism because the founders of what became the American government began their lives as British, and were more naturally influenced by, or were part of, the tradition, thereafter creating their own. The influence of a tradition that is imposed through colonial power may be expected to be less influential, and indeed one might expect the tradition to the rejected after independence. As Hyden (2010) argues, Africans in British colonies discovered rather quickly that they were treated as subjects and not as citizens.

Although at least nine European nations were involved in colonialism in Africa, Asia, Oceania, and the Americas, this chapter will focus on the impact of British and French colonial administration in Africa. These were the largest colonial powers, and given that they had markedly different administrative traditions any different outcomes may help understand the process of transferring administrative practices. Likewise, we could examine the impact of colonialism in any of a number of geographical settings, but instead will focus on the countries of Africa. This narrowed focus allows us to limit the extraneous variance affecting any observations—a version of most-similar systems design (Ankar 2020). That said, we must always be cognizant of the social and cultural differences that exist across areas of the African continent (Darbon 2004; see also Mamadani 1999).

We can also conceptualize the colonial inheritance in Africa in a somewhat different manner. Olivier de Sardan (2009) has argued that contemporary public bureaucracy in Africa represents the cumulative effects of two "ruptures." One rupture was colonization that, to varying degrees, substituted the rule of the colonial power for traditional forms of governance in the African states. The second rupture was the end of colonialism and the creation of independent governments that had to attempt to rule as states within the international system. While those governments had examples and advice from their former colonial power, they also had traditional administrative and legal structures that had not been totally supplanted by colonialism, especially at the local level. More than formal structures, customary ideas about governing and administration persisted in many areas because they had not been directly challenged by colonialism (but see Staniland 1971).

Therefore, as we examine the role of administrative traditions on contemporary administrative practices, we need to consider those two sets of traditions. One question is whether colonial powers, especially France and the United Kingdom, were successful in transferring their administrative structures to their colonies. Or in Badie's (1992) term, is there an "imported state" that can function in the post-colonial world? And is that imported state more powerful than the societies which it is meant to control (Migdal 1988)? Or is the imported state merely a facade that hides the functioning of a state that depends on more traditional ideas about governance and institutions?

A fourth and closely related question is whether any adoption of the colonial systems of administration had relatively insignificant impacts on contemporary administration, compared to the persistence of traditional social and cultural patterns within them. It is difficult to argue that there were bureaucratic patterns existing prior to colonization, but there were forms of local governance (and in some cases more centralized and powerful governance structures), which did function and which appear to have enduring influences. And, it is argued, these pre-colonial patterns of governance continue to influence contemporary governance (Vansina 2004; Foa 2016).

There may be yet a third set of influences on the development of public administration in African countries. Even after the end of colonialism there is substantial influence from European and North American countries on these administrative systems. Some of this has been through direct contact from the formal colonial power, but some has been through donor organizations and the ideas that are promoted by Northern institutions as being "modern." Thus, there have been pressures for greater isomorphism between administrative systems in African countries and those Northern countries (Dimaggio and Powell 1991). Some of the pressures are coercive, with donor countries and organizations requiring recipient governments comply with certain standards to receive loans and grants. Other pressures may be mimetic, with the desire of governments to appear as engaging in "best practice," and to appear modern.

Given the effects of the two "ruptures" in administrative performance in Africa, we may expect that the post-colonial period in Africa (and to some extent in other post-colonial areas) has been characterized by the creation of a hybrid public administration (de Waal and Ibreck 2013). These hybrids represent the confluence of colonial forms of administration with traditional practices, with ideas about administration such as New Public Management (NPM) (Engida and Bardill 2013) further complicating the mixture. And the nature of the hybrid may be different depending upon where one observes administration. In the national capital the rhetoric, and to some extent the practice, will be "modern" and post-colonial, while in decentralized administration the practices may be much more traditional.

In general terms, I will be arguing (with Darbon 2002) that merely dealing with the formal structures of government, or technical ideas such as those of the NPM, is not sufficient to understand contemporary governance and public administration in African countries. And much the same argument can be made for administration in other developing and transitional political systems. Even some countries in Central and Eastern Europe that have modernized their administrative structures to gain entry to the European Union have experienced significant "backsliding" in the direction of older forms of governance and administration (Bauer et al. forthcoming).

In addition, even within the same country there may be differences in the style of administration. Some of these may be a function of the social structure and the form of government before and during the colonial period. In addition, the nature and strength of local economies may also affect the capacity of local governments, and local leaders, to assert their power against the central government (Boone 2003). Thus, despite the appearance of much of the forms of administration derived from colonial experience, there are other factors at work that may diminish the continuing appearance of that "rupture."

Patterns of Colonial Rule

The contrast between British and French colonial rule in Africa, and elsewhere, is often drawn as a stark dichotomy. The prevailing assumption has been that British colonial administration was characterized by indirect rule, coopting and utilizing local political structures to govern. This pattern, typified by the administrative style and writing of Lord Lugard (1965), was perhaps best demonstrated in India and other Asian colonies of the United Kingdom (Braibanti 1966) but was also present in Africa. Indirect rule was not the same in every British colony, or even in different parts of the same colony (Maddox 2018), but compared to other versions of colonialism British rule was indirect.

One observer of British colonization in Africa argued that British colonial officials acted more as advisors to local village and tribal leaders than as rulers (Crowder 1964). While that observation may underestimate the amount of command and control exercised through colonial administration, especially in matters such as taxation and security, it does say something about the day-to-day workings of colonial government in those colonies. There were certainly issues about which the colonial administration would become deeply and directly involved, but many quotidian issues could be left to the traditional leadership to manage. Further, when traditional leadership structures were not readily available, British administrators would attempt to create them (Collins and Burns 2007).

The contrasting French (and also Belgian and Portuguese) pattern was assumed to involve more direct intervention in governance by colonial officials (Diouf 2002). Typically there would be a larger contingent of officials from France in the colonies, and they would be more directly involved in implementing law—generally bringing with them the code law of France. The French style of administration in the colonies, like the style of administration in France itself, was centralized and controlling, attempting to create uniformity and a thorough application of the law throughout the territory.

Further, the French style of administration was assimilationist, attempting to create millions of new Frenchmen rather than merely ruling through existing social structures (Betts 1961). The task of ruling large swathes of the world from Paris was, of course, daunting, so some mechanisms of indirect rule were employed, but the general pattern was built on an assumption that once Africans, or Vietnamese, were exposed to French culture and administration, they would naturally accept its superiority and adopt those practices.

The differences between French and the British styles of administration lead to two questions about the enduring consequences of these patterns of administration. The first is, given our interest in the persistence of administration, whether one pattern or the other has survived more fully after independence, and can be seen in existing administrative systems. After all, colonial rule in Africa was a relatively brief period in historical terms, and hence the patterns of administration may have had insufficient time to become institutionalized.

The second question is whether the differences in colonial administration appear to have had any enduring effects on the quality of administration in African countries. One argument would be that indirect rule could have prepared African subjects of colonialism more fully for governing after independence. The contrary argument has been that by "propping up" traditional structures indirect rule did not make a sufficient break with traditional administration and hence modernization would be more difficult. Both of these questions are difficult to answer in any definitive manner, but we will attempt to provide some insights into the effects of colonial administration.

Contemporary Public Administration in Africa

Public administration in contemporary Africa has continued enjoy a poor reputation, despite numerous attempts at reform, coming both from the governments themselves and from international donor organizations. The usual characterization of these administrative systems is that they are rife with corruption and inefficiency, and often indifferent to the citizens who they are intended to serve (see Moïse 2000). There are "islands of excellence" (Andrews 2013) or "pockets of effectiveness" (Roll 2009) within these administrative systems, but the general picture is portrayed as rather dismal.

The paradox of public bureaucracies in Africa, albeit less than in other developing societies, is that they are also powerful actors (Moshonas 2014) while suffering from many dysfunctional problems when viewed from the perspective of developed countries. For all the dysfunctions observed within these institutions they are central, and in some cases dominant, actors in governance. The bureaucracies tend to contain a number of highly educated individuals, although less proportionately than in Northern bureaucracies because of nepotism and patronage. They also are important links with the donor community and are responsible for administering the development projects funded by those donors. And, finally, they are to some extent decentralized and therefore represent the state throughout the country.

The transfer of administrative traditions to African countries, or indeed any other subjugated territory may involve two elements. The first, and simpler to manage, are the formal institutions of government and administration—the "dead hand" of structure (Painter and Peters 2010a: 6; see also Yesilkagit 2010: 148). The other element of tradition is more alive, and is composed of the ideas and values that affect the behavior of the current administrators. Even with the institutional elements of the tradition, there is a possibility that there is formal adherence to the procedures while the content of the decision-making is significantly different. This separation of reality from form is very much what Riggs (1964) described in his discussion of "prismatic society" (see also "double speak," discussed below).

Although the problems of contemporary governance in Africa, as well as in Asia and Latin America, are generally blamed on contemporary politicians and bureaucrats, there is also an argument that some of the dysfunctions of bureaucracy are learned behaviors from the colonial period that have been institutionalized. Olivier de Sardan (2009) has argued that the current practice of bureaucracies in Africa represent the effects of the two "ruptures" mentioned above: one caused by colonialism and the second caused by bureaucratization in the post-colonial period.[2]

---

[2] That bureaucratization may still reflect the bureaucratic patterns that were developed during the colonial period.

While colonial heritage is indeed important, we must also remember that this was a relatively brief period in African history (unlike the three centuries of Spanish and Portuguese rule in Latin America; see Hyden 2013; Foa 2016). For example, Ghana was a formal colony of Britain for ninety years, although the British and other Europeans had been involved in the slave trade and other economic activities for several centuries prior to that. And the current country of Benin was a French colony for just over sixty years. Thus, can a colonial power alter thinking about government and administration in such a relatively brief period, especially given that there were established patterns of rule within those future colonies?[3]

Following the point raised by Blundo and Le Meur (2009), we need to understand the persistence of two traditions in contemporary African administrations. One goes back to the pre-colonial period and includes both hierarchical elements from kingdoms and empires, such as Dahomey, Mali, and Songhai. It also includes decentralized local, customary rule in villages, with local elites serving as de facto executive and judicial authorities. While the hierarchical elements of the pre-colonial tradition were largely destroyed by colonialism, the decentralized elements persisted, even under direct rule (Bayart 1993). While this local governance is clearly not a state tradition, it does affect public administration.

The second tradition has been the pattern of administration inherited from the colonial period, with its linkages to the imperial center, and hence a new form of hierarchical control. These two forms of governance were not necessarily incompatible. Just as some of the consolidated democracies permit more traditional patterns of governance to exist within their boundaries (e.g., Native Americans in the United States and the Maori in New Zealand), these arrangements may be functional politically, although perhaps not administratively. That is, permitting dual patterns of governance may cause less conflict with society than attempts to create a uniform, "modern" administration. And these more traditional forms of governing may be more effective, at least in the short term.

One of the most important elements of post-colonial transformation in Africa is the shift in goals for administration. While the colonial period (and to some extent the pre-colonial governance structures) were concerned with control and extraction, the goals of administration after independence became development. As Edward Schumacher (1975: 85) wrote about the goals of administration after independence, "Central...was replacing the 'law

---

[3] The Kingdom of Dahomey in what is now Benin, for example.

and order' colonial bureaucracy with a system of public administration genuinely 'oriented to development.'" This shift in focus then involved attempting to change from public administration that mimicked the colonial past to a new style of administration (Rutake 1986).

Although politically important, that shift in goals created conflict within the administrative system. A number of colonial administrators were still in positions in government, and numerous advisors were provided by the former colonial countries. These administrators appeared to still have the "law and order" orientation of the colonial past. This internal conflict may have been less in the former French colonies because of the French experience with public sector planning, a mechanism that became important in attempts to foster economic and social development. But in most countries there has been conflict, and some continuing conflict, over how administration would be conducted in the post-colonial period (see Umeh and Andranovich 2005).

Elements of Dysfunctional Administration

There has been some general agreement among commentators that public administration in much of Africa has been less than effective (Umeh and Andranovich 2005). Much of the discussion of the failings of administration in Africa focuses on corruption and patrimonialism (Blundo et al. 2006), but there are a number of other factors that reduce the effectiveness of these bureaucracies. The dysfunctional elements of public administration in the continent have been described in a number of ways, but Olivier de Sardan (2009) has provided a rather comprehensive list. In his view, contemporary administrative failures can be defined through a number of factors (presented in Table 9.1). Berman and Tettey (2001) have a shorter but similar list, related to the failures of information technology in African bureaucracies: the limited technical capacity of bureaucrats, hierarchical decision-making by generalists in government, and the predominance of patron–client relationships in government.

Olivier de Sardan is quick to note that all of these negative features of bureaucracies exist in all administrative systems, including the ones described in other chapters of this book. For example, the corruption, patronage, and patrimonialism that are considered characteristic of many African bureaucracies can also be found in Latin American, Asian, and some Eastern European countries (Holmes 2003; Kopecký et al. 2012) The difference between those cases and most African cases is that the dysfunctions are not as pervasive in those systems as in the countries on which he based his analysis.

Table 9.1 Sources of failure in African public administration

Clientelism	Linkages between patrons and clients that undermine universality in administration
Double-speak*	Using one set of words and concepts to justify actions to those outside of government, while using another inside.
	Double-speak is especially important when dealing with donor organizations
The formal and the real	Formal institutions exist, but there are other, less formal, mechanisms in place that actually control governing and the relationships between bureaucrats and their clients
"Every man for himself"	There is a pronounced absence of teamwork within public organizations, as each employee pursues his or her own goals.
	Individuals keep their sphere of action as personal property and do not engage in exchange with others
"Privilegism"	The concept inherited to a great extent from the colonial period, that administrators should be a privileged class and need have little regard for the ordinary citizen
Generalized exchange of favors	Public services are provided differently depending upon the personal relationships, or lack thereof, between the bureaucrat and the client.
	Friends and relatives are treated very well; others are treated with indifference
Systemic corruption	Following from the pattern of exchanging favors, there has been pervasive corruption within administrative systems.
	Government business may not be accomplished without some exchange of money
Lack of motivation	The administrative system is demotivating for the individuals within it.
	Official salaries are derisory and motivate individuals to search for other sources of income, including corruption

Note: * This category is, of course, very reminiscent of Fred Riggs' (1964) work on prismatic societies. There is one language involving the usual terms of modern administration, and to some extent the inherited models from colonial times, and another language for discussing the realities of administration, especially in the field (see Lund 2006).

While to some extent colonialism may explain these negative features of African bureaucracies, there is also a strong traditional and social base. Michal Herzfeld (1992) argues, for example, that all bureaucracies may attempt to create indifference toward those who do not conform to its classifications. Therefore, the persistence of ethnicity as a strong foundation of society in Africa tends to make bureaucrats indifferent to those citizens from other ethnic groups. This is not the Weberian notion of equality and acting without regard for social characteristics; it is more a lack of interest in "outsiders." While some political systems in Africa have been able to develop consociational systems that are more inclusive (Lemarchand 2007), there are still patterns of exclusion of ethnic groups in many African countries (see Mustapha 2006).

Other scholars (e.g., Moyo 1992) have argued that even more than indifference to some groups in society, bureaucracy in Africa tends to be indifferent to clients in general. As mentioned in Table 9.1, the "privilegism" of the bureaucracy, and other rulers, sets them apart from society and leads to a culture that is the antithesis of the "public service motivation" expected in European, North American, and some other administrative systems. Akintoye (1976) blames this, in part, on the manner in which African states gained their independence. This was in most cases not through revolution but through one set of autocratic rulers replacing another.

In addition, the clientelism and generalized exchange of favors appear to be components of traditional social and economic life that cannot necessarily be attributed to colonial administrative patterns. While indirect rule may have reinforced relationships between traditional leaders and other members of their village or region, those patterns were in place long before colonial rule began. If anything, these clientelistic relationships may have been reinforced after independence, when resources available to the state were less tightly controlled than under colonial regimes attempting to extract resources from the colonies.

Perhaps the most important element of the current dysfunctions of bureaucracy in Africa that can be associated with the colonial past is what Olivier de Sardan calls "privilegism." This is the assumption by holders of positions in public administration that they are entitled to special privileges, and are set apart from the rest of society. Therefore, rather than being servants of the people—the assumption in much of Northern public administration, e.g., the public service motivation concept (Perry and Hondeghem 2008; see also p. 37 in this volume)—these public administrators feel no particular responsibility for providing public services. Nor do they appear particularly interested in providing services to the public.

Finally, it is important to consider the role of street-level bureaucracy in service delivery in Africa, as is true in all countries (Hupe 2019). The "interface" bureaucracy may be the weakest element of public administration in African countries. Many of the bureaucratic dysfunctions already mentioned are manifested particularly strongly at the local level, especially personal ties and the "economy of affection" (Hyden 1980). In addition, local government officials and officials in deconcentrated central government organizations have become adept at appropriating resources intended for distribution for themselves (Sabbi 2017).

Table 9.2   Comparison of civic and affective spaces of communication

	Action level	Interactive behavior	Claims of validity	Effects
Civic	Principles	Discursive	Universal	Enhancing citizen voice
Affective	Concrete action	Compliant	Local	Strengthening loyalty

Source: Hyden (2010).

Göran Hyden (2010) contrasted the "civic" version of communication within a society to the affective version, arguing that the latter was more powerful in African political and administrative systems (Table 9.2). Similar to the arguments from Olivier de Sardan, the power of the affection and social linkages make movement toward a more formally bureaucratic, universalistic model of service delivery difficult. Relationships among individuals remain more particularistic, as opposed to the universalistic expectations of bureaucracy. And these forces appear to have survived the brief colonial period in these countries.

Does it Matter?

The above descriptions of the influence of colonial patterns of governance on contemporary African public bureaucracy has described some clear influences, especially in terms of structure, although underlying social patterns appear to dominate the influences of colonialism. While some of the literature discusses African bureaucracies as one large group, African political systems do appear to govern differently. The obvious question which then arises is whether those differences in administrative traditions have had any impact other than differences in institutions and processes.

Substantial literature exists on the impact of colonialism on the success and failure of governance as a function of colonial experiences (see, e.g., Lange et al. 2006; Gerring et al. 2011). Much of this literature has focused on the economic well-being of countries after independence (Iyer 2010), in part because it is easier to measure the consequences of colonialism in economic than in political or social terms. There are certainly reasonable measures of success in governance, as I will discuss below, but standard economic measures such as growth in per capita GDP, are more widely accepted as definitive measures.

Two dominant lines of thought appear in the literature on the effects of colonialism (see Gerring et al. 2011; see also Bernhard et al. 2004). The first is that those colonialisms that utilized existing governance structures, such as the British did in parts of India and to a lesser extent in Africa, will be associated with greater subsequent governance success (see Smith 1978). Preserving the indigenous structures, it is argued, provides an ongoing foundation for governance than can persist and be used in the period of independence to augment, or even substitute for, governance through the state apparatus. In addition, the use of indigenous political and social structures for governance may legitimate the colonial regime more readily than those patterns of colonialism that supplant the existing structures.

The alternative argument is that breaking down and delegitimizing indigenous governance structures was necessary for successful governance in the future, meaning here governance of a "modern" variety. In this conception of governance, the persistence of customary practices of governance represents competition for state institutions, and the public may tend to maintain their commitments to traditional structures to the exclusion of the state. Implicit in this argument is that traditional structures must be broken down if more modern institutions of governance are to be successful, and, further, there is an assumption that modernity is an important goal for most African countries (Hyden 2010).

These arguments are related to the discussion of informal institutions presented by Gretchen Helmke and Steven Levistsky (2004). They are concerned with the extent to which informal institutions can contribute to, or detract from, the capacity to achieve governance, especially when the formal institutions of the state are not effective (Table 9.3). In the case of public administration in Africa, some aspects of the traditional administrative structures can complement the formal institutions of the state (Cell A), as when local traditional leaders perform important administrative and judicial functions, or the two patterns of governing may accommodate one another (Cell C). In more extreme cases the informal rules may substitute (Cell B) the formal institutions when those formal institutions are incapable of providing governance.

There is a good deal of evidence about the impact of these different styles of colonialism. For example, Iyer (2010) found that within India, the parts of the country that had been ruled indirectly have fared substantially worse economically than have those that were ruled more directly by the British Raj. Acemoglu et al. (2001) argued further that the choice of institutions was not so much a difference between colonial powers as a function of mortality rates among European settlers, with more disease-ridden parts of the continent being ruled more indirectly. Where the mortality rate was high, colonial

Table 9.3 Relationship of formal and informal institutions

Formal institutions		
	Effective	*Ineffective*
Convergent	Complementary	Substitutive
Outcomes		
Divergent	Accommodating	Competing

Source: Helmke and Levitsky (2004).

powers created extractive (indirect) institutions that continue to be associated with lower rates of economic growth. And Firmin-Sellers (2000) has identified continuing impacts of colonial patterns on policy choices by governments, especially in property rights and fundamental economic policies.

Other scholars have attempted to identify the effects of patterns of colonialism on contemporary governance. For example, Lange (2004) found that higher levels of indirect rule among British colonies were associated with more negative scores on World Bank governance indicators. This study (as was true for Iyer 2010) held at least some elements of colonialism constant, so that the effects of patterns of colonialism might be identified more clearly. Within the one style of colonialism, more direct interventions by government appeared to produce less effective governance after independence.

A study by Lange et al. (2006) contrasted the impacts of Spanish and British colonialism, with the former style of colonialism being very much direct rule that attempted to impose a distinct hierarchical pattern of control and the latter often being more indirect. Further, the Spanish style of colonialism created a more predatory state that did not support local economic development, while the more liberal British style generally fostered greater economic development within the colony. British colonialism was extractive, as have been all colonial experiences, but there was some concern for indigenous economic development.

In summary, the relationship between the colonial experience and contemporary governance is complex, and it is difficult to make definitive statements linking national patterns with outcomes. To some extent the effect of indirect rule, for example, depended upon the existence of legitimate and effective institutions within the areas to which some autonomy was delegated. But it does appear clear that in many ways colonialism was not necessarily the sole or perhaps even the major cause of governance difficulties in contemporary Africa.

Colonialism and Public Administration

The studies cited here have focused primarily on the economic and political effects of patterns of colonialism, but less on the consequences for public administration. Therefore, I have analyzed the consequences for public administration of having a British or French colonial legacy among African countries. Using data from the Quality of Governance website for overall governance capacity and several specific aspects of public administration, it appears that, in general, former British colonies have fared somewhat better than former French colonies in sub-Saharan Africa (Table 9.4). The mean score for the former colonies was higher, and the maximum scores were also superior.[4] That said, the former French colonies in North Africa appear to be performing somewhat better than the former British colonies in Africa as a whole.[5]

Another important measure for the performance of public administration in Africa (and elsewhere) is the level of corruption. In one measure, respondents to a survey were asked to estimate what percentage of tax officials will ask for bribes. The sums of money involved here are generally small, but this petty corruption often grates on the ordinary citizen and creates a very negative perception of the performance of the public sector. The other measure of corruption is more comprehensive (see Stephenson 2017). Using these

Table 9.4 Measures of administrative performance of countries based on colonial background

	British	French	French North Africa
Overall governance *	54.1	46.7	59.0
	(73–21)	(61–28)	(65–53)
Corruption perception **	0.375	0.416	0.313
	(0.56–0.19)	(0.55–0.22)	(0.40–0.23)
Bayesian corruption index ***	54.3	62.8	49.0
	(67–37)	(75–44)	(57–45)

Notes: Average scores and range* Expert survey, possible scores range 0–100; ** Expectation of bribe request from tax officer; *** Expert survey, possible scores range 0–100.

Source: Calculated using data from the Quality of Governance Institute, University of Gothenburg, https://qog.pol.gu.se/.

[4] The very low minimum scores were from the Sudan and South Sudan, which had been experiencing a long and destructive civil war.

[5] If one removes Sudan and South Sudan from the British colonies, then the score for the former British colonies is roughly the same as for the North African countries with a French legacy. This might be justified given the effects of the civil war and then break-up of Sudan.

two measures of corruption, it again appears that the former British colonies have performed better than the former French colonies, although the differences are not large.

These quantitative indicators are useful for comparing countries, but qualitative methods may provide some greater insight into the dynamics linking colonial backgrounds and contemporary government performance. For example, Lange (2009) demonstrates the different paths that, within a common British legacy of colonialism, countries have developed after independence. Again, this research does not focus on the development of the administrative system per se, but there does seem to be a significant relationship between the degree of direct rule and post-independence development, with more direct rule associated with more development. But that relationship did have important exceptions, with indirectly ruled Botswana developing rapidly, and directly ruled Guyana having a poor development record following independence.

In summary, the colonial legacy appears to have had some influence on the quality of contemporary governance and public administration in African countries, but the differences are not as stark as might be expected. This relative absence of difference is especially noticeable given the amount of past and current discussion about the various styles of colonialism. Further, there is also significant variance within groups of countries classified by their colonial background, indicating that the link is not strong, and more factors must be considered before reaching any conclusions about the influence of patterns of colonialism.

Summary and Conclusions

Scholars tend to know somewhat less about the transfer of administrative practices than we do about the transfer of substantive public policies (see Rose 1993; Dunlop 2020; but see also Sager et al. 2018). That said, the experiences of the NPM era did show that ideas about public administration can travel and can be adopted in different settings (McCourt and Martin 2001; Pollitt et al. 2001). In a wide range of settings and in a variety of interpretations, the ideas of NPM were implemented around the globe. African bureaucracies were also a target for the NPM reformers.

While for some countries the ideas of NPM were imposed by external donors, with the implied or real threat of loss of support, its imposition in colonial systems was more immediate. That said, given the emphasis on indirect rule especially in the British colonies, the patterns of administration at home for the colonial government may not have been readily apparent to the African nations. Much of the influence of the tradition therefore may have been transmitted after independence, when former colonial officers stayed on to advise the new leaders on how best to organize and manage their newly independent governments.

The alternative conceptual approach to understand contemporary African administration is path dependence, and the survival of patterns of administration that were in place, or at least implicit before colonialism, after the years of colonial rule. While the "rupture" of the colonial period was of course extremely significant, it was insufficient to undermine deeply seated social patterns, and ideas about appropriate patterns of rule. The survival of many traditional structures, and perhaps even more traditional ideas, has meant that contemporary public administration in Africa represents very much the prismatic pattern described by Riggs half a century ago.

But in spite of the various difficulties faced, administration in Africa works, after a fashion. As Olivier de Sardan (2009) argues, African states and their administrations are not "failed" or "phantoms." They exist and continue to provide public services, even if the quality is often not what one might hope for, and the style of delivery is not as public-oriented as we might prefer. Further, there are often islands of excellent performance (Crook 2010), based on individual leadership or successful reforms. And the relationship of contemporary administration to the colonial past is paradoxical. On the one hand, colonialism clearly created the pre-conditions for many of the governance failures observed in African regimes, while, on the other hand, the development of dysfunctions has been largely post-colonial and reflects social and cultural patterns that may have preceded colonialism.

As is so often the case, no single factor can account for the contemporary public administration in Africa, or elsewhere. Causation is complex and involves interactions of factors in ways that may not be readily apparent. I have spent most of this book developing the idea of administrative traditions, but have never claimed that this alone shapes the current practice of public administration. Rather, those underlying traditions—whether indigenous or imposed—are an important, but not the sole, explanation for observed patterns in contemporary governments.

10

Persistence and Change in Public Administration

To this point, I have argued that there is a continuing influence of administrative styles that were established early in the life of political systems. I believe that I have demonstrated that there are some enduring features found in the administrative systems of a number of countries, and these exist within the families of countries. This persistence is evident even when there have been significant changes in the political systems within which they function, and the policies that they are implementing. But at the same time there have been, and continue to be, important pressures toward change, and perhaps especially pressures toward convergence.

Pressures toward persistence and change in patterns of administration need to be understood in theoretical terms as well as in the more descriptive terms presented in the previous chapters. There are a variety of explanations for the persistence of and movement away from traditional patterns of administration. Using evidence from the numerous cases presented so far in this volume, and additional material, this chapter discusses alternative explanations for both persistence and change in administration. In so doing, I will highlight some of the differences among the several varieties of administrative systems. Some of these explanations are rather general, focusing on the characteristics of institutions in general, while others are more specific to public administration.

Likewise, there are a variety of alternative explanations for change in public administration. The most widely discussed has been the diffusion of the ideas of New Public Management (NPM), as well as other ideas about what the state of the art should be. There is also a presumed tendency toward convergence in the administrative systems of at least the industrialized democracies, and even more especially among European countries. Even the administrative systems of less-developed countries have been under pressure from donor organizations and the international diffusion of "ideas in good currency" to adopt more marketized versions of public administration (Schick 1998; Andrews 2013). Being more dependent upon external resources and perhaps

Administrative Traditions: Understanding the Roots of Contemporary Administrative Behavior. B. Guy Peters,
Oxford University Press (2021). © B. Guy Peters. DOI: 10.1093/oso/9780198297253.003.0010

having contested political structures these governments may be more amen-able to change, or at a minimum attempted change, than are European, North American, and Antipodean systems.

This one dominant explanation of change in the public sector—NPM and market models—can be supplemented by at least one other that focuses more on the democratic elements of public administration than on efficiency. The participatory approach to administrative reform (Peters 2010b) or New Public Governance (Aucoin 2012; Aucoin et al. 2013) has emphasized values of public involvement rather than efficiency, as well as embracing some of the older administrative values such as accountability and probity. These pressures for more democratic change can also be seen in the emphasis on collaborative governance (Ansell and Gash 2008; Peters et al. forthcoming). Although not appearing as radical a departure from traditional public administration as the NPM approach, this alternative mode of reform does challenge the legalism and formality of more traditional approaches, and even in democratic regimes may not be particularly welcome.

We should note here that neither of these approaches is entirely new in all administrative systems. For example, we have argued elsewhere that NPM was less important in the United States and Canada because many of the basic ideas concerning management had been adopted much earlier (Peters and Savoie 1994; Peters 2010a). Likewise, for the Scandinavian countries, partici-patory ideas of governance and public administration were hardly novel (Sørensen and Torfing 2007; see also Chapter 5 in this volume). Thus, an argument that there has been a total revolution in thinking about public administration is difficult to sustain, although certainly some ideas have become more prominent and generated pressures for change.

In addition, although I am discussing these various alternatives for public administration, we should also be aware that they have broader implications and represent alternative modes of governance. NPM emphasized the market and efficiency for administration, but it was one component of a broader neo-liberal movement emphasizing market principles for government as a whole. And, likewise, collaborative governance is about more than public administration, and emphasizes the importance of collaboration for policy design (Lewis et al. 2019) and governance in general terms as well as in the public bureaucracy.

I will begin by discussing concepts of reform and change in public admin-istration. Having dedicated most of this book to persistence, I will first discuss why persistence can, and often should, be sacrificed for the sake of needed change. Although there has been persistence in many administrative patterns, change is always present, and the possibilities for generating effective change need to be understood. I will then return to the theme of persistence and change, and their co-existence in public administration, at the end of this chapter.

The Fundamentals of Change

Administrative systems, like most other social systems, have a high level of inertia. Left to themselves, they tend to persist in well-established patterns until there is some good reason to change. Further, administrative systems have perhaps more reasons to persist in their established patterns than do other social systems. First, they tend to have some legal foundation that defines their purpose and provides them with the capacity to enforce and/or make law. Second, they have clients—whether individual citizens, organizations, or perhaps other parts of government—that want some predictability in the behavior of these organizations.[1] Third, members of these organizations are committed to them and may be loath to alter their ways of conducting business.

As implied above, there have been some major reform efforts during the past decades that are often argued to have produced convergence in administration (Olsen 2003). I will discuss the convergence argument in some detail below, but will begin by discussing more general questions about reform in administration, and their relationship to the administrative traditions that have been the principal focus of this book. As important for the argument here is an understanding of the ways in which administrative traditions can resist change, or integrate change into existing patterns of governing.

Perhaps most fundamentally regime change can alter the public administration that serves the regime. For example, Ian Scott (2005) described the major changes in administration in Hong Kong following the return of the former British colony to China. While some aspects of British administration have remained in place, new patterns of administration reflect the fundamental political differences in the regimes. Similarly, changes in public administration following the fall of communism in Central and Eastern Europe produced significant changes (Nunberg et al. 1999), although the nature of

---

[1] In short, bureaucracies can provide "credible commitment" on policies that may be less likely from more politicized institutions within the public sector. Even here, however, some public sector organizations such as central banks and regulatory agencies may have greater demand for long-term credibility than do other public organizations.

the new administrative systems differed significantly across the political systems there.[2]

The above examples of regime change would certainly fit any criterion of fundamental, but seemingly less significant changes in political regimes can also alter public administration significantly, and permanently. For example, Margaret Thatcher's government did not enact massive institutional change at the political level, but it did produce large-scale and enduring reform for public administration (Savoie 1994; Burton 2013).

In addition to fundamental regime change, administrative changes appear to have a number of other drivers. For the period following roughly the 1970s onward, one of the major drivers has been failure, due to perceptions that government as a whole was failing and public administration was a major component of that failure (see Stoker forthcoming). While, objectively, there have been some major failures (along with some major successes) in the public sector, the use of the failure idea to promote administrative change has also been a construction of the political right (and also to some extent from the political left) that has reduced the legitimacy of government and of public administration. But this characterization of failure has been more successful within the Anglo-American tradition than in others, perhaps because of the general distrust of the public sector in that approach to governing.

One factor that has not arisen among these drivers of change has been that the administrative system is fundamentally unsuited for the political system within which it functions—the most extreme form of failure. While some NPM critiques of government border on that type of argument, most reform efforts involve tweaking the existing model of administration and attempting to make it work better while maintaining the fundamental values and practices of the system. Even the most fundamental reforms of administration have paid some obeisance to the underlying traditions and history of the administrative system.

As well as being driven by political pressures, and the sense that existing administrative systems are unsuited for the tasks at hand, change in public administration has also been influenced by technology, and especially by "e-government" (see Homburg 2008). While the potential of technology to totally transform government has been significantly overstated, at least at the time of this writing, there is little doubt that information technology has been altering the ways in which governments work.

---

[2] Some of the systems appeared to recapture some aspects of their previous administrative patterns under the Austro-Hungarian Empire, while others were more innovative or copied patterns from Western European systems.

Some of these changes have been internal, involving the capacity to manage information more quickly and efficiently, but more important changes may appear in the relationships between government and citizens. Rather than having a civil service employing large numbers of "street-level bureaucrats" who meet with citizens and decide about individual claims, much of contact of citizens with government would be electronic. This style of governance, while appealing perhaps for economic reasons, may also undermine the more participatory styles of governing that are characteristic of the Scandinavian tradition, and at least in part of the Anglo-American traditions (Chadwick and May 2003).

Even if the intended, or presumed, result is not convergence, diffusion and learning can be a powerful driver of change in public administration (Toonen 2003; Radaelli and Dunlop 2013). The rather simplistic model of learning often applied assumes that a single administrative system learns from another that it deems to be more successful, or more admirable, in some other dimension. That simplistic model, however, is now largely eclipsed by more complex models of organizations or whole administrative systems attempting to import ideas from a range of different examples, and create less piecemeal reforms (Dwyer and Ellison 2009).

The above paragraph purposefully said "attempting to import" ideas because learning, and especially cross-national learning, is difficult. Although often phrased in rather generic terms—especially for NPM—administrative reforms often have a clear cultural and normative foundation that may make simply moving them from one setting to another difficult. Indeed, moving reforms outside their natural homes may produce exactly the opposite effects of those intended. Moving NPM reforms into settings lacking a managerialist culture and a large employment base may create more inefficiency and potential corruption rather than the improvement in public sector performance advertised.

In terms of historical institutionalist approaches to change, the common pattern of change has not been a complete "punctuation" in the pattern but more things like layering, drift, and displacement. That is, rather than a complete transformation, most change involves gradual movements away from the status quo, or perhaps adding some elements to the administrative system, while retaining much of the existing framework for administering public programs. This pattern of reform also means that understanding the nature of an organization, or group of organizations, at any one time involves an almost archeological unpacking of several waves of reform and the continuing interactions of the initial organizational DNA and the various reforms that have been added.

The Convergence of Administrative Systems

Change occurs in all public administrative systems, and may move in a variety of different directions depending upon the time and the political system. That said, it has been argued that reforms over the past several decades have produced convergence among administrative systems, with all changes tending to move in a particular direction (Meyer-Sahling and Van Stolk 2015; but see also Pollitt 2001). The ideas of NPM, and more recently the ideas of governance, as alternatives to historical patterns of administration have been assumed to produce substantial uniformity in administrative systems. Fritz Sager and colleagues (2018) have examined the spread of ideas and convergence across the Atlantic, finding more commonality than might have been expected. The assumption of increased uniformity might be expected to be true, given the powerful forces that have been behind the adoption of those ideas for reforming the public sector.

Several factors have tended to encourage a push toward greater convergence. In the first place, the ideas motivating NPM reforms themselves were powerful, even if somewhat disparate, and appeared to have substantial plausibility to government leaders (Hood 1991). If, indeed, private sector management appeared more successful than did public administration, then perhaps it made sense for public administration to adopt those ideas. This was especially true given the prevalence of ideas about the failure of public administration, and of government considered more generally (Peters 2015).

The apparent success of the private sector was in contrast to the perceived failure of the public sector. Despite the development and implementation of the welfare state, the preservation of peace (at least within Europe) and the widespread economic growth of much of the postwar period, there was a dominant zeitgeist in the latter part of the twentieth century that emphasized crisis (Crozier et al. 1975), "ungovernability," bankruptcy (Rose and Peters 1976), and the end of late capitalism (O'Connor 1973). This sense of failure of the public sector was reiterated with the 2008 financial crisis, and a sense that governments had failed to control the private sector and had failed their publics. Given all of that, it is not surprising that one might think that market-based ideas would come to be extremely influential in the design of public sector policies and administration.

In addition to the power of the ideas themselves, powerful political figures fostered these reforms and helped to diffuse the ideas. This was especially true within the Anglo-American world where Margaret Thatcher, Ronald Reagan, and Brian Mulroney, inter alia, advocated market-based reforms within government in general and public administration in particular (Savoie 1994). While these proponents were from the political right, others from the political left such as Tony Blair (Cutler and Waine 2000) and Bill Clinton implemented their own, somewhat less extreme, versions of market-based management within government.[3]

There is a much larger literature on the diffusion of policy ideas than there is on the spread of ideas about institutions, other than perhaps those of democracy. While the evidence about the success and failure of policy transfers is, at best, mixed, policymakers continue to borrow ideas from other (presumably) successful programs and attempt to implement them in new settings. Transplanting ideas about institutions may be even more problematic, given that they depend upon a collection of "myths, symbols, routines," that make implementing them in different settings extremely problematic (see Meyer and Rowan 1977; March and Olsen 1989).

Public administration systems also learn from one another, even when they originate in different traditions and continents. Fritz Sager et al. (2018) point out the extent to which learning has occurred between European and American administrative systems, and argue that the distinctiveness of these systems is less than usually assumed. However, that learning may still occur in a context of a dominant paradigm of administration which is not significantly altered by learning some useful elements from other administrative traditions.[4]

Finally, the ideas of reforming public administration (and doing so especially by using market-based instruments) have been diffused by international organizations. Many international donor organizations became enamored of the ideas of NPM, and saw them as a means of enhancing the efficiency and effectiveness of administration in poorly performing governments in less-developed countries; in some cases receiving aid from donors became contingent upon adopting these reforms. This contingency was in place no matter how appropriate or inappropriate the ideas of NPM were for the countries in question (Schick 1998).

This spread of forms of administration can be seen within the framework of Dimaggio and Powell's (1991) institutional isomorphism. Their argument

---

[3] Interestingly, many of these ideas were initially fostered by the Labour government in New Zealand, but then became mantras for the political right.

[4] Speaking of the practices of imperial Germany, Woodrow Wilson (1887) wrote: "If I see a murderous fellow sharpening a knife cleverly I can borrow his way of sharpening the knife without borrowing his probable intention...." By this he meant that he, or the United States, could learn about efficient administration without having to adopt other aspects of the political system.

was, in a simple form, that organizations operating in the same functional domains would over time resemble one another. This isomorphism was assumed to result through one of three processes: mimesis, coercion, or learning. In the case of assumed convergence among administrative systems it appears that any of these three processes could be relevant. For example, there is certainly some level of simple copying going on—to be a modern administrative system one needs to have implemented NPM (see Hood 1991). In other cases there may be some real learning occurring, with governments seeing that other systems are being successful through the adoption of certain ideas about administration. Finally, as argued above, with the case of many less-developed countries there is a significant amount of coercion being applied by donor organizations to accept reforms based on NPM.

Europeanization as a Special Case

One of the more important forces presumed to be creating isomorphism among public administrations, at least within Europe, was the development of the European Union and the process of "Europeanization" (Börzel 2002). Although the exact meaning of this term has been debated, the general argument is that being a member of the EU placed pressures on governments to develop structures and procedures that corresponded to a general European model. Some of this pressure was coercive, especially for accession countries, but some of it was simply mimesis. With the Union now six decades old, we should expect a good deal of convergence in patterns of administration.

   Although Europeanization might appear to be a powerful force, one of the strongest arguments against the powers of convergence appears within the European Union. In many ways this is the easiest case for a convergence argument, given that individual countries have joined a proto-state which imposes numerous administrative demands on them, and which has its own administrative style to which members must adapt.[5] Again, this demand for conformity was greatest for accession countries who had to develop the capacity to administer the *acquis* before they were admitted to the Union. But even for countries that joined the EU in its early days, the demands of

---

[5] That adaptation is, of course, mutual and the Union must also take into account the administrative styles of the member states. As I pointed out in Chapter 7, there is continuing interaction between the national bureaucracies and the Brussels bureaucracy.

transposition of regulations and the subsequent imposition of those regulations placed pressures for convergence on a common European model.

The problem with this idea of the Europeanization of administration is that the evidence that this has occurred is rather weak. In an extensive work, Christoph Knill (2005) argued that Europeanization of administration appears to be a plausible argument, but his study focused on only two administrative systems—Germany and the United Kingdom. Both of these systems have well-developed administrative patterns that might be expected to resist change, and come from relatively powerful countries that also would have greater capacity to resist pressures toward uniformity.[6]

Edward Page (2003) has also contrasted pressures for Europeanization with pressures for persistence of national administrative patterns. Page finds that although there are a variety of forces that may lead to the homogenization of administration among the member states of the EU, there are perhaps even more powerful forces that prevent the convergence predicted by some scholars and European advocates. As Page points out, the actors in Brussels continue to function *through* the member states, and those states continue to perform their tasks much as they did before the creation of the Union.

Even for the accession countries of Central and Eastern Europe there are marked differences in the extent to which Europeanization has occurred. Some of these differences reflect the historical patterns of public administration in these countries, with those countries with a more bureaucratic tradition (e.g., those having a background in the Hapsburg imperial style) finding adaptation perhaps easier than others (Verheijen and Rabrenovic 2007). But other countries have developed their own approaches to administration after gaining independence from the Soviet era (e.g., Estonia adopting a more NPM, marketized style of governing) than that found in the countries usually considered the heartland of NPM (Bouckaert et al. 2011).

Resisting Convergence

The arguments about isomorphism and other pressures for convergence make a strong case that we should expect to find substantial movement toward a common model of administration, especially among the more developed

---

[6] The desire of the United Kingdom to resist Europeanization might be expected to be especially high, given the rather pronounced differences of its administrative tradition (see Chapter 6) from the Continental pattern, and its relatively late membership in the Union. This sense of distinctiveness was manifested in part by the vote in favor of Brexit in 2016.

systems. But the evidence, even among European countries, is not very strong in that direction. Indeed, one can make an equally strong case for the persistence of national patterns in the face of homogenization, and further that in some cases there has been divergence as well as convergence. Much of the discussion of administrative change has been based on the assumption of convergence and widespread change, but the empirical reality of the patterns of change is more confusing.

Interpretive Lenses

One of the first reasons for the failure of convergence arguments is that the perceived needs for change, and the repertoire of possible changes, differs across countries. Even if there were agreement within a society that something was wrong with government and with public administration, there have been a variety of different diagnoses of the problems (see Peters 2010b). In the 1990s, the logic driving change in the public sector, when considered across a range of countries, was that something was wrong and needed to be done, but not necessarily that the same things were wrong and needed a common remedy (see Pollitt and Bouckaert 2017). Analyses ranged from neo-Marxist arguments about late capitalism to conservative arguments on behalf of markets.

For example, for those countries that adopted the NPM, market-driven approaches to reform, the prevailing diagnosis was that governments were failing because of inefficient administration resulting from an excessively bureaucratic (in the connotative sense of the term) administrative system (Gualmini 2008). This emphasis on efficiency was perhaps the most common pattern of reform motivation in public administration, albeit often driven by perceptions rather than any hard evidence of the success or failure of public bureaucracies. Indeed, most objective studies of public bureaucracies find about the same level for success as one finds for the services provided by large private sector organizations ('t Hart and Compton 2019).

The other aspect of the interpretive lenses that affect administrative change is what is considered the right way to administer the public sector, and the appropriate linkages with political leaders. Further, what is the appropriate link of government to society? These "logics of appropriateness" are components of the administrative traditions we have been outlining, and tend to have a significant influence over behaviors. Further, if problems are identified in the public sector, the tendency is often to apply more of the familiar pattern of governing rather than to look for new solutions to the problems. That pattern of bounded rationality may be found in the private sector as well (Cyert and March 1967).

Changes in the public sector have also tended to generate a perceived need for yet more change. NPM was to some extent successful in many countries, but it also ran its course and its dysfunctional consequences became more apparent to practitioners and to academics. The quest then began for the justification for the next round of reform, with a variety of labels applied to change such as New Public Governance (Aucoin et al. 2013), the neo-Weberian state (Lynn 2008), and New Public Service (Denhardt and Denhardt 2003).

Path Dependency

While the institutionalist approach of Dimaggio and Powell would argue for convergence and isomorphism, the historical institutionalist approach (Steinmo 2008) would emphasize path dependency and persistence. This version of institutional analysis argues simply that once patterns of policy or administration are created, they will persist unless there are significant forces to divert them from their paths. In the simplest form of the argument, there is little dynamic explaining this persistence, other than perhaps habit.

There can, however, be more explicit explanations for persistence of administrative patterns. For example, Pierson (2000) has argued that path dependency depends upon positive feedbacks arising from the existing patterns. These positive returns accrue to political and administrative leaders, and perhaps also to the recipients of public programs. Especially when both political and administrative elites and their clients believe they are receiving positive rewards from an existing policy and its implementation, it may be difficult to alter the pattern. This is perhaps especially true because of the segmentation of governments and failures to consider alternative uses of resources outside of specific "silos."

Administrative convergence also tends to be restricted because of the nature of the training and the patterns of personnel management reflected in various countries. These patterns of training and the recruitment of personnel, tend to reinforce one another and to prevent significant movements away from a status quo of existing national patterns. For example, the legalism of administration in Germany, even leaving aside some of the excessive stereotyping, is more difficult to change because the hiring of new civil servants tends to be of lawyers who will fill positions that involve the use of law. All organizations tend to hire people that replicate existing patterns.[7] Thus, moving toward the NPM model in Germany or similar countries would be more difficult because there are relatively few civil servants with management training or managerial inclinations.

Functional Demands

Regardless of the administrative system in question, some aspects of public administration are more amenable to reform, whether of the NPM or "governance" style than are others. The central legal "defining functions" of the state (Rose 1976a) are more likely to require a more traditional form of administration than is service delivery to the public or to groups (including firms) within society. On the other hand, actually delivering services to the public may be more amenable to implementation through the more managerialist mechanisms of NPM, or the participatory mechanism associated with governance.

The effects of these functional requirements for governing can be seen readily in the German case. While characterizing administration in Germany as remaining legalistic at the central government level appears accurate, it is also clear that at lower levels of government there is a good deal of reform that follows the general direction of NPM. While not as extensive as those found in the Anglo-American or even Scandinavian cases, there are important transformations of the manner in which local and even *Land* governments perform their tasks (Reichard 2003).

The German case discussed above also points to the differences between public administrators playing roles as policymakers and policy advisors and those public administrators functioning as implementers. The roles played at the center of ministries and in central agencies require a range of skills and processes that are not amenable to promoting efficiency as a central value, while at lower levels of implementation there can well be efficiency gains. Likewise, at the center, much of the engagement and empowerment of civil servants that has been a significant component of participatory styles of reform have been in place for decades.[8]

---

[7] Universities are certainly following this pattern, reinforcing existing disciplinary patterns even when there are increasing demands for programs that cross those traditional boundaries.

[8] Indeed, the NPM reforms appear to have undermined that participation in some systems as political leaders distrusted their civil servants and attempted to remove them from the loop of policymaking.

Another of the functional differences among components of the public sector that may influence convergence or divergence is the extent to which the public employees are involved with actors in the economy and society. Organizations within the public sector that have significant contacts with the public will have a different manner of functioning than will those which perform more technical tasks, or which are central agencies mainly charged with internal control of other public organizations (Dahlström et al. 2011). All of these characteristics of public organizations may make organizations performing similar functions in different countries more similar than those performing different functions within the same administrative system (Freeman 1985).

Eroding of Reforms: Back to the Future?

Another important consideration in the understanding of the convergence of administrative systems is the extent to which countries may have chosen to back away from reforms and to some extent return to the status quo *ante*. The argument here, very similar to that underlying this book, is that there are deeply ingrained patterns of administration that may be disturbed in the short term but which will reassert themselves after time. The assumption is that reformed patterns of governing simply do not feel right to the participants and to citizens, or in some cases may even be illegal, and there are then pressures to return to the older patterns.

To some extent, the logic of Dimaggio and Powell can be run in reverse to understand the return of administrative systems to their long-established patterns. For example, we can conceptualize some of the pressures to return to historical patterns of administration as bordering on coercive, given that there may be legal practices that must be followed that are simply not possible when adhering to the more managerialist approaches (see Dunn and Miller 2007). Likewise, the learning aspect involved in returning to previous patterns of administration may be recognizing that the old system did work, and perhaps worked better than many of the "modern" patterns of administration central to NPM thinking.

New Zealand is the usual example provided of an administrative system that returned to its previous patterns after a period of reform. New Zealand had been one of the principal innovators of NPM (Boston 1996), adopting a range of market-oriented programs and separating administration from policymaking in a manner that became known as "agencification" in other settings. After a decade or more of these reforms there was some movement back toward a traditional Whitehall style of management, although the extent of that movement has been contested by scholars and practitioners (e.g., Lodge and Gill 2011).

The New Zealand experience can be used to argue that even if administrative systems do return to their underlying patterns of governing, they may still have been transformed through the reform process (Chapman and Duncan 2007). Even in the most extreme cases, the older patterns of administration were not abandoned completely, and vestigial elements continued to function alongside newer reformed elements. As with the model of "layering" of institutional change in the new institutionalism (Mahoney and Thelen 2010a), administrative systems may contain a number of layers of structures and practices that reflect the fads and fashions of various times in their development, and which are rarely totally erased.

For our fundamental argument here, there is an integral set of norms, structures, and procedures that is laid down early in the formation of an administrative system that continue to influence subsequent patterns of development. As argued elsewhere, the components of the administrative DNA of these systems not only create pressures for reversion once the equilibrium of the system has been altered, but they also may inhibit certain types of change. For example, as noted in Chapter 4 on the Germanic system, the strong legal foundation of administration, and of the state more generally, made the market-oriented reforms associated with NPM less palatable than in administrative traditions that did not emphasize legalism so strongly.

Institutionalizing and Deinstitutionalizing Change

In Chapter 1, I argued that we can conceptualize administrative traditions in institutional terms. They are, in terms of the normative institutionalism, "myths, symbols, routines…" that shape the behavior of members of the institution—in this case the public bureaucracy (March and Olsen 1989: 14). That capacity to shape behavior is a product of having institutionalized those values within the structure, so that the structure has meaning for its participants (Selznick 1957). The socialization process uses ideas, and places pressures on individual members of the institution to learn and internalize those ideas, as a way of replicating behaviors.

The institutionalization process can also be seen in functional terms (see Oliver 1992). Samuel Huntington (1968) argued that political systems confront challenges from their environment and need to develop institutional capacities at at least the same rate as those challenges develop. Although he was writing about development of political systems as a whole, the same logic would apply to administrative systems facing both external challenges and perhaps internal challenges to their own ways of performing public administration. If organizations are able to maintain these processes of institutionalization (in value terms), then they will be able to counter pressures for change.

The nature of pressures for change from outside and within organizations may affect the capacity of the institution to maintain its internal equilibrium. If those pressures for change are highly congruent with general values in the society and within administration, then it will be difficult for an organization (or the bureaucracy as a whole) to resist the pressures. Likewise, if the values driving change are incongruent, then persistence is more likely. Thus, it is difficult to predict *ex ante* how individual organizations, or administrative systems as a whole, will respond to pressures for change.

But just as institutionalization is an important process for change (and for resistance to change) so, too, can be deinstitutionalization (Oliver 1992). That is, organizations and institutions can break down and become less effective and persistent. Indeed, all institutions can be seen as involved in continuing processes of institutionalization and deinstitutionalization. And if the institution deinstitutionalizes, it may have the opportunity to reinstitutionalize in a new and more effective form that better matches the challenges being faced in its contemporary environment.

Layering and Paradox

Perhaps the simplest explanation of the persistence of administrative traditions is that administrative systems, and many other social systems, can be characterized as layers of ideas, laws, practices, and people who have been dominant within the institution at one time and then have been supplanted by others. But, having been institutionalized at one point, they continue to have some enduring influence. For example, although NPM became popular, if not dominant, in the last quarter of the twentieth century, many members of public bureaucracies continued in their jobs, including those committed to "old-fashioned" administration rather than public management.

These layers represent not only changing ideas about public administration, but they may also represent changing politics within the state. For example, politics in the Scandinavian countries was dominated by social democratic parties for a number of decades. However, beginning in the

1990s, parties of the political right began to have more success in elections.[9] This success meant not only changes in substantive public policies but also the creation of a more market-oriented approach to governance in general. Civil servants hired during the period of social democratic dominance were therefore in the somewhat awkward position of having to deal with very different ways of thinking about governing. The layer of leaders brought into manage the center-right governments may have been doing one thing, while many people under them were continuing to do what they had always done.

The presence of multiple layers and multiple sets of values within public organizations creates potential paradoxes about the functioning of these organizations (Hood and Peters 2004). Some public employees who think they are hired to be autonomous managers may find themselves more politicized because political leaders fear losing control over the organization (Maor 1999). Also, given that some levels of an organization are functioning with managerial values and other are functioning with more traditional administrative and legal values, internal control may be more difficult, rather than easier, as those emphasizing management might assume.

A Simple Dichotomy?

The discussion of layering and paradox above brings me to the conclusion of this discussion. And that conclusion is that it is probably wrong to think of persistence and change as a simple dichotomy. Critics of "traditions logic" point to the changes that occur even in the most resilient of administrative traditions (see, e.g., Sager et al. 2018),[10] and they are correct to do so. Advocates of the "traditions perspective" will point to the persistence of structural and behavioral features of administrative systems, and they are likewise correct to do so.

What I have been attempting to do in this book is to emphasize the persistence of many features of administrative systems, while not denying the presence of change. Attempting to understand the nuances of change and persistence leads in turn to several points that will help move the stark

---

[9] There were other short-lived breakthroughs from the right prior to that; e.g., coalitions led by the Centre Party in Sweden in the 1970s.
[10] The mere existence of change within administrative systems does not negate the viability of the traditions concept, however. The question is what remains as well as what is changed, and secondly what types of changes appear most possible within the particular tradition.

dichotomy that is sometimes presented into more of a dimension. First, we should consider individual organizations as well as administrative systems as a whole. Some organizations may be more subject to pressures for change than are others. For example, economic ministries and agencies may be more subject to pressures for Europeanization than are organizations delivering social services or education.

In addition, the nature of the pressures for change may affect the degree of change that occurs. NPM has been a major force for change in public administration and its ideas are more congruent with those of Anglo-American administration than with the values of Continental European administration, or administration in Latin America. Likewise, more collaborative approaches to making and implementing policy (Ansell and Gash 2008) appeared more compatible with administration in the Scandinavian countries, and perhaps in Islamic states, than in many others. And the Napoleonic states appeared to resist, albeit not completely, both of these forms of change. Thus, the question is not change, but what change, if we want to understand better persistence and change.

Table 10.1 presents a listing of the four major administrative traditions and their possible affinity for significant patterns of reform. Even within NPM and more participatory versions of reform, there are several individual reforms that may have different levels of compatibility with the several traditions. For example, although the Napoleonic tradition has in general resisted NPM, one element of that version of reform—performance management—has been introduced with some success (Bruntiere 2006). And even within each of these traditions, there are cases which do not match the general profile, for example the relatively weak acceptance of agencies within the Canadian government.

Table 10.1 Administrative traditions and administrative reforms: levels of compatibility

Reforms	Traditions			
	Napoleonic	Germanic	Scandinavian	Anglo-American
NPM	Low	Low	Medium to high	High
Participation	Low	Medium	High	Medium
Neo-Weberian state	High	High	Medium	Low

Making Traditions Work: Social Mechanisms

The final theoretical question that arises concerning traditions is, how do they work? That is, we have been assuming throughout the discussion that the traditions influence contemporary patterns of administration, but what basic mechanisms are available that have both allowed for the persistence of patterns of administration, and also for them to influence administration even when there are significant attempts to impose other patterns? Very much as we assume that policy instruments are the mechanisms through which policies influence the economy and society (Hood 1984), what tools or mechanisms translate the traditions into action? There, of course, one crucial difference lies in that policy tools are designed and implemented purposefully, while the influence of traditions generally lacks agency.

Ideas are perhaps the most important of the mechanisms involved in the persistence of traditions (Beland and Cox 2011). Although much of contemporary political science and public administration tends to reject the importance of ideas as causal mechanisms (but see Rodrik 2014), preferring to focus on interests, that is, rational choice, it is difficult to argue that traditions do not reflect ideas. Further, the persistence of those ideas even in the face of attempts to alter the style of governing, often based on alternative ideas, is indicative of the power of deeply embedded ideas to shape behavior.

We must remember that the persistence of ideas and structures in the public sector is not necessarily functional. There is a long-standing assumption that public organizations—the components of the bureaucracy—survive long after their utility has been exhausted (Kaufman 1974; Olsen 2009). Although there is more organizational termination (Lewis 2002) than usually assumed, government organizations do tend to have long lives. Ideas may also survive longer than their functional existence, becoming "zombies" that continue to influence public policy long after they have been proven invalid (Peters and Nagel 2019).

But that, to some extent, raises other questions, the most important being the role of conflict—overt or more likely covert—over the dominance of contending sets of ideas. Why are some new ideas adopted even when there is a well-established style of governing and administration, and others are not? And even within one country with contending political ideas (e.g., France; see Mastor 2018) what determines which ideas dominate? One answer to the dominance of certain ideas may come from the institutionalism literature

(Dimaggio and Powell 1991), which argues that the environment of any one institution—the public bureaucracy for example—is other institutions. And, further, there are pressures for isomorphism among those institutions. This may be true across types of institutions, (e.g., the economy, bureaucracy, and law), or it may be true for different versions of the same institution (e.g., bureaucracies in different sectors or in different countries).

An additional question is why some ideas are more powerful than others in shaping the behavior of public sector institutions. For example, the ideas of NPM were extremely significant in a number of settings, and apparently much more pervasive than other attempts at reform over the past century. Other ideas, such as the neo-Weberian state, did have some influence, but did not sweep across the public sectors of many countries, nor did they gain the support of major international organizations.

Authority and power are perhaps the antithesis of ideas as the means of making traditions perform as intended, but they nonetheless have the capacity to replicate behavior over time and enforce patterns of behavior. These mechanisms, perhaps operating through rules (law or internal organizational rules), will produce the behaviors required by the organization, and will tend to reproduce over time. But power and authority are not the same thing (Dahl 1957) and they do not operate in a similar manner. Authority depends on the acceptance of the actions of public sector actors as legitimate, while power involves the ability to produce action even with opposition and illegitimacy. Thus, authority may depend to some extent on ideas, while power may depend more on coercion.

Amitai Etzioni (1975) argued that organizations with a normative (ideas) base, as well as those with a coercive base, could survive. So, too, could organizations based on remuneration, in which individuals joined and complied in order to be paid or receive other material benefits. Any of these organizations could be successful so long as the incentives being offered to the members matched the motivations of the members when they join. Thus, an individual in a coercive institution (a prison, for example) is unlikely to be motivated effectively by values or by monetary incentives—he or she did not choose to be there and mostly just wants to leave the organization.

That said, the basis of compliance of individuals may change over time. Individuals may join an organization simply to earn a living but may become attached to the organization and think of it in normative terms—much like the idea of institutionalization for Selznick. Even some coercive organizations may be able to alter the means of motivation of their members. The military may use largely coercive means for training its inductees, but then must make those new soldiers committed to the military and its values if the organization is to be effective in extreme situations.

Etzioni also mentions remuneration as a means of producing compliance within organizations. While a simple notion of remuneration as salary may be insufficient to maintain an administrative tradition in the face of challenges, an expanded version of remuneration certainly may be. As Pierson (2000) argued concerning path dependence, positive feedback and increasing (or at least stable) returns may preserve an administrative tradition. This is, in essence, a rational choice perspective on the maintenance of a tradition, with the anticipated (or feared) losses of change being greater than the gains, and their net benefit being less than the status quo.

For administrative systems this mechanism of remuneration would imply that those individuals seeking to maintain the administrative tradition have something to gain by maintaining it. The extent of the rewards of remaining in the status quo would be dependent upon a number of factors, such as the job market for individuals with their skill set. For administrative systems with high levels of patronage appointments, for example, finding positions with equal rewards may be difficult if the individuals have attained their positions merely through "jobs for the boys" (Grindle 2012).

The various traditions I have discussed throughout this book may not differ much in terms of the motivations of their members. The literature on public service motivation shows some differences among these groups, but most display rather high levels of motivations. For example, the evidence presented in Table 2.3 shows that public servants in Southern European countries (essentially Napoleonic cases) appear to have the highest levels of public service motivation among the groups of countries discussed here.[11] This might not have been the expectation given the image of an aloof and autonomous public service in these countries, but does make clear the prevalence of some common administrative values among European systems.

We can also consider the levels of remuneration offered to public employees working within different traditions as an indication of the perceived importance of that source of motivation. For example, public servants in Scandinavian countries are paid relatively little given their responsibilities, reflecting an egalitarian culture and the importance attached to working for the public good (Brans and Peters 2012). On the other hand, salaries for

---

[11] The relatively low level of purposive involvement of their members with the administrative systems in Northern and Western Europe may reflect the higher status of civil servants in these systems, and a more "solidary" commitment to the organization (Clark and Wilson 1961).

civil servants in the Anglo-American countries tend to be relatively high, reflecting the "instrumental" nature of the public bureaucracy in these countries (Knill 1999) and the assumption that these are managers much like those in the private sector.

Summary and Conclusions

The emphasis on traditions in this book implies some continuity in the underlying patterns of public administration in most governments. The argument is that contemporary administration reflects to some degree the persistence of historical ideas and structures. There may have been overlays of other ideas and different interpretations of underlying ideas over time, but yet there is some DNA in administrative systems that continues to influence contemporary behaviors. Perhaps because the usual stereotype of bureaucracy is excessively stable, most of the theoretical discussion around this institution has been about change, but we do also need to understand the sources of stability.

However, arguing that there is some level of persistence of traditions does not negate the possibility of change. One could not expect the practice of administering public policies to remain stagnant over centuries, or even over decades. Administrative systems do, of course, respond to changing demands (e.g., administering an expanded welfare state), and to changing ideas about what constitutes good administration, but the underlying traditions comprise lenses through which the actors responsible for making any reforms interpret the pressures for change and develop responses to those pressures.

This book has demonstrated both persistence and change within public administration in a number of different settings. By looking at these patterns of change and stability in a comparative manner we can understand better what forces contribute to change, and what forces may inhibit change. The basic patterns of persistence and change we have identified are viable in a number of settings, but they manifest in different ways given the institutionalized patterns of behavior within bureaucracies. These varied patterns of response to pressures for change have provided the opportunity to understand better the rich variety that exists within what is often thought to be a stable and even boring public sector institution.

References

Aberbach, J. D., R. D. Putnam and B. A. Rockman (1987), *Bureaucrats and Politicians in Western Democracies* (Cambridge, MA: Harvard University Press).

Acemoglu, D., S. Johnson and J. A. Robinson (2001), The Colonial Origins of Comparative Development: An Empirical Investigation, *American Economic Review* 91, 1369–401.

Adam, C., S. Hurka, C. Knill, B. G. Peters and Y. Steinbach (2019), Introducing Vertical Coordination to Comparative Policy Analysis: The Missing Link Between Policy Production and Implementation, *Journal of Comparative Policy Analysis* 21, 499–517.

Adams, P. S. (2008), The Europeanization of the Social Partnership: The Future of Neo-Corporatism in Germany and Austria, unpublished Ph.D. dissertation, University of Massachusetts, Amherst.

Adelman, J. (1999), *Colonial Legacies: The Problem of Persistence in Latin American History* (New York: Routledge).

Afonso, A. and Y. Papadopoulos (2013), Europeanization or Party Politics: Explaining Government Choice for Corporatist Concentration, *Governance* 26, 5–29.

Agh, A. (2003), Public Administration in Central and Eastern Europe, in B. G. Peters and J. Pierre, eds., *Handbook of Public Administration* (London: Sage).

Ahlbäck-Öberg, S. (2012), Rewards for High Public Office in Sweden, in M. Brans and B. G. Peters, eds., *Rewards for High Public Office in Europe and North America* (London: Routledge).

Ahn, B. M. (1980), Korean Political Culture and Bureaucracy [in Korean], quoted in Y.-P. Kim, The South Korean Administrative System, in J. P. Burns and B. Bowornwathana, eds., (2001), *Asian Civil Service Systems* (Cheltenham: Edward Elgar).

Ahonen, P. (2015), Aspects of the Institutionalization of Evaluation in Finland: Basic, Agency, Process and Change, *Evaluation* 21: 308–24.

Ahonen, P. and K. Palonen (1999), *Disembalming Max Weber* (Jyvaskyla: Sophi).

Aja, E. (2003), *El Estado Autonómico: Federalismo y Hechos Diferenciales* (Madrid: Alianza Editorial).

Akintoye, S. A. (1976), *Emergent African States: Topics in Twentieth-Century African History* (London: Longman).

Alasuutari, P. (2015), The Discursive Side of the New Institutionalism, *Cultural Sociology* 9, 162–84.

Alba, C. R. and C. Navarro (2011), Administrative Tradition and Reform in Spain: Adaptation versus Innovation, *Public Administration* 89, 783–800.

Alberts, S., M. Dávila and A. Valenzuela (2020), Chile, in B. G. Peters, C. Alba and C. Ramos, eds., *Handbook of Public Administration in Latin America* (Bingley: Emerald).

Alcaras, J.-R., G. Marrel, C. Marchand and M. Nonjon (2016), The Managerial Conversion of Senior Civil Servants: A Convenient Myth About the French Local Welfare State?, *International Review of Administrative Sciences* 82, 190–207.

Aliabadi. A. (1998), *Administrators in Islamic Society* (Tehran: Ramin Publications).

Allison, G. T. (1980), Public and Private Management: Are They Fundamentally Alike in All Unimportant Respects?, *Proceedings of the Public Management Research Conference* (Washington, DC: Office of Personnel Management).

Allison, G. T. and P. Zelikow (1999), *Essence of Decision: Explaining the Cuban Missile Crisis*, 2nd ed. (New York: Addison Wesley Longman).

Andersen, J. G., M. A. Schoyen and B. Hvinden (2017), Changing Scandinavian Welfare States: Which Way Forward?, in P. Taylor-Gooby, B. Leruth and H, Chung, *After Austerity: Welfare State Transformation in Europe after the Great Recession* (Oxford: Oxford University Press).

Andersen, L. (1987), The State in the Middle East and North Africa, *Comparative Politics* 20, 1–18.

Anderson, C. W. (1970), *The Political Economy of Modern Spain: Policymaking in an Authoritarian System* (Madison: University of Wisconsin Press).

Andrews, M. (2013), *The Limits of Institutional Reform in Development: Changing Rules for Realistic Solutions* (Cambridge: Cambridge University Press).

Anechiarico, F. (1998), Administrative Culture and Civil Society, *Administration and Society* 30, 13–34.

Anell, A. (2005), Swedish Healthcare Under Pressure, *Health Economics* 14, S237–54.

Ankar, C. (2020), The Most Similar and Most Different Systems Design in Comparative Policy Analysis, in B. G. Peters and G. Fontaine, eds., *Handbook of Methodology for Comparative Policy Analysis* (Cheltenham: Edward Elgar).

Ansell, C. and A. Gash (2008), Collaborative Governance in Theory and Practice, *Journal of Public Administration Research and Theory* 18, 543–71.

Anter, A. (2005), Max Weber, in W. Bleek and H. J. Lietzman, eds., *Klassiker der Politikwissenschaft. Von Aristotle bis David Easton* (Munich: Beck).

Argyris, C (1990 [1964]), *Integrating the Individual and the Organization* (New Brunswick, NJ: Transaction Books).

Armstrong, J. A. (1973), *The European Administrative Elite* (Princeton, NJ: Princeton University Press).

Arnold, P. (1986), *Making the Managerial Presidency* (Princeton, NJ: Princeton University Press).

Askim, J., R. Karlsen and K. Kollveit (2017), Political Appointees in Executive Government: Exploring and Explaining Roles Using a Large-N Survey in Norway, *Public Administration* 95, 342–58.

Askim, J., K. Kolltveit and E. Smith (2019), Studying Horizontal Coordination in the Core Executive: Formal Institutions and Practices in the Core Executive, paper presented at Conference on Policy Coordination in the Scandinavian Countries, Copenhagen Business School, December.

Athanasaw, Y. A. (2003), Team Characteristics, and Team Member Knowledge, Skills and Ability Relationships to the Effectiveness of Cross-Functional Teams in the Public Sector, *International Journal of Public Administration* 26, 1165–203.

Auby, J.-B. and M. Morabito (2017), Evolution and Gestalt of the French State, in P. M. Huber, A. Bogdandy and S. Cassese, eds., *The Administrative State* (Oxford: Oxford University Press).

Aucoin, P. (2012), New Political Governance in Westminster Systems: Impartial Public Administration and Management at Risk, *Governance* 25, 177–99.

Aucoin, P., H. Bakvis and M. Jarvis (2013), Constraining Executive Power in an Era of New Political Governance, in J. Bickerton and B. G. Peters, eds., *Governing: Essays in Honour of Donald J. Savoie* (Montreal: McGill/Queens University Press).

Auyero, J. (2012), *Patients of the State: The Politics of Waiting in Argentina* (Durham, NC: Duke University Press).

Ayres, D. W. (2014), A Remembrance of Louis Brownlow, *Public Administration Review* 74, 12–14.

Bach, S. and R. K. Givan (2011), Varieties of New Public Management: The Reform of Public Service Employment Relations in the UK and USA, *The International Journal of Human Resource Management* 22, 2349–66.

Bach, T. (2014), The Autonomy of Government Agencies in Germany and Norway: Explaining Variations in Management Autonomy Across Countries and Agencies, *International Review of Administrative Sciences* 80, 341–61.

Bach, T. and S. Veit (2017), The Determinants of Promotion to High Public Office in Germany: Partisan Loyalty, Political Craft, or Managerial Competencies?, *Journal of Public Administration Research and Theory* 28, 254–69.

Baczko, B. (1987), The Social Contract of the French: Sieyès and Rousseau, *Journal of Modern History* 60, 98–115.

Badie, B. (1992), *L'État importé* (Paris: Fayard).

Bakvis, H. and M. Jarvis (2012), *From New Public Management to New Public Governance: Essays in Honour of Peter C. Aucoin* (Montreal: McGill/Queens University Press).

Balboa, C. M. (2018), *The Paradox of Scale: How NGOs Build, Maintain and Lose Authority in Environmental Governance* (Cambridge, MA: MIT Press).

Baldini, G. and B. Baldi (2014), Decentralization and the Troubles of Federalization in Italy, *Regional & Federal Studies* 24, 87–108.

Baldwin, R. (1996), *Rules and Government* (Oxford: Oxford University Press).

Balla, S. J. and J. R. Wright (2001), Interest Groups, Advisory Committees, and Congressional Control of the Bureaucracy, *American Journal of Political Science* 45, 798–812.

Ban, C. (2013), *Management and Culture in an Enlarged European Commission: From Diversity to Unity* (Basingstoke: Macmillan).

Banfield, E. C. (1967), *The Moral Basis of a Backward Society* (New York: Free Press).

Barilari, A. and M. Bouvier (2010), La LOLF et la nouvelle gouvernance financière de l'État (Paris: LGDJ).

Bauer, M., S. Becker, B. G. Peters, J. Pierre and K. Yesilkagit (forthcoming), *Liberal Democratic Backsliding and Public Administration*.

Bauer, M. W. and J. Ege (2013), Commission Civil Servants and Politics: De-Politicized Bureaucrats in an Increasingly Political Organization, in C. Nneuhold, S. Vanhooonacker and L. Verhey, eds., *Civil Servants and Politics: A Delicate Balance* (Basingstoke: Macmillan).

Bayart, J.-F. (1993), *The State in Africa: The Politics of the Belly* (Harlow: Longman).

Beck, J. (2008), Patterns of Administrative Culture in Cross-Border Cooperation, in J. Beck and F. Thedieck, eds., *The European Dimension of Administrative Culture* (Baden-Baden: Nomos).

Beck, U. (2001), La fin du neoliberalisme, *Le Monde*, November 10.

Becker, S. O., K. Boeckh, C. Hainz and L. Woessmann (2016), The Empire Is Dead, Long Live the Empire! Long-Run Persistence of Trust and Corruption in the Bureaucracy, *The Economic Journal* 126(590): 40–74.

Beer, S. (1969), *British Politics in the Collectivist Age* (New York: Vintage Books).

Beland, D. and R. H. Cox (2011), *Ideas and Politics in Social Science Research* (New York: Oxford University Press).

Bendixsen, S., M. B. Bringslid and H. Vike (2018), *Egalitarianism in Scandinavia: Historical and Contemporary Perspectives* (London: Macmillan).

Benz, A. (2001), *Der moderne Staat* (Munich: Oldenbourg).

Bergman, T. and K. Strøm (2011), *The Madisonian Turn: Political Parties and Parliamentary Democracy in Northern Europe* (Ann Arbor: University of Michigan Press).

Berman, B. J. (1984), Structure and Process in the Bureaucratic States of Colonial Africa, *Development and Change* 15, 161–202.

Berman, B. J. and W. J. Tettey (2001), African States, Bureaucratic Culture and Computer Fixes, *Public Administration and Development* 21, 1–13.

Bernhard, M., C. Reenock and T. Nordstrom (2004), The Legacy of Western Overseas Colonialism on Democratic Survival, *International Studies Quarterly* 48, 225–50.

Bersch, K., S. Praça and M. M. Taylor (2017), State Capacity, Bureaucratic Politicization, and Corruption in the Brazilian State, *Governance* 30(1), 105–24.

Besancon, M. (2003), *Good Governance Rankings: The Art of Measurement* (Cambridge, MA: World Peace Foundation).

Betts, R. F. (1961), *Assimilation and Association in French Colonial Theory 1890–1914* (New York: Columbia University Press).

Bezes, P. (2008), Le tournant neomanagerial de l'administration française, *Politiques publiques* 1, 215–54.

Bezes, P. (2009), *Réinventer L'État: Les réformes de l'administration française (1962–2008)* (Paris: PUF).

Bezes, P. and S. Parrado (2013), Trajectories of Administrative Reform: Institutions and Timing and Choices in France and Spain, *West European Politics* 36, 22–50.

Biela, J., A. Hennl and A. Kaiser (2013), *Policymaking in Multi-Level Systems: Federalism, Decentralization and Performance in OECD Countries* (Colchester: ECPR Press).

Bierschenk, T. (2008), The Everyday Functioning of an African Public Service: Informalization, Privatization and Corruption in Benin's Legal System, *Journal of Legal Pluralism and Unofficial Law* 57, 101–39.

Binderkrantz, A. and J. G. Christensen (2009), Governing Danish Agencies by Contract: From Negotiated Freedom to the Shadow of Hierarchy, *Journal of Public Policy* 29, 55–78.

Binderkrantz, A. S. and P. M. Christensen (2015), From Classic to Modern Corporatism: Interest Group Representation in Danish Public Committees in 1975 and 2000, *Journal of European Public Policy* 22, 1022–39.

Bioy, X., J.-M. Eymeri-Douzans and S. Mouton (2016), *La règne des entourages: Cabinets et conseillers de l'exêcutif* (Paris: Presses de Sciences Po).

Bjørna, H. and S. Jenssen (2006), Prefectoral Systems and Central-Local Government Relations in Scandinavia, *Scandinavian Political Studies* 29, 308–22.

Blais, A. and S. Dion (1991), *The Budget-Maximizing Bureaucrat: Appraisals and Evidence* (Pittsburgh, PA: University of Pittsburgh Press).

Blake, S. P. (2011), The Patrimonial-Bureaucratic Empire of the Mughals, *The Journal of Asian Studies* 39, 77–94.

Blau, P. M. and W. R. Scott (2003 [1962]), *Formal Organizations: A Comparative Approach* (Stanford, CA: Stanford University Press).

Blundo, G. (2006), Dealing with the Local State: The Informal Privatization of Street-Level Bureaucracies in Senegal. *Development and Change* 37, 799–819.

Blundo, G. and P.-Y. Le Meur (2009), *The Governance of Daily Life in Africa: Ethnographic Explorations of Public and Collective Service Services* (Leiden: Brill).

Blundo, G. and J.-P. Olivier de Sardan, with N. Bako Arifari and M. Tidjani Alou (2006), *Everyday Corruption and the State: Citizens and Public Officials in Africa* (London: Zed Books).

Bochsler, D. and K. S. Bousbah (2015), Competitive Consensus: What Comes After Consociationalism in Switzerland, *Swiss Political Science Review* 21, 654–79.

Bogdanor, V. (2001), *Devolution in the United Kingdom* (Oxford: Oxford University Press).

Bogumil, J. and W. Jann (2009), *Verwaltung und Verwaltungswissenschaft in Deutschland* (Heidelberg: Springer).

Boone, C. (2003), *Political Topographies of the African State: Territorial Authority and Institutional Choice* (Cambridge: Cambridge University Press).

Booth, P. (2009), Planning and the Culture of Governance: Local Institutions and Reform in France, *European Planning Studies* 17, 677–95.

Börzel, T. (1997), Organizing Babylon–On the Different Conceptions of Policy Networks, *Public Administration* 76, 253–73.

Börzel, T. A. (2002), Member States' Responses to Europeanization, *Journal of Common Market Studies* 40, 193–214.

Boston, J. (1996), *Public Management: The New Zealand Model* (Oxford: Oxford University Press).

Bouchard, G. and B. W. Carroll (2008), Policymaking and Administrative Discretion: The Case of Immigration in Canada, *Canadian Public Administration* 45, 239–57.

Bouckaert, G. (2012), Trust and Public Administration, *Administration* 60(1): 91–115.

Bouckaert, G. and J. A. Halligan (2008), *Managing Performance: International Comparisons* (Abingdon: Routledge).

Bouckaert, G., V. Nakrosis and J. Nemec (2011), Public Administration and Management Reforms in CEE: Main Trajectories and Results, *NISPACEE Journal of Public Administration and Policy* 4, 9–29.

Bouckaert, G., B. G. Peters and K. Verhoest (2010), *The Coordination of Public Sector Organizations: Shifting Patterns of Public Management* (Basingstoke: Macmillan).

Bouckaert, G. and C. Pollitt (2009), *Continuity and Change in Public Policy and Management*, 2nd edn (Oxford: Oxford University Press).

Bourmaud, D. (2001), Les Ves republiques: Monarchie, dyarchie, polyarchie: Variations autour du pouvoir sous la Ve Republique, *Pouvoirs* 99, 7–17.

Bovens, M. A. P. (2007), Analyzing and Assessing Accountability: A Conceptual Framework, *European Law Journal* 13, 447–68.

Bovens, M. A. P., P. 't Hart and B. G. Peters (2001), *Success and Failure in Public Governance* (Cheltenham: Edward Elgar).

Bozeman, B. (2000), *Bureaucracy and Red Tape* (Upper Saddle River, NJ: Prentice-Hall).

Braendle, T. and A. Sturtzer (2010), Public Servants in Parliament: Theory and Evidence on its Determinants in Germany, *Public Choice* 145, 223–52.

Braendle, T. and A. Sturtzer (2013), Political Selection of Public Servants and Parliamentary Oversight, *Economics of Governance* 14, 45–76.

Braibanti, R. (1966), *Asian Bureaucratic Systems Emergent from the British Imperial Tradition* (Durham, NC: Duke University Press).

Branine, M. and D. Pollard (2010), Human Resource Management with Islamic Management Principles: A Dialectic for a Reverse Diffusion in Management, *Personnel Review* 39(6), 712–27.

Brans, M., C. Pelgrims and D. Hoet (2006), Comparative Observations on Tensions Between Professional Policy Advice and Political Control in the Low Countries, *International Review of Administrative Sciences* 72(1), 57–71.

Brans, M. and B. G. Peters (2012), *Rewards for High Public Office in Europe and North America* (London: Routledge).

Braun, C. (2012), Captive or Broker? Explaining Public Agency-Interest Group Interactions, *Governance* 25, 291–314.

Brehm, J. and S. Gates (1997), *Working, Shirking and Sabotage: Bureaucratic Response to a Democratic Public* (Ann Arbor: University of Michigan Press).

Brewer, P. and S. Venaik (2014), The Ecological Fallacy in National Culture Research, *Organization Studies* 35, 1063–86.

Brunet, E. (1998), *La Bêtise Administrative* (Paris: Albin Michel).

Bruntiere, J.-R. (2006), Les indicateurs de la loi organique relative aux lois de finances (LOLF): une occasion de débat démocratique? *Revue française d'administration publique* 117, 95–111.

Bruun F. (2000), Den professionelle forvaltning: Fra embede til direktør. in P. Bogason, ed., *Stat, forvaltning og samfund efter 1950* (København: Jurist- og Økonomforbundets Forlag).

Bullock, J. B., J. M. Stritch and H. G. Rainey (2015), International Comparison of Public and Private Employees' Work Motives, Attitudes and Perceived Rewards, *Public Administration Review* 75, 479–89.

Burns, J. P. and B. Bowornwathana, eds. (2001), *Civil Service Systems in Asia* (Cheltenham: Edward Elgar).

Burton, M. (2013), *The Politics of Public Sector Reform: From Thatcher to the Coalition* (London: Macmillan).

Bussell, J. (2012), *Corruption and Reform in India: Public Service in the Digital Age* (Cambridge: Cambridge University Press).

Bussmeyer, M. R. (2019), Bildung, Kontinuatät und Wandel in der Politik der Großen Koalition (2013–17), in R. Zohnhöfer and T. Sallfeld, eds., *Zwischen Stillstand, Politikwandel und Krisenmanagement* (Wiesbaden: Springer).

Butler, D., A. Adonis and T. Travers (1994), *Failure in British Government: The Politics of the Poll Tax* (Oxford: Oxford University Press).

Cai, Y. (2014), Managing Group Interests in China, *Political Science Quarterly* 129, 107–31.

Cairney, P. and N. McGarvey (2013), *Scottish Politics* (London: Palgrave).

Callaghan, J. and S. Tunney (2001), The End of Social Democracy, *Politics* 21, 63–72.

Campbell, C. and G. K. Wilson (1995), *The End of Whitehall* (Oxford: Blackwell).

Capano, G. (2003), Administrative Traditions and Policy Change: When Policy Paradigms Matter. The Case of Italian Administrative Reform During the 1990s, *Public Administration* 81, 781–801.

Capano, G. (2018), Reconceptualizing Layering—From Mode of Institutional Change to Mode of Institutional Design: Types and Outputs, *Public Administration* 97, 590–604.

Caranta, R. and A. Gerbrandy (2012), *Tradition and Change in European Administrative Law* (np: European Law Publishing).

Carl, S. (2013), Prisoner Welfare, Human Rights and the North Rhine-Westphalisn Prison Ombudsman, *Journal of Social Welfare and Family Law* 35, 365–77.

Carlsson, P. (2010), Priority Setting in Health Care: Swedish Efforts and Experiences, *Scandinavian Journal of Public Health* 38, 561–4.

Castles, F. G. (1993), *Families of Nations: Patterns of Public Policy in Western Democracies* (Aldershot: Dartmouth Publishing).

Chadwick, A. and C. May (2003), Interaction between States and Citizens in the Age of the Internet: 'E-Government' in the United States, Britain and the European Union, *Governance* 16, 271–300.

Chanlat, J.-F. (2003), *Le managérialisme et l'éthique du bien commune: la question et la motivation au travail dans les services publics* (Paris: DRM, Université Paris Dauphine).

Chanlat, J.-F., E. Davel and J. P. Dupuis (2013), *Cross-Cultural Management: Culture and Management Across the World* (London: Routledge).

Chapman, J. and G. Duncan (2007), Is There Now a New "New Zealand Model?," *Public Management Review* 9, 1–25.

Cheung, A. B. L. (2013), Can There be an Asian Model of Public Administration?, *Public Administration and Development* 33, 249–61.

Chevallier, J. (2003), *Le service publique* (Paris: Presses Universitaires de France).

Christiansen, T. and S. Vanhoonacker (2008), At a Critical Juncture?: Change and Continuity in the Institutional Development of the Council Secretariat, *West European Politics* 31, 754–70.

Christensen, J. G. (2004), Political Responsiveness in a Merit Bureaucracy, in B. G. Peters and J. Pierre, eds., *Politicization of the Civil Service in Comparative Perspective: The Quest for Control* (London: Routledge).

Christensen, J. G. (2009), Danish Public Management Reform Before and After NPM, in S. Goldfinch and J. Wallis, eds., *International Handbook of Public Management Reform* (Cheltenham: Edward Elgar).

Christensen, T. (2003), Narratives of Governance: Elaborating the Norwegian Strong State Tradition, *Public Administration* 81, 163–90.

Christensen, T. and P. Laegreid (1998), Administrative Reform Policy: The Case of Norway, *International Review of Administrative Sciences* 64, 457–75.

Christensen, T. and P. Laegreid (2009), Living in the Past?: Continuity and Change in the Norwegian Central Civil Service, *Public Administration Review* 69, 951–61.

Christensen, T. and P. Laegreid (2010), *Ashgate Companion to the New Public Management* (Farnham: Ashgate).

Christensen, T., A. Lie and P. Laegreid (2008), Beyond New Public Management: Agencification and Regulatory Reform in Norway, *Financial Accountability & Management* 24, 15–30.

Church, C. H. (2007), *Switzerland and the European Union: A Close, Contradictory and Misunderstood Relationship* (London: Routledge).

Cini, M. (1997), Administrative Culture in the European Commission: The Cases of Competition and Environment, in N. Nugent, ed., *At the Heart of the Union* (London: Macmillan).

Clark, C. (2006). *Iron Kingdom: The Rise and the Downfall of Prussia 1600–1947* (London: Penguin).

Clark, P. B. and J. W. Wilson (1961), Incentive Systems: A Theory of Organizations, *Administrative Science Quarterly* 6, 129–66.

Clifford, C. and V. Wright (1997), Politicization of the British Civil Service (unpublished paper, Nuffield College, Oxford).

Codato, A., A. P. Lopes Ferreira and L. Domingos Costa (2015), Do Serviço Público à Câmara Dos Deputados: Os Parlamentares Originários Do Funcionalismo Público No Brasil, *Revista do Serviço Público* 66, 605–26.

Colomer, J. M. (1998), The Spanish State of Autonomies: Non-institutional Federalism, *West European Politics*, 21, 40–52.

Cohn, M. (2001), Fuzzy Legality in Regulation: The Legislative Mandate Revisited, *Law and Policy* 23, 469–97.

Collins, R. O. and J. M. Burns (2007), *A History of Sub-Saharan Africa* (Cambridge: Cambridge University Press).

Common, R. (2004), Public Management and Policy Transfer in Southeast Asia, in M. Evans, ed., *Policy Transfer in Global Perspective* (London: Routledge).

Conklin, A. L., S. Fishman and R. Zaretsky (2011), *France and its Empire Since 1870*, 2nd edn (Oxford: Oxford University Press).

Connaughton, B. (2015), Developing a Hybrid Identity?: The Europeanization of Public Servants at the Continent's Far West, in F. Sager and P. Overeem, eds., *The European Public Servant: A Shared Administrative History* (Colchester: ECPR Press).

Connell, J. (2005), *Papua New Guinea: The Struggle for Development* (London: Routledge).

Cook, B. J. (2014), *Bureaucracy and Self-Government: Reconsidering the Role of Public Administration in American Politics*, 2nd edn (Baltimore, MD: Johns Hopkins University Press).

Copus, C., M. Roberts and R. Wall (2017), *Local Government in England: Centralisation, Autonomy and Control* (London: Palgrave).

Cotta, M. and P. Tavares de Alameda (2007), From Servants of the State to Elected Representatives: Public Sector Background of Members of Parliament, in M. Cotta and H. Best, *Democratic Representation in Europe* (Oxford: Oxford University Press).

Craft, J. (2015), Revisiting the Gospel: Appointed Political Staff and Core Executive Policy Coordination, *International Journal of Public Administration* 38, 56–65.

Cretu, G. (2014), Reform Trajectories in Southeastern Europe: Greece and Romania in Comparative Perspective, *Sfera Politicii* 2, 39–45.

Crook, R. (2010), Rethinking Civil Service Reform in Africa: "Islands of Effectiveness" and Organisational Commitment, *Commonwealth and Comparative Politics* 48, 479–504.

Crossman, R. H. S. (1976), *Diaries of a Cabinet Minister* (London: Hamish Hamilton).

Crouch, C. (1986), Sharing Public Space: States and Organized Interests in Western Europe, in J. A. Hall, ed., *States in History* (Oxford: Blackwell).

Crowder, M. (1964), Indirect Rule: French and British Style, *Africa: Journal of the International African Institute* 34, 197–205.

Crowther, W. and G. Flores (1984), Problemas latinoamericanos en administración pública y dependencia de soluciones desde Estados Unidos, in Gilberto Flores and Jorge Nef, eds., *Administración Publica: Perspectivas Criticas* (San José, Costa Rica: ICAP).

Crozier, M., S. P. Huntington and J. Watanuki (1975), *Crisis of Democracy: Report on the Governability of Democracies to the Trilateral Commission* (New York: New York University Press).

Culpepper, P. (2008), Capitalism, Coordination and Economic Change, in B. Palier, P. Clpepper and P. A. Hall, eds., *Changing France: The Politics that Markets Make* (London: Macmillan).

Cutler, T. and B. Waine (2000), Managerialism Reformed?: New Labour and Public Sector Management, *Social Policy and Administration* 34, 318–32.

Cyert, R. and J. G. March (1967), *A Behavioral Theory of the Firm* (Englewood Cliffs, NJ: Prentice-Hall).

d'Arcy, F. (1996), L'administration territoriale de la Republique ou le maintien de la spécificité française, in F. D'Arcy and L. Rouban, eds., *De la Ve Republique à l'Europe* (Paris: Presses de Sciences Po).

Dahl, R. A (1957), The Concept of Power, *Behavioral Science* 2, 201–15.

Dahlström, C. and M. Holmgren (2019), The Political Dynamics of Bureaucratic Turnover, *British Journal of Political Science* 49, 823–39.

Dahlström, C. and B. Niklasson (2013), The Politics of Politicization in Sweden, *Public Administration* 91, 891–907.

Dahlström, C., B. G. Peters and J. Pierre (2011), *Governing From the Centre: Strengthening Political Control in Western Democracies* (Toronto: University of Toronto Press).

Daly, G. (1968), Prolegomena on the Spanish American Political Tradition, *Hispanic American Historical Review* 48, 37–58.

Damaska, M. R. (1986), *The Faces of Justice and Authority: A Comparative Approach to the Legal Process* (New Haven, CT: Yale University Press).

Darbon, D. (2002), La culture administrative en Afriques: la construction historique de significations di "phénomène bureaucratique," *Cadernos de Estudos Africanos* 3, 65–92.

Darbon, D. (2004), Pour une socio-anthropologie de l'administration en Afrique, *Politique africaine* 96, 163–76.

Davis, J. (2006), Meritocracy in the Civil Service, 1853–1970, *The Political Quarterly* 77, 27–35.

Day, P. and R. Klein (1987), *Accountabilities* (London: Tavistock).

De Graaf, G. (2011), The Loyalties of Top Public Administrators, *Journal of Public Administration Research and Theory* 21, 285–306.

De Montricher, N. (1990), The Prefect and State Reform, *Public Administration* 78, 657–78.

de Waal, A. and R. Ibreck (2013), Hybrid Social Movements in Africa, *Journal of Contemporary African Studies* 31, 303–24.

Denhardt, R. B. and J. V. Denhardt (2003), The New Public Service: An Approach to Reform, *International Review of Public Administration* 8, 3–10.

Derlien, H.-U. (1999), On the Selective Interpretation of Max Weber's Theory of Bureaucracy, in P. Ahonen and K. Palonen, eds., *Disembalming Max Weber* (Jyvaskyla: Sophi).

Derlien, H. U. and B. G. Peters (2000), *The State at Work* (Cheltenham: Edward Elgar).

Di Maschio, F. and A. Natalini (2013), Fiscal Retrenchment in Southern Europe: Changing Patterns of Public Management in Greece, Italy, Spain and Portugal, *Public Management Review* 17, 129–48.

Diamant, A. (1968), Tradition and Innovation in French Administration, *Comparative Political Studies* 1, 251–74.

Dienstag, J. F. (1996), Between History and Nature: Social Contract Theory in Locke and the Founders, *Journal of Politics* 58, 985–1009.

Diez-Picazo, L. M. (2013), La générosité de la responsibilité "objective" de l'administration en droit espagnole, *Revue francaise d'administration publique* 147, 653–64.

Dimaggio, P. and W. Powell (1991), The Iron Cage Revisited: Institutional Isomorphism and Collective Rationality in Organizational Fields, *American Sociological Review* 48, 147–60.

Diouf, M. (2002), The French Colonial Policy of Assimilation and the Civility of the Originaires of the Four Communities (Senegel), *Development and Change* 29, 671–96.

Donahue, J. D and R. J. Zeckhauser (2012), Collaborative *Governance: Private Roles for Public Goals in Turbulent Times* (Princeton, NJ: Princeton University Press).

Dowding, K. (2013), The "Prime Ministerialisation" of the British Prime Minister, *Parliamentary Affairs* 66, 617–35.

Drechsler, W. (2013a), Islamic Public Administration: The Missing Dimension in NISPAcee Public Administration Research?, in M. Vintar et al., eds., *The Past, Present and Future of Public Administration in Central and Eastern Europe: Twenty Years of NISPAcee, 1992–2012* (Bratislava: NISPAcee Press).

Drechsler, W. (2013b), Three Paradigms of Governance and Administration: Chinese, Western and Islamic, *Society and Economy* 35, 319–42.

Drechsler, W. (2015) Paradigms of Non-Western Public Administration and Governance, in A. Massy and K. Johnston, eds., *The International Handbook of Public Administration and Governance* (Cheltenham: Edward Elgar).

Drechsler, W. (2018), Beyond the Western Paradigm: Confucian Public Administration, in S. Bice, A. Poole and H. Sullivan, eds., *Public Policy in the Asian Century* (London: Macmillan).

Dreyfus, F. (2013), Far Beyond the "Napoleonic Model": Richness of the French Administrative History, in J.-M. Eymeri-Douzans and G. Bouckaert, eds., *La France et ses Administrations: Un etat des savoirs* (Brussels: Bruylant).

Drezner, D. (2018), The Infectious Incompetence of the Populists, *The Washington Post*, July 18.

Dubois, V. (2010), *La vie au guichet: Relation administrative et traitemente de la misère* (Paris: Economic).

Dubois, V. (2012), Le rôle des street-level bureaucrats dans la conduite de l'action publique en France, in J.-M. Eymeri-Douzans and G. Bouckaert, eds., *La France et ses administrations. Un état des savoirs* (Bruxelles: Bruylant-De Boeck).

Duffy, D. P. (1995), The Northwest Ordinance as a Constitutional Document, *Columbia Law Review*, 95, 929–68.

Dunham, D. (1999), Civil Lives: Leadership and Accomplishment in Botswana, in J. L. Comaroff and J. Comaroff, eds., *Civil Society and the Political Imagination in Africa* (Chicago, IL: University of Chicago Press).

Dunlop, C. A. (2020), *Policy Learning and Policy Failure* (Bristol: Bristol University Press).

Dunn, W. N. and D. Y. Miller (2007), A Critique of the New Public Management and the Neo-Weberian State: Advancing a Critical Theory of Administrative Reform, *Public Organization Review* 7, 345–58.

Duran, P. (2000), *Penser l'action sociale* (Paris: LGDJ).

Durán, I. P. (2018), Interest Group Representation in the Formal Design of European Union Agencies, *Regulation & Governance* 12, 238–62.

Durant, R. F. (2016), Federal Administrative Leadership in the American Political System, in D. H. Rosenbloom, P. S. Malone and B. Valdez, eds., *The Handbook of Federal Government Leadership and Administration* (New York: Routledge).

Duryea, S., A. Olgiati and L. Stone (2006), *The Under-Registration of Children in Latin America* (Washington, DC: Inter-American Development Bank).

Dwyer, P. and N. Ellison (2009), "We nicked stuff from all over the place": Policy Transfer or Muddling Through? *Policy & Politics* 37(3), 389–407.

Dyson, K. H. F. (1980), *The State Tradition in Western Europe: A Study of an Idea and an Institution* (Oxford: Oxford University Press).

Ebbinghaus, B. (2010), Reforming Bismarckian Corporatism: The Changing Role of Social Partnership in Continental Europe, in B. Palier, ed., *A Long Goodbye to Bismarck* (Amsterdam: Amsterdam University Press).

Egeberg, M. (2004), An Organizational Approach to European Integration: Outline of a Complementary Perspective, *European Journal of Political Research* 43, 100–219.

Egeberg, M. and A. Heskestad (2010), The Denationalization of Cabinets in the European Commission, *Journal of Common Market Studies* 48, 775–86.

Egeberg, M. (2013), How Bureaucratic Structure Matters: An Organizational Perspective, in B. G. Peters and J. Pierre, eds., *Handbook of Public Administration* (London: Sage).

Eichbaum, C. and R. Shaw (2008), Revisiting Politicization: Political Advisers and Public Servants in Westminster Systems, *Governance* 21, 337–63.

Eisenstadt, S. N. (1964), Continuity of Modernization and Development of Administration (CAG Occasional Paper) (Bloomington: Indiana University Press).

Ekiert, G. and S. E. Hanson (2003), *Capitalism and Democracy in Central and Eastern Europe* (Cambridge: Cambridge University Press).

Eliason, S. (2000), Max Weber's Methodology: An Ideal Type, *Journal of the History of the Behavioral Sciences* 36, 241–63.

Elkins, D. J. and R. E. B. Simeon (1979), A Cause in Search of An Effect; Or What Does Elite Political Culture Explain?, *Comparative Politics* 11, 117–46.

Ellinas, A. and E. N. Suleiman (2008), Reforming the Commission: Between Modernization and Bureaucratization, *Journal of European Public Policy* 15, 708–25.

Engida, T. G. and J. Bardill (2013), Reform of the Public Sector in Light of New Public Management: Cases of Sub-Saharan Africa, *Journal of Public Administration and Policy Research* 5, 1–7.

Englebert, P. (2000), Pre-Colonial Institutions, Post-Colonial States, and Economic Development in Tropical Africa, *Political Research Quarterly* 53, 7–36.

Erk, J. (2004), Austria: A Federation without Federalism, *Publius* 34, 1–20.

Erkkilä, T. (2012), *Government Transparency: Impacts and Unintended Consequences* (Basingstoke: Macmillan).

Esping-Andersen, G. (1990), *The Three Worlds of Welfare Capitalism* (Princeton, NJ: Princeton University Press).

Esplugas-Labatut, P. (2018), *Le service public*, 4th edn (Paris: Dalloz).

Etzioni, A. (1975), *A Comparative Analysis of Complex Organizations: On Power, Involvement and their Correlates*, rev. edn (New York: Free Press).

Evans, P. and J. Rauch (1999), Bureaucracy and Growth: A Cross-National Analysis of the Effects of Weberian State Structures on Economic Growth, *American Sociological Review* 64, 748–65.

Eymeri-Douzanes, J. M. (2001), *Pouvoir politique et haute administration: Une comparison européene* (Maastricht: European Institute of Public Administration).

Fabbrini, S. (2010), *Compound Democracies: Why the Europe and the United States Are Becoming More Similar* (Oxford: Oxford University Press).

Falleti, T. (2010), *Decentralization and Subnational Politics in Latin America* (Cambridge: Cambridge University Press).

Fan, R. (2011), *The Renaissance of Confucianism in Contemporary China* (Heidelberg: Springer).

Farazmand, A. (2002), Administrative Legacies of the Persian World-State Empire: Implications for Modern Public Administration, *Public Administration Quarterly* 25, 280–316.

Fenna, A. and T. Hueglin (2010), *Comparative Federalism: A Systematic Inquiry* (North York, ON: University of Toronto Press).

Fenton, B. (2006), How Whitehall was beaten to the punch by the Crossman Diaries, *Daily Telegraph*, January 2.

Filleule, O. (2003), France, in C. Rootes, ed., *Environmental Protest in Western Europe* (Oxford: Oxford University Press).

Firmin-Sellers, K. (2000), Institutions, Context, and Outcomes: Explaining French and British Rule in West Africa, *Comparative Politics* 32, 253–72.

Fisch, S. (2008), Mechanisms Creating a European Administrative Culture, in J. Beck and F. Thedieck, eds., *The European Dimension of Administrative Culture* (Baden-Baden: Nomos).

Fischer, M. E. (1989), *Nicolae Ceausecu: A Study in Political Leadership* (Boulder, CO: Lynne Rienner).

Fisher, L. E. (1928), The Intendant System in Spanish America, *Hispanic American Historical Review* 8, 3–13.

Fizot, S. (2007), Le contrôle des gestionnaires publics par les Cours des Comptes, *Politiques et management public* 25, 141–56.

Fleischer, J. (2011), Steering from the German Centre: More Policy Coordination and Fewer Policy Initiatives, in C. Dahlström, B. G. Peters and J. Pierre, eds., *Steering from the Centre: Strengthening Political Control in Western Democracies* (Toronto: University of Toronto Press).

Flinders, M. (2004), Distributed Public Governance in the European Union, *Journal of European Public Policy* 11, 530–44.

Foa, R. (2016), *Ancient Polities, Modern States*, unpublished dissertation, Graduate School of Arts and Sciences, Harvard University.

Forest, V. (2008), Rémunération au mérite et motivation au travail: perspectives théoretique et empiriques pour la fonction publique française, *Revue internationale des sciences administratives* 74, 345–59.

Fournier, J. (1998), Administrative Reforms in Commission Opinions Concerning the Accession of Central and Eastern European Countries, in SIGMA, *Preparing Public Administration for the European Administrative Space* (Paris: Sigma).

France, P. and A. Vauchez (2017), *Sphère publique, intérêts privé: Enquête sur un grand brouillage* (Paris: Presses de Science Po).

Frank, S. A. and G. B. Lewis (2004), Government Employees: Working Hard or Hardly Working?, *American Review of Public Administration* 34, 36–51.

Freedman, J. O. (1980), *Crisis and Legitimacy* (Cambridge: Cambridge University Press).

Freeman, G. P. (1985), National Styles and Policy Sectors: Explaining Structured Variation. *Journal of Public Policy* 5(4): 467–96.

Freeman, S (2009), *Justice and the Social Contract: Essays on Rawlsian Political Philosophy* (Oxford: Oxford University Press).

Fried, R. C. (1963), *The Italian Prefects: A Study in Administrative Politics* (New Haven, CT: Yale University Press).

Gailmard S. and J. W. Patty (2012), Formal Models of Bureaucracy, *Annual Review of Political Science* 15, 353–77.

Gaman-Golutvina, O. (2008), The Changing Role of the State and State Bureaucracy in the Context of Public Administration Reforms: Russian and Foreign Experience, *Journal of Communist Studies and Transition Politics* 25, 37–53.

Gandhi, J. (2008), *Political Institutions Under Dictatorship* (Cambridge: Cambridge University Press).

Gargarella, R. (2004), Latin American Constitutionalism 1810–1860, *Latin American Research Review* 39, 141–53.

Gauthier, D. (1986), *Morals by Agreement* (Oxford: Oxford University Press).

Genieys, W. and P. Hassenteufel (2012), Qui gouverne les politiques publiques?, *Gouvernement et action publique* 1, 89–115.

Gerring, J., D. Ziblatt, J. Van Gorp and J. Arévalo (2011), An Institutional Theory of Direct and Indirect Rule, *World Politics* 63, 377–43.

Gersen, J. E. and M. C. Stephenson (2014), Over-Accountability, *Journal of Legal Analysis* 6, 185–243.

Gilley, B. (2009), *The Right to Rule: How States Win and Lose Legitimacy* (New York: Columbia University Press).

Go, J. (2011), *Patterns of Empire: The British and American Empires 1688 to the Present* (Cambridge: Cambridge University Press).

Goldsmith, S. and D. F. Kettl (2009), *Unlocking the Power of Networks* (Washington DC: The Brookings Institution).

Goncharov, D. and A. Shirikov (2013), Public Administration in Russian, in S. Liebert, S. E. Condrey and D. Goncharov, eds., *Public Administration in Post-Soviet Countries* (Boca Raton, FL: CRC Press).

Goodsell, C. T. (2011), *Mission Mystique: Belief Systems in Public Agencies* (Washington, DC; CQ Press).

Goodsell, C. T. (2014), *The Case for Bureaucracy: A Public Administration Polemic* (Washington, DC: CQ Press).

Gormley, W. T. and S. J. Balla (2013), *Bureaucracy and Democracy: Accountability and Performance* (Washington, DC: CQ Press).

Gravier, M. and C. Roth (2016), Practices of Representative Bureaucracy in the European Commission, Paper presented at Midwest Political Science Association Convention, Chicago, IL.

Green, J. F. (2016), *Rethinking Private Authority: Agents and Entrepreneurs in Global Environmental Governance* (Princeton, NJ: Princeton University Press).

Gregory, R. (2003), All the King's Horses and All the King's Men: Putting New Zealand's Public Sector Back Together Again, *International Public Management Review* 4, 42–58.

Gregory, R. and J. G. Christensen (2004), Similar Ends, Differing Means: Contractualism and Civil Service Reform in Denmark and New Zealand, *Governance* 17, 59–82.

Gremion, P. (1976), *Le pouvoir périphérique: Bureaucrates et notables dan le systeme politique français* (Paris: Seuil).

Greve, C., N. Ejersbo, P. Lægreid and L. Rykkja (2019), Unpacking Nordic Administrative Reform: Agile and Adaptive Governments, *International Journal of Public Administration* 43(8), 697–710.

Grindle, M. S. (2012), *Jobs for the Boys: Patronage and the State in Latin America* (Cambridge, MA: Harvard University Press).

Grønegård Christensen, J. (2004), Political Responsiveness in a Merit Bureaucracy: Denmark, in B. G. Peters and J. Pierre, eds., *Politicization of the Civil Service in Comparative Perspective: The Quest for Control* (London: Routledge).

Grønegård Christensen, J., R. Klemmensen and N. Ostrup (2014), Politicization and Replacement of Top Civil Servants in Denmark, *Governance* 27, 215–41.

Grube, D. C. and C. Howard (2016), Is the Westminster System Broken Beyond Repair?, *Governance* 29, 467–81.

Gualmini, E. (2008), Restructuring Weberian Bureaucracy: Comparing Managerial Reforms in Europe and the United States, *Public Administration* 86, 75–94.

Guichard, S., G. Montagnier, A. Varinard and T. Debard (2011), *Institutions juridictionelles* (Paris: Dalloz).

Gunlicks, A. B. (2003), *The Länder and German Federalism* (Manchester: Manchester University Press).

Gupta, A. (2012), *Red Tape:* Bureaucracy, Structural Violence and Poverty in India (Durham, NC: Duke University Press).

Hajnal, G. and S. Boda (forthcoming), The Anatomy of Illiberal Transformation of Government Bureaucracy: An Empirical Test of a Conceptual Model, in M. Bauer, B. G. Peters, J. Pierre, A. K. Yesilkagit and S. Becker, eds., *Liberal-Democratic Backsliding and Public Administration*.

Hall, P. (2016), The Swedish Administrative Model, in J. Pierre, ed., *The Oxford Handbook of Swedish Politics* (Oxford: Oxford University Press).

Halligan, J. A. (2004), *Civil Service Systems in Anglo-American Countries* (Cheltenham: Edward Elgar).

Hammerschmid, G., R. E. Meyer and C. Demmke (2007), Public Administration Modernization: Common Reform Trends or Different Paths, in K. Schedler. and I. Proeller, eds., *Cultural Aspects of Public Management Reform* (Amsterdam: JAI).

Hampton, J. (1986), *Hobbes and the Social Contract Tradition* (Cambridge: Cambridge University Press).

Handy, C. B. (2005), *The Age of Paradox* (Cambridge, MA: Harvard Business Press).

Hansen, H. F. (2011), NPM in Scandinavia, in T. Christensen and P. Laegreid, eds., *The Ashgate Research Companion to the New Public Management* (Avebury: Ashgate).

Hansen, M. B. and H. H. Salomonsen (2011), The Public Service Bargains of Danish Permanent Secretaries, *Public Policy and Administration* 26, 189–208.

Hoque, N., M. A. Khan and M. M. Mowla (2013), Organizational Culture: Features and Framework from Islamic Perspective, *Humanomics* 29(3), 202–19.

Hoque, S. (1996), The Contextless Nature of Public Administration in Third World Countries, *International Review of Administrative Sciences* 62, 315–29.

Hardiman, N. and M. MacCarthaigh (2011), The UnPolitics of New Public Management in Ireland, in J.-M. Eymeri-Douzans and J. Pierre, eds., *Administrative Reform and Democratic Governance* (London: Routledge).

Hargreaves, A. G. (2005), *Memory, Empire and Postcolonialism: Legacies of French Colonialism* (Lanham, MD: Rowman & Littlefield).

Hashmi, S. H. (2002), *Islamic Political Ethics: Civil Society, Pluralism, and Conflict* (Princeton, NJ: Princeton University Press).

Hassel, A. (2009), Policies and Politics of Social Pacts in Europe, *European Journal of Industrial Relations* 15, 7–26.

Hattenhauer, H. (1993), *Geschichte des Deutschen Beamtentums* (Cologne: Carl Heymanns Verlag).

Häusermann, S., A. Mach and Y. Papadopoulos (2004), Social Policymaking Under Strain in Switzerland, *Swiss Political Science Review* 10, 33–59.

Häusermann, S., G. Picot and D. Gerring (2013), Review Article: Rethinking Party Politics and the Welfare State, *British Journal of Political Science* 43, 221–40.

Hay, C. (2006), Constructivist Institutionalism, in R. A. W. Rhodes, S. A. Binder and B. A. Rockman, eds., *Oxford Handbook of Political Institutions* (Oxford: Oxford University Press).

Hayward, J. E. S. (1983), *Governing France: The One and Indivisible Republic*, 2nd edn (London: Weidenfeld and Nicolson).

Hayward, J. E. S. and V. Wright (2002), *Governing from the Centre: Core Executive Coordination in France* (Oxford: Oxford University Press).

Hazareesingh, S. (1994), *Political Traditions in Modern France* (Oxford: Oxford University Press).

Hazareesingh, S. (2005), *The Legend of Napoleon* (London: Granta Books).

Heady, F. (1996), Configurations of Civil Service Systems, in A. G. M. Bekke, J. L. Perry and T. A. J. Toonen, eds., *Civil Service Systems in Comparative Perspective* (Bloomington: Indiana University Press).

Heady, F. (2001), *Public Administration: A Comparative Perspective*, 6th edn (Boca Raton, FL: CRC Press).

Heider, D. S. and J. T. Heider (2003), *Manifest Destiny* (Westport, CT: Greenwood Press).

Heisler, M. O. (1978), The European Polity Model, in M. O. Heisler, ed., *Politics in Europe* (New York: Longmans).

Helmke, G. and S. Levitsky (2004), Informal Institutions and Comparative Politics: A Research Agenda, *Perspectives on Politics* 2, 725–40.

Henderson, K. M. (2005), American Administrative Culture: An Evolutionary Perspective, in J. G. Jabbra and O, P. Dwivedi, eds., *Administrative Culture in Global Context* (Whitby, ON: de Sitter Publications).

Henderson, K. M. (2006), The Quest for Indigenous Administration, Asian Communist, Islamic Revivalist and Other Models, *Public Organization Review* 6, 55–67.

Hendrych, D. (1993), Transforming Czechoslovakian Public Administration: Traditions and New Challenges, *Public Administration* 71, 41–54.

Hennessy, P. (1989), *Whitehall* (New York: Free Press).

Hennessy, P. (2005), Rulers and Servants of the State: The Blair Style of Government 1997–2004, *Parliamentary Affairs* 58, 6–16.

Henriksen, J. B. (2008), The Continuous Process of Recognition and Implementation of the Sami People's Right to Self-Determination, *Cambridge Review of International Affairs* 21, 27–40.

Henstridge, M. (2020), Cases, Deaths and Lockdowns: The Variety of Pandemic Data and the Uniformity of Responses, Oxford Policy Management May, 2020. https://www.opml. co.uk/blog/cases-deaths-and-lock-downs-the-variety-of-pandemic-data-and-uniformity-of-response

Heper, M. (1987), *The State and Public Bureaucracies* (Westport, CT: Greenwood Press).

Heper, M. (2000), The Ottoman Legacy and Turkish Politics, *Journal of International Affairs* 54, 63–82.

Herbst, J. (2014), *States and Power in Africa: Comparative Lessons in Authority and Control* (Princeton, NJ: Princeton University Press).

Herzfeld, M. (1992), *The Social Production of Indifference: Explaining the Symbolic Roots of Western Bureaucracy* (New York: Berg).

Hinnebusch, R. (2006), Authoritarian Persistence, Democratization Theory and the Middle East: An Overview and Critique, *Democratization* 13, 373–95.

Hirschl, R. (2008), The Judicialization of Politics, in R. E. Goodin, ed., *Oxford Handbook of Political Science* (Oxford: Oxford University Press).

Hodgetts, J. E. (2007), Royal Commission and Public Service Reform: Personal Reflections, *Canadian Public Administration* 50, 525–40.

Hofstede, G. (1984), *Culture's Consequences: International Differences in Work-Related Values*, rev. edn (London: Sage).

Hofstede, G., G. J. Hofstede and M. Mirkov (2010), *Culture and Organizations: Software of the Mind* (New York: McGraw-Hill).

Hogwood, B. W., D. Judge and M. McVicar (2000), Agencies and Accountability, in R. A. W. Rhodes, ed., *Transforming British Government, Vol 1: Changing Institutions* (Basingstoke: Macmillan).

Holmes, L. (2003), Corruption in Central and Eastern Europe, in M. J. Bull and J. L. Newell, eds., *Corruption in Contemporary Politics* (London: Palgrave Macmillan).

Hollibaugh, G. E. (2015), Naïve Cronyism and Neutral Competence: Patronage. Performance and Policy Agreement in Executive Appointments, *Journal of Public Administration Research and Theory* 25, 341–72.

Homburg, V. (2008), *Understanding E-government: Information Systems in Public Administration* (London: Routledge).

Hongbo, L. (2014), Human Rights, Good Administration, and Democracy: Ombudsman in the Process of Law and Social Development in Europe, *Journal of Comparative Law*.

Hood, C. (1984), *The Tools of Government* (Chatham, NJ: Chatham House).

Hood, C. (1991), A Public Management for all Seasons? *Public Administration* 69, 3–19.

Hood, C. (2000), *The Art of the State: Culture, Rhetoric, and Public Management* (Oxford: Oxford University Press).

Hood, C. (2011), *The Blame Game: Spin, Bureaucracy and Self-Preservation in Government* (Princeton, NJ: Princeton University Press).

Hood, C., O. James, B. G. Peters and C. Scott (2004), *Controlling Modern Government: Variety, Commonality and Change* (Cheltenham: Edward Elgar).

Hood, C., O. James, C. Scott, G. W. Jones and T. Travers (1999), *Regulation Inside Government* (Oxford: Oxford University Press).

Hood, C. and M. Lodge (2006), *The Politics of Public Service Bargains: Reward, Competency, Loyalty—and Blame* (Oxford: Oxford University Press).

Hood, C. and B. G. Peters (2004), The Middle-Aging of New Public Management: Into the Age of Paradox, *Journal of Public Administration Research and Theory* 14, 267–82.

Hood, C. and B. G. Peters, with Grace O. M. Lee (2002), *Reward for High Public Office in Asia and Pacific Rim Countries* (London: Routledge).

Hooghe, L. (1999), Consociationalists vs. Weberians? Top Commission Officials on Nationality, *Governance* 12, 397–424.

Horton, S. (2008), History and Persistence of an Idea and an Ideal, in J. L. Perry and A, Hondeghem, eds., *Motivation in Public Management: The Call of Public Service* (Oxford: Oxford University Press).

Horton, S. (2011), Contrasting Anglo-American and Continental European Civil Service Systems, in A. Massey, ed., *International Handbook of Civil Service Systems* (Cheltenham: Edward Elgar).

Houck, O. A. (2002), *The Clean Water Act TMDL Program: Law, Policy and Implementation*, 2nd edn (Washington, DC: Environmental Law Institute).

House, R. J., P. J. Hanges, M. Javidan, P. W. Dorfman and V. Gupta (2009), *Culture, Leadership and Organization: The GLOBE Study of 62 Countries* (Thousand Oaks, CA: Sage).

Houston, D. J. (2011), Implications of Occupational Locus and Focus for Public Service Motivation: Attitudes Toward Work Motives Across Nations, *Public Administration Review* 71, 761–71.

Howlett, M. (2003), Administrative Styles and the Limits of Administrative Reform: A Neo-Institutional Analysis of Administrative Culture, *Canadian Public Administration* 46, 471–94.

Howlett, M. and J. Tosun (2019), *Policy Styles and Policy-Making: Exploring the Linkages* (London: Routledge).

Huber, J. G. and C. R. Shipan (2006), Politics, Delegation and Bureaucracy, in B. R. Weingast and D. A. Witman, eds., *Oxford Handbook of Political Economy* (Oxford: Oxford University Press).

Hueglin. T. and A. Fenna (2016), *Comparative Federalism: A Systematic Inquiry*, 2nd edn (Toronto: University of Toronto Press).

Humphrey, C. and D. Sneath (2017), Shanghaied by the Bureaucracy: Bribery and Post-Soviet Officialdom in Russia and Mongolia, in I. Pardo, ed., *Between Morality and the Law: Corruption, Anthropology and Comparative Society* (London: Routledge).

Huntington, S. P. (1968), *Political Order in Changing Societies* (New Haven, CT: Yale University Press).

Hupe, P. (2019), *Research Handbook on Street-Level Bureaucracy* (Cheltenham: Edward Elgar).

Hupe, P., M. Hill and A. Buffat (2015), *Understanding Street-Level Bureaucracy* (Bristol: Policy Press).

Hyden, G. (1980), *Beyond Ujaama in Tanzania: Underdeveloped and an Uncaptured Peasantry* (Berkeley: University of California Press).

Hyden, G. (2010), Where Administrative Traditions are Alien: Implications for Reform in Africa, in M. Painter and B. G. Peters, eds., *Tradition and Public Administration* (Basingstoke: Macmillan).

Hyden, G. (2013), Culture, Administration and Reform in Africa, *International Journal of Public Administration* 36, 922–31.

Hysing, E. and E. Lundberg (2016), Making Government Networks More Democratic: Lessons from Swedish Government Commissions, *Critical Policy Studies* 10, 21–38.

Im, T. (2014), Bureaucracy in Three Different Worlds: The Assumptions of Failed Public Sector Reforms in Korea, *Public Organization Review* 14, 577–96.

Im, T. J. W. and S. Cha (2013), Revisiting Confucian Bureaucracy: Roots of the Korean Government's Culture and Competitiveness, *Public Administration and Development* 33, 286–96.

Immergut, E. (1992), *Health Care Politics: Ideas and Institutions in Western Europe* (Cambridge: Cambridge University Press).

Ingraham, P. W. (1995), *The Foundations of Merit: Public Service in American Democracy* (Baltimore, MD: Johns Hopkins University Press).

Ingraham, P. W., J. R. Thompson and E. F. Eisenberg (1995), Political Management Strategies and Political/Career Relationships, *Public Administration Review* 55, 263–72.

Iyer, L. (2010), Direct and Indirect Colonial Rule in India: Long-Term Consequences, *Review of Economics and Statistics* 92, 693–713.

Jacobs, H. (1967), *German Administration Since Bismarck: Central Authority versus Local Autonomy* (New Haven, CT: Yale University Press).

Jacobsson, B., J. Pierre and G. Sundström (2016), *Governing the Embedded State: The Organizational Dimension of Governing* (Oxford: Oxford University Press).

Jäger, W. (1988), Von der Kanzlerdemokratie zur Koordinationsdemokratie, *Zeitschrift für Parlamentsfragen* 35, 15–32.

Jann, W. (2003), State, Administration and Governance in Germany: Competing Traditions and Dominant Narratives, *Public Administration* 87, 95–118.

Jerome-Forget, M., J. White and J. M. Wiener (1995), *Health Care Through Internal Markets* (Montreal: Institute for Research on Public Policy).

Jessop, B. (1982), *The Capitalist State: Marxist Theories and Methods* (Oxford: Martin Roberstson).

Jewell, C. J. (2007), *Agents of the Welfare State: How Caseworkers Respond to Need in The United States, Germany and Sweden* (Basingstoke: Palgrave Macmillan).

Jobert, B. (2004), *Estado, sociedad, politicas publicas* (Santiago: LOM).

Jobert, B. and P. Muller (1987), *L'Etat en action: politique publiques et corporatismes* (Paris: Presses Universitaires de France).

Johns, C. M., P. L. O'Reilly and G. J. Inwood (2006), Intergovernmental Innovation and the Administrative State in Canada, *Governance* 19, 627–49.

Johnson, B. (2017), Bureaucrats as Activists: A Revisionist Take, *Process: A Blog on American History*, May 23, http://www.processhistory.org/bureaucrats-as-activists/.

Johnson, J. J. (1964), *The Military and Society in Latin America* (Stanford, CA: Stanford University Press).

Johnson, N. (2000), State and Society in Britain: Some Contrasts with the German Tradition, in H. Wollmann and E. Schröter, eds., *Comparing Public Sector Reform in Britain and Germany* (Aldershot: Ashgate).

Johnston, M. (2014), The Emerging Agenda for Corruption Research, in P. Heywood, ed., *Routledge Handbook of Political Corruption* (London: Routledge).

Jones, M. L. (2007), Hofstede—Culturally Questionable. https://ro.uow.edu.au/commpapers/370.

Jørgensen, O. (2014), *Access to Information in the Nordic Countries* (Gothenburg: Nordicom).

Kada, N. (2012), Les institutions locales et la décentralisation, in L. Verpeaux, ed., *Institutions et vie politique sous la Cinquième République*, 4th edn (Paris: La Documentation Française).

Kagan, R. A. (2001), *Adversarial Legalism—The American Way of Law* (Cambridge, MA: Harvard University Press).

Kahn, R. L., D. Katz and B. Gutek (1976), Bureaucratic Encounters—An Evaluation of Government Services, *Journal of Applied Behavioral Science* 12, 178–98.

Kamisar, B. (2017), Republicans Impatient with Anti-Trump Civil Servants, *The Hill*, February 2, http://thehill.com/homenews/administration/317651-gop-lawmakers-impatient-with-anti-trump-civil-servants.

Kanyane, M. (2017), Interfacing Interplay of Local Government, Traditional Leaders and Society, *Journal of Contemporary African Studies* 35, 212–20.

Karlhofer, F. (2006), The Long Shadow of Corporatism: Scope and Limits of Think Tank Activities in Austria, *German Policy Studies* 3, 347–81.

Kassim, H., B. G. Peters and V. Wright (2000), *National Coordination of EU Policy: The Domestic Level* (Oxford: Oxford University Press).

Kassim, H., J. Peterson, M. W. Bauer, S. Connolly, R. Dehousse, L. Hooghe and A. Thompson (2013), *The European Commission of the Twenty-First Century* (Oxford: Oxford University Press).

Kassim, H. (2018), The European Commission as an Administration, in E. Ongaro and S. Van Thiel, eds., *The Palgrave Handbook of Public Administration and Management in Europe* (London: Palgrave).

Katzenstein, P. (1987), *Politics and Policy in West Germany: The Growth of a Semisovereign State* (Philadelphia, PA: Temple University Press).

Katzenstein, P. J. (2005), Conclusion: Semisovereignty in Unified Germany, in S. Green and W. Patterson, eds., *Governance in Contemporary Germany: The Semisovereign State Revisited* (Cambridge: Cambridge University Press).

Kaufman, H. A. (1974), *Are Government Organizations Immortal?* (Washington, DC: The Brookings Institution).

Keeler, J. T. S. (1997), *The Politics of Neocorporatism in France: Farmers, the State and the Politics of Agriculture Policymaking in the Fifth Republic* (Oxford: Oxford University Press).

Keogh, D. (2005), *Twentieth-Century Ireland: Revolution and State-Building*, rev. edn (Dublin: Gill & Macmillan).

Kerwin, C. M. and S. R. Furlong (2019), *Rulemaking: How Government Agencies Write Law and Make Policy*, 5th edn (Washington, DC: CQ Press).

Kettl, D. F. (2000), Public Administration at the Millennium: The State of the Field, *Journal of Public Administration Research and Theory* 10, 7–34.

Kettl, D. F. (2006), Modernizing Government: The Way Forward, *International Review of Administrative Sciences* 72, 313–17.

Kickert. W. J. M. (1997), Public Governance in the Netherlands: An Alternative to Anglo-American "Managerialism," *Public Administration* 75, 731–52.

Kim, Y.-P. (2001), The South Korean Civil Service System, in J. P. Burns and B. Bowornwathana, eds., *Asian Civil Service Systems* (Cheltenham: Edward Elgar).

Kingsley, J. D. (1944), *Representative Bureaucracy* (Yellow Springs, OH: Antioch Press).

Kiser, E. (1987), The Formation of State Policy in Western European Absolutisms: A Comparison of England and France, *Politics & Society* 15, 259–95.

Kitschelt, H. (2003), What Accounts for Post-Communist Regime Diversity?: What Counts as a Good Cause?, in G. Ekiert and S. E. Hanson, eds., *Capitalism and Democracy in Central and Eastern Europe* (Cambridge: Cambridge University Press).

Knapp, A. (1983), The *Cumul des mandats*, Local Power and Political Parties in France, *West European Politics* 14, 18–39.

Knill, C. (1999), Explaining Cross-National Variance in Administrative Reform: Autonomous versus Instrumental Bureaucracies, *Journal of Public Policy* 19, 113–39.

Knill, C. (2001), *The Europeanization of National Administrations: Patterns of Institutional Change and Persistence* (Cambridge: Cambridge University Press).

Knill, C. (2005), *The Europeanization of National Administration: Patterns of Institutional Change and Persistence* (Cambridge: Cambridge University Press).

König, K. (1996), Unternehmerisches oder exekutives Management—die Perspektive der klassischen öffentlichen Verwaltung, *Verwaltungs-Archiv*, 87, 19–37.

König, T. and L. Mäder (2014), The Strategic Nature of Compliance: An Empirical Examination of Law Implementation in the European Union, *American Journal of Political Science* 58, 246–53.

Kopecký, P., P. Mair and M. Spirova (2012), *Party Patronage and Party Government in European Democracies* (Oxford: Oxford University Press).

Kotchegura, A. (1999), The Russian Civil Service: Legitimacy and Performance, in T. Verheijen, ed., *Civil Service Systems in Central and Eastern Europe* (Cheltenham: Edward Elgar).

Kriesi, H. and A. H. Treschel (2008), *The Politics of Switzerland: Continuity and Change in a Consensus Democracy* (Cambridge: Cambridge University Press).

Kristinsson. G. H. (2012), Party Patronage in Iceland: Rewards and Control Appointments, in P. Kopecký, P. Mair and M. Spirova, eds., *Party Patronage and Party Government in European Democracies* (Oxford: Oxford University Press).

Kristinsson, G. H. (2016), Specialists, Spinners and Networkers: Political Appointees in Iceland, *Acta Politica* 51, 413–32.

Kuhlmann, S. (2010), New Public Management for the "Classical Continental European Administration": Modernization at the Local Level in Germany, France and Italy, *Public Administration* 88, 1116–30.

Kuhlmann, S., J. Bogumil and S. Grohs (2008), Evaluating Administrative Modernization in German Local Government: Success or Failure of the "New Steering Model," *NISPAcee Journal of Public Administration and Policy* 1, 31–54.

Kumlin, S. and B. Rothstein (2003), Staten och det sociala kapitalet, in J. Pierre and B. Rothstein, eds., *Välfärdstat i otakt* (Malmö: Liber).

Laborde, C. (2000), The Concept of the State in British and French Political Thought, *Political Studies* 48, 540–57.

Lægreid. P and P. Roness (2012), Rewards for High Public Office: The Case of Norway, in M. Brans and B. G. Peters, eds., *Rewards for High Public Office in Europe and North America* (London: Routledge).

Lægreid. P., R. S. Steinhorssen and B. Thorallsson (2004), Europeanization of Central Government Administration in the Nordic States, *Journal of Common Market Studies* 42, 347–69.

Lange, M. K. (2004), British Colonial Legacies and Political Development, *World Development* 32, 905–22.

Lange, M. K. (2009), *Lineages of Despotism and Development: British Colonialism and State Power* (Chicago, IL: University of Chicago Press).

Lange, M. K., J. Mahoney and M. Von Hau (2006), Colonialism and Development: Comparative Analysis of Spanish and British Colonies, *American Journal of Sociology* 111, 1412–62.

Lalenis, K. (2003), The Evolution of Local Administration in Greece, in M. de Jong, K. Lalenis and V. Mamadouh, *The Theory and Practice of Institutional Transplantation* (Dordrecht: Kluwer).

LaPalombara, J. (1965), *Bureaucracy and Political Development* (Princeton, NJ: Princeton University Press).

LaPalombara, J. (1968), Macrotheories and Microapplications in Comparative Politics: A Widening Chasm, *Comparative Politics* 1, 52–78.

Lawrence, B., E. L. Osborn and R. Roberts (2006), *Intermediaries, Interpreters and Clerks: African Employees in the Making of Colonial Africa* (Madison: University of Wisconsin Press).

Le Gales, P. and N. Vizinat (2014), *L'État recomposé* (Paris: PUF).

Le Grand, J. (2003), *Motivation, Agency and Public Policy: Of Knights and Knaves, Pawns and Queens* (Oxford: Oxford University Press).

Le Lidec, P. (2005), La Relance de la decéntralization en France, *Politiques et management publique* 23, 101–25.

Lee, K.-H. and J. C. Raadschelders (2008), Political-Administrative Relations: Impacts of, and Puzzles, in Aberbach, Putnam and Rockman, *Governance* 21, 419–38.

Legay, M.-L. (2009), The Beginnings of Public Management: Administrative Science and Political Choices in the Eighteenth Century in France, Austria and the Austrian Netherlands, *The Journal of Modern History* 81, 243–93.

Lehmbruch, G. (2003), Proporzdemokratie: Politisches System und politisches Kulturr in der Schweiz und Österreich in *Verhandlungsdemokratie* (Wiesbaden: Springer).

Lemarchand, R. (2007), Consociationalism and Power Sharing in Africa: Rwanda, Burundi, and the Democratic Republic of the Congo, *African Affairs* 106, 1–20.

Lewansky, R. (2000), The Development and Current Features of the Italian Civil Service System, in A. J. G. M. Bekke and F. Van der Meer, eds., *Civil Service Systems in Western Europe* (Cheltenham: Edward Elgar).

Lewis, D. E. (2002), The Politics of Agency Termination: Confronting the Myth of Agency Immortality, *Journal of Politics* 64, 89–107.

Lewis, D. E. (2007), Testing Pendleton's Premise: Do Political Appointees Make Worse Bureaucracts?, *Journal of Politics* 69, 1073–88.

Lewis, J. M., M. McGann and E. Blomkamp (2019), When Design Meets Power Design Thinking, Public Sector Innovation and the Politics of Policymaking, *Policy & Politics* 48, 111–30.

Light, P. C. (1995), *Thickening Government* (Washington, DC: The Brookings Institution).

Lijphart, A. (2012), *Patterns of Democracy: Government Forms and Performance in Thirty-Six Countries*, 2nd edn (New Haven, CT: Yale University Press).

Lindenfeld, D. (1997), *The Practical Imagination: German Science of the State in the 19th Century* (Chicago, IL: University of Chicago Press).

Linder, W. and A. Vatter (2001), Institutions and Outcomes of Swiss Federalism: The Rose of the Cantons in Swiss Politics, *West European Politics* 24, 95–122.

Lindvall, J. and B. Rothstein (2006), Sweden: The Fall of the Strong State, *Scandinavian Political Studies* 29, 47–63.

Ling, L. H. M. and C.-Y. Shih (1998), Confucianism with a Liberal Face: The Meaning of Democratic Politics in Postcolonial Taiwan, *Review of Politics* 60, 558–82.

Lipsky, M. (2010), *Street Level Bureaucracy: Dilemmas of the Individual in Public Service*, updated edn (New York: Russell Sage).

Lodge, M. and D. Gill (2011), Toward a New Era of Administrative Reform?: The Myth of Post-NPM in New Zealand, *Governance* 24, 141–66.

Loriaux, M. (1999), The French Developmental State as Myth and Moral Ambition, in M. Woo-Cumings, ed., *The Developmental State* (Ithaca, NY: Cornell University Press).

Loughlin, J. (2001), *Subnational Democracy in the European Union* (Oxford: Oxford University Press).

Loughlin, J. and B. G. Peters (1997), State Traditions, Administrative Reform and Regionalization, in M. Keating and J. Loughlin, eds., *The Political Economy of Regionalism* (London: Routledge).

Louvaris, A. (2019), Whither the French Model of Dual Jurisdictions? Sketched Observations on "un illustre vieillard" (an Illustrious Old Man). *Administrative Law, Administrative Structures, and Administrative Decision making* (London: Hart), hal-02156465.

Lu, X. (1999), From Rank-Seeking to Rent-Seeking: Changing Administrative Ethos and Corruption in Reform China, *Crime, Law and Social Change* 32, 347–70.

Lugard, F. D. (1965), *The Dual Mandate in British Tropical Africa*, 5th edn (London: Frank Cass).

Lund, C. (2006), Twilight Institutions: Public Authority and Local Politics in Africa, *Development and Change* 37, 685–705.

Lund, C. (2007), *Twilight Institutions: Public Authority and Local Politics in Africa* (Oxford: Blackwell).

Lynn, L. E. (2008), What Is the Neo-Weberian State?: Reflections on the Concept and Its Implications, *NISPACEE Journal of Public Administration and Policy* 2, 17–30.

McConalogue, J. (2020), A Great Resettlement?: Parliamentary Sovereignty After Brexit, in J. McConalogue, ed., *The British Constitution Resettled* (London: Palgrave).

McConnell, G. (1966), *Private Power & American Democracy* (New York: Knopf).

McCourt, W. and M. Martin (2001), *The Internationalization of Public Management: Reinventing the Third World* (Cheltenham: Edward Elgar).

McFarland, A. S. (2004), *Neopluralism: The Evolution of Political Process Theory* (Lawrence: University Press of Kansas).

McKenna, B. (2017), What's Wallonia's Deal?: A Primer on its Role in the CETA Crisis, *The Globe and Mail*, January 5.

Maddox, G. (2018), *The Colonial Epoch in Africa* (London: Routledge).

Madsen, P. K. (2006), How Can it Possibly Fly?: The Paradox of a Dynamic Labor Market in a Scandinavian Welfare State, in J. L. Campbell, J. A. Hill and O. K. Pedersen, eds., *National Identities and a Variety of Capitalism: The Case of Denmark* (Montreal: McGill/Queens University Press).

Mahoney, J., M. Lange and M. Vom Hau (2006), Colonialism and Development: A Comparative Analysis of Spanish and British Colonialism, *American Journal of Sociology* 111, 1412–62.

Mahoney, J. and K. Thelen (2010a), A Theory of Gradual Institutional Change, in J. Mahoney and K. Thelen, eds., *Explaining Institutional Change: Ambiguity, Agency and Power* (Cambridge: Cambridge University Press).

Mahoney, J. and K. Thelen (2010b), *Explaining Institutional Change: Ambiguity, Agency and Power* (Cambridge: Cambridge University Press).

Mamdani, M. (1999), *Citizen and Subject: Contemporary Africa and the Legacy of Late Colonialism* (Princeton, NJ: Princeton University Press).

Mann, M. (1984), The Autonomous Power of the State: Its Origins, Mechanisms and Results, *European Journal of Sociology* 25, 185–213.

Mann, M, (2008), Infrastructural Power Revisited, *Studies in Comparative International Development* 43, 355–74.

Maor, M. (1999), The Paradox of Managerialism, *Public Administration Review* 59, 5–18.

March, J. G. and J. P. Olsen (1989), *Rediscovering Institutions* (New York: Free Press).

Marin, A. (2016), Aligning the General Secretariat of the Government and the General Secretariat of European Affairs: What Perspective for Interministerial Coordination in France?, *Revue française d'administration publique* 158, 373–88.

Martí-Henneberg, J. (2005), A Map of Europe: Continuity and Change in Administrative Boundaries (1850–2000), *Geo-Politics* 10, 791–815.

Martin, B. (1995), Fatal Affinities: The German Role in the Modernization of Japan in the Early Meiji Period (1868–95) and its Aftermath, in B. Martin, ed., *Japan and Germany in the Modern Era* (Oxford: Oxford University Press).

Mashaw, J. L. (1985), *Due Process in the Administrative State* (New Haven, CT: Yale University Press).

Mastor, W. (2018), Les présidents de la Ve Reublique: Jacobins ou Girondins?, *Pouvoirs* 166, 81–96.

Matei, Lucica (2011), Arhitectura administratiei publice: Conexiuni si complementaritate: Japonia si Romania [The architecture of public administration: Connections and complementarities: Japan and Romania], http://www.admpubl.snspa.ro/fisiere/japonia/ Arhitectura%20administratiei%20publice.%20Conexiuni%20si%20complementaritate %20Japonia%20-%20 Romania%20-%20Lucica%20Matei.pdf [last accessed December 2019].

Mattson, I. (2016), Parliamentary Committees, in J. Pierre, ed., *The Oxford Handbook of Swedish Politics* (Oxford: Oxford University Press).

Mayntz, R. and F. W. Scharpf (1975), *Policy-Making in the German Federal Bureaucracy* (Amsterdam: Elsevier).

Mazur, S., M. Możdżen and M. Oramus (2018), The Instrumental and Ideological Politicisation of Senior Positions in Poland's Civil Service and its Selected Consequences, *NISPAcee Journal of Public Administration and Policy* 11, 63–89.

Mazur, S. (2020), *Public Administration in Central Europe: Ideas as a Source of Reform* (London: Routledge).

McSweeny, B. (2002), Hofstede's Model of National Cultures: A Triumph of Faith—A Failure of Analysis, *Human Relations* 56, 89–118.

Mead, W. R. (2002), *Special Providence* (New York: Routledge).

Meininger, M. C. (2000), The Development and Current Features of the French Civil Service System, in A. J. G. H. Bekker and F. Van der Meer, *Civil Service Systems in Western Europe* (Cheltenham: Edward Elgar).

Mendez, J. L. (2019), Personnel Systems in Latin America, in C. Ramos, B. G. Peters and C. Alba, eds., *The Handbook of Public Administration in Latin America* (Bingley: Emerald).

Mesa-Lago, C. (2008), *Reassembling Social Security: A Survey of Pensions and Health Care Reforms in Latin America* (Oxford: Oxford University Press).

Meseguer, C. (2005), Policy Learning, Policy Diffusion and the Making of a New Order, *The ANNALS of the American Academy of Political and Social Science* 598, 67–82.

Metzger, G. E. (2017), 1930s Redux: The Administrative State Under Siege, *Harvard Law Review* 131, 1–95.

Meyer, J. and B. Rowan (1977), Institutionalizing Organizations: Formal Structure as Myth and Ceremony, *American Journal of Sociology* 83, 340–63.

Meyer, J. W., J. Boli, G. M. Thomas and F. O. Ramirez (1997), World Society and the Nation State, *American Journal of Sociology* 103, 141–81.

Meyer-Sahling, J.-H. (2009), Varieties of Legacies: A Critical Review of Legacy Explanations of Public Administration Reform in East Central Europe, *International Review of Administrative Sciences* 75, 509–28.

Meyer-Sahling, J.-H. (2011), The Durability of EU Civil Service Policy in Central and Eastern Europe After Accession, *Governance* 24, 231–60.

Meyer-Sahling, J.-H. and C. Van Stolk (2015), A Case of Partial Convergence: The Europeanization of Central Government in Central and Eastern Europe, *Public Administration* 93, 230–47.

Meyer-Sahling, J.-H. and K. Yesilkagit (2011), Three Propositions on the Impact of Administrative Traditions on Public Administration Reform in Europe East and West, *Journal of European Public Policy* 18, 311–22.

Meyers, M. K. and V. L. Nielsen (2011), Street-Level Bureaucrats and the Implementation of Public Policy, in B. G. Peters and J. Pierre, eds., *The Sage Handbook of Public Administration*, 2nd edn (London: Sage).

Migdal, J. S. (1988), *Strong Societies and Weak States: State–Society Relations and State Capabilities in the Third World* (Princeton, NJ: Princeton University Press).

Migdal, J. S. (2009), Researching the State, in M. I. Lichbach and A. S. Zuckerman, eds., *Comparative Politics: Rationality, Culture and Structure*, 2nd edn (Cambridge: Cambridge University Press).

Minkov, M. (2011), *Cultural Differences in a Globalizing World* (Bingley: Emerald).

Mirow, M. C. (2000), The Power of Codification in Latin America: Símón Bolívar and the Code Napoléon, *Tulane Journal of International and Comparative Law* 8, 83–116.

Moïse, N. (2000), *Le glas doe la fonction publique dans les états d'afriue francophone* (Paris: L'Harmattan).

Molina, O. and M. Rhodes (2002), Corporatism: The Past, Present and Future of a Concept, *Annual Review of Political Science* 5, 305–31.

Momdani, M. (1999), *Citizen and Subject: Contemporary Africa and the Legacy of Late Colonialism* (Princeton, NJ: Princeton University Press).

Moreno, F. J. (1969), *Legitimacy and Stability in Latin America: A Study of Chilean Political Culture* (Boston, MA: Beacon Press).

Moshonas, S. (2014), The Politics of Civil Service Reform in the Democratic Republic of the Congo, *Journal of Modern African Studies* 52, 251–76.

Moyo, J. M. (1992), *Politics of Administration: Understanding Bureaucracy in Africa* (Harare: Sapes Books).

Müller, W. C. (2007), The Changing Role of the Austrian Civil Service: The Impact of Politicization, Public Sector Reform and Europeanization, in E. C. Page and V. Wright, eds., *From the Active to the Enabling State* (Basingstoke: Palgrave).

Müller-Rommel, F. (1994), The Role of German Ministers in Cabinet Decision-Making, in R. Calvert, M. Laver and K. A. Shepsle, eds., *Cabinet Ministers and Parliamentary Government* (Cambridge: Cambridge University Press).

Murtazashvili, J. B. (2016), *Informal Order and the State in Afghanistan* (Cambridge: Cambridge University Press).

Mustapha, A. R. (2006), *Ethnic Structure, Inequality and Governance of the Public Sector in Nigeria* (New York: United Nations Research Institute for Social Development).

Nagel, M. and B. G. Peters (2018), Representative Bureaucracy and a "Failed" Public Policy: The Case of the Berlin Police, paper presented at International Public Policy Workshops, University of Pittsburgh, June.

Nakamura, A. and N. Dairokuno (2003), Japan's Pattern of Rewards for High Public Officials: A Cultural Perspective, in C. Hood, B. G. Peters and G. O. M. Lee, eds., *Reward for High Public Office in Asia and Pacific Rim Countries* (London: Routledge).

Naschold, F. and J. Bogumil (2013), *Modernisierung des Staates: New Public Management in deutscher und internationaler Perspektive* (Heidelberg: Springer).

Nef, J. (1998), Administrative Culture in Latin America: Historical and Structural Outline, *Africanus* 28, 19–32.

Neto, J. V. (2018), When the Bureaucracy Legislates: An Analysis of Civil Servants' Socio-Demographic, Career, and Ideological Profiles in Latin American Legislatures, unpublished paper, Department of Political Science, University of Pittsburgh.

Neuhold, C., S. Vanhoonacker and L. Verhey (2013), *Civil Servants and Politics: The Delicate Balance* (Basingstoke: Macmillan).

Newbold, S. P. and D. H. Rosenbloom (2007), Brownlow Committee Retrospective, *Public Administration Review* 67, 1006–9.

Newman, P. and A. Thornley (1996), *Urban Planning in Europe: International Competition, National Systems and Planning Projects* (London: Routledge).

Niclauß, K. (1988), *Kanzlerdemokratie. Bonner Regierungspraxis von Konrad Adenauer bis Helmut Kohl* (Stuttgart: Kohlhammer).

Nishikawa, Y. (2007), Public Administration Between Western Model and Eastern Tradition: A Historical and Comparative Sketch, in J. J. Hesse, J.-E. Lane and Y, Nishikawa, eds., *The Public Sector in Transition* (Baden-Baden: Nomos).

Niskanen, W. (1971), *Bureaucracy and Representative Government* (Chicago, IL: Aldine Atherton).

Nordlinger, E. (1981), *On the Autonomy of the Democratic State* (Cambridge, MA: Harvard University Press).

Nørgaard, O. and S. S. Winding (2007), The Impact of Administrative Traditions on Public Administration Reform: The Baltic Case, in B. G. Peters, G. Sootla and B. Connaughton, eds., *Politico-Administrative Dilemma: Old Traditions, New Solutions* (Bratislava: NISPACEE Press).

Nunberg, B., L. Barbone and H.-U. Derlien (1999), *The State after Communism: Administrative Transitions in Central and Eastern Europe* (Washington, DC: The World Bank).

OECD (2018), *OECD Labour Force Statistics* (Paris: OECD).

O'Connor, J. R. (1973), *The Fiscal Crisis of the State* (New York: St. Martin's Press).

O'Donnell, G. (1988), *Bureaucratic Authoritarianism: Argentina 1966–73 in Comparative Perspective* (Berkeley: University of California Press).

O'Leary, R. (2013), *The Ethics of Dissent: Managing Guerilla* Government (Washington, DC: CQ Press).

Oberdorff, H. and J. C. Fromont (1995), L'institution préfectoral entre tradition et modernité, in J.-J. Gleizal, ed., *Le retour des préfets* (Grenoble: Presses Universitaires de Grenoble).

Oberdorff, H. and N. Kada (2016), *Les institutions administratives*, 8th edn (Paris: Dalloz).

Öberg, P. (2016), Interest Groups in the Policy Process, in J. Pierre, ed., *The Oxford Handbook of Swedish Politics* (Oxford: Oxford University Press).

Öberg, P., T. Svensson, P. M. Christiansen, A. S. Nørgaard, H. Rommeyvedt and G. Thesesn (2011), Disrupted Exchange and Declining Corporatism: Government Authority and Interest Group Capability in Scandinavia, *Government and Opposition* 46, 365–91.

Oleinik, A. (2008), Existing and Potential Constraints Limiting State Servant's Opportunism: The Russian Case, *Journal of Communist Studies and Transition Politics* 24, 156–89.

Oliver, C. (1992), The Antecedents of Deinstitutionalization, *Organization Studies* 13, 563–88.

Olivier de Sardan, J.-P. (2009), State Bureaucracy and Governance in Francophone West Africa: An Empirical Diagnosis and Historical Perspective, in G. Blundo and P.-Y. Le Meur eds., *The Governance of Daily Life in Africa* (Leiden: Brill).

Olsen, J. P. (2003), Towards a European Administrative Space, *Journal of European Public Policy* 10, 506–31.

Olsen, J. P. (2009), Democratic Government, Institutional Autonomy and the Dynamics of Change, *West European Politics* 32, 439–65.

Olsson, J. (2016), *Subversion in Institutional Change and Stability: A Neglected Mechanism* (London: Palgrave).

Ongaro, E. (2009), *Public Management Reform and Modernization: Trajectories of Administrative Change in Italy, France, Greece, Portugal and Spain* (Cheltenham: Edward Elgar).

Ongur, H. O. (2015), Identifying Ottomanisms: The Discursive Evolution of Ottoman Pasts in the Turkish Presents, *Middle Eastern Studies* 51, 416–32.

Østerud, Ø., F. Engelstad and P. Selle (2003), *Makten og demokratiet* (Oslo: Glydendal).

Ostrom. E. (1990), *Governing the Commons: The Evolution of Institutions of Collective Action* (Cambridge: Cambridge University Press).

Ott, J. S. and A. M. Baksh (2005), Understanding Organizational Climate and Culture, in Stephen E. Condrey, ed., *Handbook of Human Resource and Management in Government* (New York: Wiley).

Page, E. C. (1985), *Bureaucratic Authority and Bureaucratic Power: A Comparative Analysis* (Brighton: Wheatsheaf).

Page, E. C. (1989), *Political Authority and Bureaucratic Power—A Comparative Analysis* (Knoxville: University of Tennessee Press).

Page, E. C. (1990), The Political Origins of Self-Government and Bureaucracy: Otto Hintze's Conceptual Map of Europe, *Political Studies* 38, 39–55.

Page, E. C. (1992), *Political Authority and Bureaucratic Power: A Comparative Analysis*, 2nd edn (London: Routledge).

Page, E. C. (2001), *Governing by Numbers: Delegated Legislation and Everyday Policymaking* (Oxford: Hart).

Page, E. C. (2003), Europeanization and the Persistence of Administrative Systems, in J. E. S. Hayward and A, Menon, eds., *Governing Europe* (Oxford: Oxford University Press).

Page, E. C. (2010), *Policy without Politicians: Bureaucratic Influence in Comparative Perspective* (Oxford: Oxford University Press).

Painter, M. (2003), Public Administration Reform in Vietnam: Problems and Prospects, *Public Administration and Development* 23, 259–71.

Painter, M. (2010), Legacies Remembered, Lessons Forgotten: The Case of Japan, in M. Painter and B. G. Peters, eds., *Tradition and Public Administration* (Basingstoke: Macmillan).

Painter, M. and B. G. Peters (2010a), *Traditions and Public Administration* (Basingstoke: Macmillan).

Painter, M. and B. G. Peters (2010b), Administrative Traditions in Comparative Perspective: Groups, Families and Hybrids, in M. Painter and B. G. Peters, *Traditions and Public Administration* (Basingstoke: Macmillan).

Palermo, F. and A. Wilson (2014), The Multi-Level Dynamics of State Decentralization in Italy, *Comparative European Politics* 12, 510–30.

Palme, J. H. (2015), Sustainable is the Swedish Model, in B. Marin, ed., *The Future of Welfare in a Global Europe* (London: Routledge).

Pandey, S. K and E. C. Stazyk (2008), Antecedents and Correlates of Public Service Motivation, in J. L. Perry and A. Hondeghem, eds., *Motivation in Public Management: The Call of Public Service* (Oxford: Oxford University Press).

Panizza, F. and R. Miorelli (2009), Populism and Democracy in Latin America, *Ethics & International Affairs* 23, 39–46.

Panizza, F., B. G. Peters and C. Ramos (2017), Technopols, Technos, Apparatchiks and Agents: Towards a Typology of Modalities of Patronage in Latin America and Central and Eastern Europe, unpublished paper, Montevideo, National University of Uruguay.

Panizza, F., B. G. Peters and C. Ramos (2019), Party Professionals, Programmatic Technocrats, Apparatchiks, and Agents: A Typology of Modalities of Patronage in Comparative Perspective, *Public Administration* 97, 147–61.

Parrado, S. (2000), The Development and Current Features of the Spanish Civil Service System, in A. J. G. H. Bekker and F. Van der Meer, *Civil Service Systems in Western Europe* (Cheltenham: Edward Elgar).

Peers, S. and M. Costa (2012), Accountability for Delegated and Implemented Acts after the Treaty of Lisbon, *European Law Journal* 18, 427–60.

Pepinsky, T. B., J. H. Pierskalla and A. Sacks (2017), Bureaucracy and Service Delivery, *Annual Review of Political Science* 20, 249–68.

Perrow, C. (1972), *Complex Organizations: A Critical Essay* (Glenview, IL: Scott, Foresman).

Perry, J. L. and A. Hondeghem, eds. (2008), *Motivation in Public Management: The Call of Public Service* (Oxford: Oxford University Press).

Peters, B. G. (1987), Politicians and Bureaucrats in the Politics of Policymaking in J.-E. Lane, ed., *Bureaucracy and Public Choice* (London: Sage).

Peters, B. G. (1992), Bureaucratic Politics and the Institutions of the European Community, in A. Sbragia, ed., *Euro-Politics: Institutions and Policy-Making in the "New" European Community* (Washington, DC: The Brookings Institution).

Peters, B. G. (1997), Policy Transfers Between Governments: The Case of Administrative Reforms, *West European Politics* 20, 71–88.

Peters, B. G. (1999), *Comparative Politics: Theory and Method* (Basingstoke: Macmillan).

Peters, B. G. (2000), *The Future of Governing: Four Emerging Models*, 2nd edn (Lawrence: University Press of Kansas).

Peters, B. G. (2001a), *The Future of Governing: Four Emerging Models*, 2nd edn (Lawrence: University Press of Kansas).

Peters, B. G. (2001b), The United States, in J. J. Hesse, C, Hood and B. G. Peters, eds., *Paradoxes of Public Sector Reform* (Berlin: Duncker & Humblot).

Peters, B. G. (2010a), Bureaucracy and Democracy, *Public Organization Review* 10, 209–22.

Peters, B. G. (2010b), *The Future of Governing*, 2nd edn (Lawrence: University Press of Kansas).

Peters, B. G. (2014), Politicisation: What Is It and Why Should We Care?, in C. Neuhol, S. Vanhoonacker and L. Verhey, eds., *Civil Servants and Politics: A Delicate Balance* (London: Macmillan).

Peters, B. G. (2015), State Failure, Governance Failure and Policy Failure: Exploring the Linkages, *Public Policy & Administration* 30, 261–76.

Peters, B. G. (2017), Management, Management Everywhere: Whatever Happened to Governance?, *International Journal of Public Sector Management* 30, 606–14.

Peters, B. G. (2018a), *Institutional Theory in Political Science: The New Institutionalism*, 4th edn (Cheltenham: Edward Elgar).

Peters, B. G. (2018b), *The Politics of Bureaucracy*, 7th edn (New York: Routledge).

Peters, B. G. (2020), Politicians and Bureaucrats in Central and Eastern Europe: Governance with Increased Politicization, in S. Mazur and P. Kopyciński, eds., *Public Administration in Central Europe* (London: Routledge).

Peters, B. G. and M. Nagel (2019), Zombie Ideas: Why Failed Policy Ideas Persist, paper presented at IPPC-4, Montreal, Canada, June 27.

Peters, B. G. and J. Pierre (2004a), Politicization of the Civil Service: Concepts, Causes, Consequences, in B. G. Peters and J. Pierre, eds., *Politicization of the Civil Service in Comparative Perspective: The Quest for Control* (London: Routledge).

Peters, B. G. and J. Pierre (2004b), *Politicization of the Civil Service in Comparative Perspective: The Quest for Control* (London: Routledge).

Peters, B. G. and J. Pierre (2016), *Governance and Comparative Politics* (Cambridge: Cambridge University Press).

Peters, B. G. and J. Pierre (2019), Populism and Public Administration: Confronting the Administrative State, *Administration & Society* 51, 1521–43.

Peters, B. G., J. Pierre and D. S. King (2005), The Politics of Path Dependency: Political Conflict in Historical Institutionalism, *Journal of Politics* 67, 1275–300.

Peters, B. G., J. Pierre, E. Sørensen and J. Torfing (forthcoming), *A Research Agenda for Collaborative Governance* (Cheltenham: Edward Elgar).

Peters, B. G. and D. J. Savoie (1994), Civil Service Reform: Misdiagnosing the Patient, *Public Administration Review* 54, 418–26.

Peters, B. G. and D. J. Savoie (1996), Managing Incoherence: The Coordination and Empowerment Conundrum, *Public Administration Review* 56, 281–6.

Peters, B. G. and D. J. Savoie (1998), *Taking Stock: Assessing Public Sector Reforms* (Montreal: McGill/Queens University Press).

Peters, B. G., P. Von Maravić and E. Schröter (2015), *The Politics of Representative Bureaucracy: Power, Legitimacy and Performance* (Cheltenham: Edward Elgar).

Petersen, O. H. and U. Hjelmar (2014), Marketization of Welfare Services in Scandinavia: A Review of Danish and Swedish Experiences, *Scandinavian Journal of Public Administration* 17, 2–20.

Pierre, J. (1995), *Bureaucracy in the Modern State: An Introduction to Comparative Public Administration* (Cheltenham: Edward Elgar).

Pierre, J. (2004), Politicization of the Swedish Civil Service: Necessary Evil, or Just Evil?, in B. G. Peters and J. Pierre, eds., *Politicization of the Civil Service in Comparative Perspective: The Quest for Control* (London: Routledge).

Pierre, J. (2010), Administrative Reform in Sweden: The Resilience of Administrative Tradition, in M. A. Painter and B. G. Peters, eds., *Tradition and Public Administration* (London: Macmillan).

Pierre, J. and B. G. Peters (2017), The Shirking Bureaucrat: Theory in Search of Evidence, *Policy & Politics* 45, 157–72.

Pierre, J. and B. G. Peters (2018), *Governance, Politics and the State*, 2nd edn (London: Macmillan).

Pierson, P. (2000), Increasing Returns, Path Dependence, and the Study of Politics, *American Political Science Review* 94(2), 251–67.

Pierson, P. (2001), Coping with Permanent Austerity: Welfare State Restructuring in Affluent Democracies, in P. Pierson, ed., *The New Politics of the Welfare State* (Oxford; Oxford University Press).

Pinto, A. C. (2014), Fascism, Corporatism and the Crafting of Authoritarian Institutions in Inter-War European Dictatorships, in A. C. Pinto and A. Kallis, eds., *Rethinking Fascism and Dictatorships in Europe* (London: Macmillan).

Pochet, P. and G. Fajertag (2000), A New Era for Social Pacts in Europe, in G. Fajertag and P. Pochet, eds., *Social Pacts in Europe—New Dynamics* (Brussels: European Trade Union Institute).

Poguntke, T. and P. Webb, eds. (2007), *The Presidentialization of Politics: A Comparative Study of Modern Democracies* (Oxford: Oxford University Press).

Pollitt, C. (2001), Convergence: The Useful Myth?, *Public Administration* 79, 933–47.

Pollitt, C. (2015), Not Odious but Onerous: Comparative Public Administration, Public Administration 89, 114–27.

Pollitt, C. and G. Bouckaert (2017), *Public Management Reform: A Comparative Analysis into the Age of Austerity* (Oxford: Oxford University Press).

Pollitt, C., J. Caulfield, J. Smullen and C. Talbot (2001), Agency Fever? Analysis of an International Fashion, *Journal of Comparative Policy Analysis*, 3, 271–90.

Przeworski, A. (1999), On the Design of the State: A Principal Agent Perspective, in L. C. Bresser Pereira and P. Spink, eds., *Reforming the State: Managerial Public Administration in Latin America* (Boulder: Lynne Reiner).

Pressman, J. L. and A. Wildavsky (1973), *Implementation* (Berkeley: University of California Press).

Pronin, K. (2020), Voice but not a Veto: Information and Dissent in Advisory Committees, Ph.D. thesis, Department of Political Science, University of Pittsburgh.

Putnam, R. D. (1994), *Making Democracy Work: Civic Traditions in Modern Italy* (Princeton, NJ: Princeton University Press).

Pye, L. (1965), Political Culture and Political Development, in L. Pye and S. Verba, eds., *Political Culture and Political Development* (Princeton, NJ: Princeton University Press).

Qazbir, H. (2015), Le mandat parliamentaire face au un nouveau régime du cumul, *Révue francaise de droit constitutionelle* 103, 633–56.

Quitkatt, C. and B. Finke (2008), The EU Commission Consultation Regime, in B. Kohler-Koch, D. De Bievre and W. Maloney, eds., *Opening EU Governance to Civil Society Gains and Challenges* (Mannheim: MZES).

Radaelli, C. M. (2002), The Domestic Impact of European Union Public Policy: Notes on Concepts, Methods, and the Challenge of Empirical Research, *Politique europénne* 5, 105–36.

Radaelli, C. M. and C. A. Dunlop (2013), Learning in the European Union: Theoretical Lenses and Meta-Policy, *Journal of European Public Policy* 29, 923–40.

Rainey, H. G. and P. Steinbauer (1999), Galloping Elephants: Developing Elements of a Theory of Effective Government Organizations, *Journal of Public Administration Research and Theory* 9, 1–32.

Ramio, C. and M. Salvador (2002), La configuracion de las administraciones de las Comunidades Autonomas: entre la inercia y la innovacion institucional, in J. Subirats and R. Gallego, eds., *Veinte Años de Autonomias en España* (Madrid: CIS).

Ramirez, M. F. (2009), State Reforms, Public Administration in Latin America, and Attempts to Apply New Public Management, Estudios Politcos 8, 247–70.

Ramos, C. (2019), Public Administration in Uruguay: Modernization in Slow Motion, in B. G. Peters, C. Ramos and C. Alba, eds., *The Handbook of Public Administration in Latin America* (Bingley: Emerald).

Ramos, C. and A. Milanesi (2020), The Latin American Public Administration Model, in B. G. Peters, C. Alba and C. Ramos, eds., *The Handbook of Public Administration in Latin America* (Bingley: Emerald).

Ramos, C., A. Milanesi and D. G. Ibarra (2020), Public Administration in Uruguay: Modernization in Slow Motion, in B. G. Peters, C. Alba and C. Ramos, eds., *The Handbook of Public Administration in Latin America* (Bingley: Emerald).

Randma-Liiv, T. (2008), New Public Management vs. Neo-Weberian State in Central and Eastern Europe, NISPAcee *Journal of Public Administration and Policy* 1, 69–81.

Rawls, J. (1971), *A Theory of Justice* (Cambridge, MA: Harvard University Press).

Reichard, C. (2003), Local Public Management Reforms in Germany, *Public Administration* 81, 345–63.

Rhinard, M. and A. Boin (2009), European Homeland Security: Bureaucratic Politics and Policymaking in the EU, *Journal of Homeland Security and Emergency Management* 6. https://doi.org/10.2202/1547-7355.1480.

Rhodes, R. A. W. (2011), Everyday Life in British Government (Oxford: Oxford University Press).

Rhodes, R. A. W., J. Wanna and P. Weller (2009), *Comparing Westminster* (Oxford: Oxford University Press).

Richardson, J. J. (1982), *Policy Styles in Western Europe* (London: Allen &Unwin).

Riggs, F. W. (1964), *Administration in Developing Countries: The Theory of Prismatic Society* (Boston, MA: Houghton Mifflin).

Rodrik, D. (2014), When Ideas Trump Interests: Preferences, Worldviews and Policy Innovations, *Journal of Economic Perspectives* 28, 189–208.

Rokkan, S. (1967), Norway: Numerical Democracy and Corporate Pluralism, in R. A. Dahl, ed., *Political Oppositions in Western Democracies* (New Haven, CT: Yale University Press).

Roland, G. (2004), Understanding Institutional Change: Fast-Moving and Slow-Moving Institutions, *Studies in Comparative International Development* 38(4), 109–31.

Roll, M. (2009), *Pockets of Effectiveness: Public Sector Performance in Developing Countries*.

Rommetvedt, H., G. Thesen, P. M. Christensen and A. S. Nørgaard (2013) Coping with Corporatism in Decline and the Revival of Parliament: Interest Group Lobbying in Denmark and Norway, 1980–2005, *Comparative Political Studies* 46, 457–85.

Rose, R. (1976a), On the Priorities of Government: A Developmental Analysis, *European Journal of Political Research* 4, 247–78.

Rose, R. (1976b), *The Problem of Party Government* (London: Macmillan).

Rose, R. (1993), *Lesson-Drawing in Public Policy: A Guide to Learning Across Time and Space* (Chatham, NJ: Chatham House).

Rose, R. and B. G. Peters (1976), *Can Government Go Bankrupt?* (New York: Basic Books).

Rosanvallon, P. (2004), *Le Modèle politique francais: La société civile contre le jacobinisme de 1789 à nos jours* (Paris: Seuil).

Rosenbloom, D. H. (2001), "Whose Bureaucracy Is This, Anyway?": Congress' 1946 Answer, *PS: Political Science and Politics* 34, 773–7.

Rothstein, B. (2000), Trust, Social Dilemmas and Collective Memory, *Journal of Theoretical Politics* 12, 477–501.

Rothstein, B. (2004), Social Trust and Honesty in Government: A Causal Mechanisms Approach, in J. Kornai, B. Rothstein and S. Rose-Ackerman, eds., *Creating Social Trust in Post-Socialist Transitions* (Basingstoke: Macmillan).

Roux, C. (2008), Italy's Path to Federalism: Origins and Paradoxes, *Journal of Modern Italian Studies* 13, 325–39.

Rouban, L. (2008), Reform without Doctrine: Public Management in France, *International Journal of Public Sector Management* 21, 133–49.

Rouban, L. (2010), L'Inspection générale des Finances 1958–2008: Pantouflage et reneouveau des stratégies élitaires, *Sociologies pratiques* 21, 19–34.

Rouban, L. (2011), Politicization of the Civil Service, in B. G. Peters and J. Pierre, eds., *The Sage Handbook of Public Administration*, 2nd edn (London: Sage).

Ruin, O. (1990), *Tage Erlander: Serving the Welfare State, 1946–69* (Pittsburgh, PA: University of Pittsburgh Press).

Rutake, P. (1986), De l'administration mimétique á l'administration de devéloppement, *Administration, Formation, Gestion* 1, 7–31.

Saalfeld, T. (1998), The German Bundestag: Influence and Accountability in a Complex Environment, in P. Norton, ed., *Parliaments and Government in Western Europe* (London: Frank Cass).

Saam, N. J. and W. Kerber (2013), Policy Innovation, Decentralized Experimentation and Laboratory Federalism, *Journal of Artificial Societies and Social Simulation* 16(1), http://jasss.soc.surrey.ac.uk/16/1/7.html.

Sabbi, M. (2017), Strategic Bureaucracies: Transnational Funding and Mundane Practices of Ghanaian Local Governments, *Third World Quarterly* 38, 939–55.

Saeidem, A. (2018), The Role of *Waqf* in Iranian Social Policy: The Challenge of Faith-Based Welfare Organizations, paper presented at Conference on Social Policy in the Islamic World, Allameh Tabataba'i University, Tehran, Iran.

Sager, F., C. Rosser, P. Y. Hurni and C. Mavrot (2012), How Traditional are the American, French and German Traditions of Public Administration: A Research Agenda, *Public Administration* 90, 129–43.

Sager, F., C. Rosser, C. Mavrot and P. Y. Hurni (2018), *A Transatlantic History of Public Administration: Analyzing the USA, France and Germany* (Cheltenham: Edward Elgar)

Salamon, L. M. (1981), The Search for Efficiency, in P. Szanton, ed., *Federal Reorganization: What Have We Learned?* (Chatham, NJ: Chatham House).

Salvati, M. (2006), The Long History of Corporatism in Italy: A Question of Culture or Economics?, *Contemporary European History* 15, 223–44.

Samaratunge, R., Q. Alam and J. Teicher (2008), New Public Management Reforms in Asia: A Comparison of South and Southeast Asian Countries, *International Review of Administrative Sciences* 74, 25–46.

Samier, E. (2017), Islamic Public Administration Tradition: Theoretical and Practical Dimensions, *Administrative Culture* 18, 53–71.

Sartori, G. (1969), Politics, Ideology and Belief Systems, *American Political Science Review* 63, 398–411.

Savoie, D. J. (1994), *Reagan, Thatcher, Mulroney: In Search of the New Bureaucracy* (Pittsburgh, PA: University of Pittsburgh Press).

Savoie, D. J. (2008), *Court Government and the Collapse of Accountability in Canada and the United Kingdom* (Toronto: University of Toronto Press).

Sbragia, A. (2000), The European Union as Coxswain: Governance as Steering, in J. Pierre ed., *Debating Governance: Authority, Steering and Democracy* (Oxford: Oxford University Press).

Schachter, H. L. (2007), Does Frederick Taylor's Ghost Still Haunt the Halls of Government? A Look at the Concept of Government Efficiency in Our Time, *Public Administration Review* 67, 800–10.

Schaffer, B. (1973), *The Administrative Factor* (London: Frank Cass).

Schaffer, B. (1978), Administrative Legacies and Links in the Post-Colonial State, *Development and Change* 9, 175–201.

Schedler, K. and I. Proeller (2007), *Cultural Aspects of Public Management Reform* (Amsterdam: JAI).

Schick, A. (1998), Why Most Developing Countries should not Try New Zealand's Reforms, *World Bank Research Observer (International)* 13, 23–31.

Schiller, C. (2016), *The Politics of Welfare State Transformation in Germany: Still a Semi-Sovereign State?* (London: Macmillan).

Schmidt, M. G. (2002), Germany: The Grand Coalition State, in J. M. Colomer, ed., *Political Institutions in Europe*, 2nd edn (London: Routledge).

Schmidt, V. (1990), *Democratizing France: The Political and Administrative History of Decentralization* (Cambridge: Cambridge University Press).

Schmidt, V. (2010), Taking Ideas and Discourses Seriously: Explaining Change Through Discursive Institutionalism as the Fourth New Institutionalism, *European Political Science Review* 2, 1–25.

Schmitter, P. C. (1974), Still the Century of Corporatism?, *Review of Politics* 36, 85–131.

Schumacher, E. J. (1975), *Politics, Bureaucracy and Rural Development in Senegal* (Berkeley: University of California Press).

Schön-Quinlivan, E. (2011), *Reforming the European Commission* (London: Palgrave).

Schütz, H. (2012), Neue und alte regelsteuerung in der deutschen arbeitsverwaltung, in S. Bothfeld, W. Sesselmeier and C. Bogedan, eds., *Arbeitsmarktpolitik in der sozialen Marktwirtschaft* (Wiesbaden: Springer).

Sciarini, P., M. Fischer and D. Traber (2015), *Political Decision-Making in Switzerland: The Consensus Model Under Pressure* (London: Macmillan).

Scott, I. (2005), *Public Administration in Hong Kong: Regime Change and its Impact on the Public Sector* (Singapore: Marshall Cavendish).

Seerden, R. and F. Stroink (2002), *Administrative Law of The European Union, Its Member States and the United States* (Antwerp: Intersentia).

Segrestin, D. (1984), *Le phenomène corporatiste* (Paris: Fayard).

Seibel, W. (2010), Beyond Bureaucracy: Public Administration as Political Integrator and Non-Weberian Thought in Germany, *Public Administration* 70, 719–30.

Seidman, H. B. (1999), *Politics, Power and Position*, 3rd edn (New York: Oxford University Press).

Seigfried, A. (1940), *France: A Study in Nationality* (New York: Knopf).

Self, P. (1973), *Administrative Theories and Politics: An Inquiry into the Structure and Processes of Modern Government* (Toronto: University of Toronto Press).

Self, P. (1993), *Government by the Market?* (London: Macmillan).

Selle, P., K. Strømsnes and J. Lega (2018), State and Civil Society: A Regime Change?, in B. Enjolras and K. Strømsnes, eds., *Scandinavian Civil Society and Social Transformation* (Heidelberg: Springer).

Seller, J. M and A. Lindström (2007), Decentralization, Local Government and Welfare State, *Governance* 20, 609–32.

Selznick, P. (1957), *Leadership in Administration: A Sociological Interpretation* (Berkeley: University of California Press).

Sen, S. N. (1976), *Administrative System of the Marathas*, 3rd edn (Calcutta: K. P. Bacchi).

Sharma, R. D. (2000), *Administrative Culture in India* (Delhi: Anamika Publishers).

Sharpe, L. J. (1988), The Growth and Decentralisation of the Modern Democratic State, *European Journal of Political Research*, 16, 365–80.

Shaw, C. K. Y. (1992), Hegel's Theory of Modern Bureaucracy, *American Political Science Review* 86, 381–9.

Shaw, M. (1997), The State of Globalization: Toward a Theory of State Transformation, *Review of International Political Economy* 4, 497–513.

Shepsle, K. A. (2006), Rational Choice Institutionalism, in R. A. W. Rhodes, S. A. Binder and B. A Rockman, eds., *Oxford Handbook of Political Institutions* (Oxford: Oxford University Press).

Sieber, S. (1981), *Fatal Remedies* (New York: Plenum).

Silberman, B. S. (1993), *Cages of Reason: The Rise of the Rational State in France, Japan, the United States and Great Britain* (Chicago, IL: University of Chicago Press).

Simmie, J. (1991), *Yugoslavia in Turmoil After Self-Management* (Leicester: Leicester University Press).

Sisson, C. H. (1959), *The Spirit of British Administration and Some European Comparisons* (New York: Praeger).

Skelcher, C. (1997), *The Appointed State: Quasi-Governmental Organizations and Democracy* (Buckingham: Open University Press).

Skocpol, T. (1979), *States and Social Revolutions* (Cambridge: Cambridge University Press).

Skowronek, S. (1982), *Building a New American State: The Expansion of National Administrative Capacities, 1877–1920* (Cambridge: Cambridge University Press).

Smith, B. C. (1986), *Decentralization: The Territorial Dimension of the State* (London: George Allen & Unwin).

Smith, T. (1978), A Comparative Study of French and British Decolonization. *Comparative Studies in Society and History* 20, 70–102.

Smithey, S. I. (1996), The Effects of the Canadian Supreme Courts' Charter Interpretation on Regional and Intergovernmental Tensions, *Publius* 26, 83–100.

Smyrl, M. E. (1997), Does European Community Regional Policy Empower the Regions?, *Governance* 10, 287–309.

Solomon, P. H. Jr. (2008), Law in Public Administration: How Russia Differs, *Journal of Communist Studies and Transition Politics* 24, 115–35.

Sørensen, E. (1998), New Forms of Democratic Empowerment: Introducing User Influence in the Primary School System in Denmark, *Statsvetenskapliga Tidskrift* 101, 129–43.

Sørensen, E. and J. Torfing (2007), The Democratic Anchorage of Governance Networks, *Scandinavian Political Studies* 28, 195–218.

Soros, G. (1998), *The Crisis of Global Capitalism: Open Society Endangered* (London: Little, Brown).

Spulbar, N. (1995), *The American Economy: The Struggle for Supremacy in the 21st Century* (Cambridge: Cambridge University Press).

Stack, L. (2016), Wildlife Refuge Occupied in Protest of Oregon Ranchers' Prison Terms, *The New York Times*, January 2.

Stacy, H. (2002), Relational Sovereignty, *Stanford Law Review* 55, 2029–58.

Staniland, M. (1971), Colonial Government and Populist Reform: The Case of the Ivory Coast, Part 1, *Journal of Administration Overseas* 10, 33–42.

Stegarescu, D. (2005), Public Sector Decentralization: Measurement Concepts and Recent International Trends, *Fiscal Studies* 26, 301–33.

Steinmo, S. (2008), Historical Institutionalism, in D. Della Porta and M. Keating, eds., *Approaches and Methodologies in the Social Sciences* (Cambridge: Cambridge University Press).

Steinmo, S., K. Thelen and F. Longstreth (1992), *Structuring Politics: Historical Institutionalism in Comparative Analysis* (Cambridge: Cambridge University Press).

Stephenson, M. (2017), The Bayesian Corruption Index: A New and Improved Method for Aggregating Corruption Perceptions *The Global Anticorruption Blog*, March 18, https://globalanticorruptionblog.com/2017/03/28/the-bayesian-corruption-index-a-new-and-improved-method-for-aggregating-corruption-perceptions/.

Stilles, A. (1992), *Sweden and the Baltic: 1523–1721* (London: Hodder & Stoughton).

Stillman, R. (1996), *The American Bureaucracy* (Chicago, IL: Nelson-Hall).

Stoker, G. (forthcoming), Public Administration: How to Respond to Populism and Democratic Backsliding, in M. Bauer, B. G. Peters, J. Pierre, K. Yesilkagit and S. Becker, eds., *Democratic Backsliding and Public Administration* (Cambridge: Cambridge University Press).

Stokes, S. C. (2007), Political Clientelism, in R. E. Goodin, ed., *Oxford Handbook of Political Science* (Oxford: Oxford University Press).

Streeck, W. (1995), *Staat und Verbände* (Wiesbaden: Verlag für Socialwissenschaft).

Streeck, W. and L. Kenworthy (2005), Theories and Practices of Neocorporatism, in T. Janoski, R. R. Alford, A. M. Hicks and M. A. Schwartz, eds., *The Handbook of Political Sociology: States, Civil Societies, and Globalization* (Cambridge: Cambridge University Press).

Strobel, B. and S. Veit (forthcoming), Democratic Backsliding, Systems Transformations and the Civil Service: A Case Study on the Weimar Republic and the Nazi Regime in Germany, in M. Bauer, B. G. Peters, J. Pierre, K. Yesilkagit and S. Becker, eds., *Democratic Backsliding and Public Administration* (Cambridge: Cambridge University Press).

Strøm, K. (2000), Delegation and Accountability in Parliamentary Democracies, *European Journal of Political Research* 37, 261–90.

Suvarierol, S., M. Busuioc and M. Groenleer (2013), Working for Europe?: Socialization in the European Commission and the Agencies of the European Commission, *Public Administration* 91, 908–27.

Swanstrom, T. (1985), *The Crisis in Growth Politics* (Philadelphia, PA: Temple University Press).

Swenden, W. and M. T. Jans (2016), "Will It Stay or Will It Go?": Federalism and Sustainability in Belgium, *West European Politics* 29, 877–94.

't Hart, P. and M. Compton (2019), *Great Policy Successes* (Oxford: Oxford University Press).

Taagepera, R. (1993), *Estonia: Return to Independence* (New York: Routledge).

Taggart, P. (1996), *The New Populism and the New Politics* (London: Macmillan).

Taggart, P. (1998), A Touchstone of Dissent: Euroscepticism in Contemporary West European Party Systems, *European Journal of Political Research* 33, 363–88.

Talos, E. and B. Kittel (1999), Austria in the 1990s: The Routine of Social Partnership in Question, in S. Berger and H. Compston, eds., *Social Partnership in Europe* (Oxford: Berghahn Books).

Tanguy, G. (2013), Les hafts functionaries au service de d'état ou du pouvoir?, in J.-M. Eymeri-Douzanes and G. Bouckaert, eds,. *France and Its Public Administrations: A State of the Art* (Brussels: Bruylant).

Tarschys, D. (1975), *Petita: Hur svenska myndigheter argumnterar för högre anslag* (Stockholm: Liber).

Tayeb, M. R. (1988), *Organizations and National Culture: A Comparative Analysis* (London: Sage).

Temmes, M. (1998), Finland and New Public Management, *International Review of Administrative Sciences* 64(3), 441–56.

Temmes, M. and A. Salminen (1994), The Evolution of Public Administration and Administrative Research in Finland, in T. Modeen, *Public Administration in Finland* (Helsinki: Ministry of Finance).

Terneyre, P. and D. de Béchillon (2007), Le Conseil d'état: Enfin juge, *Pouvoirs* 123, 61–72.

Teune, H. and A. Przeworski (1970), *The Logic of Comparative Social Inquiry* (New York: John Wiley).

Thedieck, F. (1992), *Verwaltungskultur in Frankreich und Deutschland* (Baden-Baden: Nomos).

Thelen, K., F. Longstreth and S. Steinmo (1992), *Structuring Politics: Historical Institutionalism in Comparative Analysis* (Cambridge: Cambridge University Press).

Thelen, K. and S. Steinmo (1992), Historical Institutionalism in Comparative Politics, in S. Steinmo, K. Thelen and F. Longstreth, eds., *Structuring Politics: Historical Institutionalism in Comparative Analysis* (Cambridge: Cambridge University Press).

Thoenig, J.-C. (2005), Territorial Administration and Political Control: Decentralization in France, *Public Administration* 83, 685–708.

Thunman, E. and M. Persson (2015), Justifying the Authentic Self: Swedish Public Workers Talk about Work Stress, *Forum: Qualitative Social Research* 16, https://www.qualitative-research.net/index.php/fqs/article/view/2158/3750.

Tignor, R. L. (1999), Colonial Africa Through the Lens of Colonial Latin America, in J. Adelman, ed., *Colonial Legacies: The Problem of Persistence in Latin American History* (New York: Routledge).

Tilly, C. (1985), *Big Structures, Large Processes, Huge Comparisons* (New York: Russell Sage).

Tilly, C. (1986), *The Contentious French* (Cambridge, MA: Harvard University Press).

Titeca, K. and T. De Herdt (2011), Real Governance Beyond the "Failed State": Negotiating Education in the Democratic Republic of the Congo, *African Affairs* 110, 213–31.

Toonen, T. A. J. (2003), Administrative Reforms: Analytics, in B. G. Peters and J. Pierre, eds., *Handbook of Public Administration* (London: Sage).

Torfing, J., B. G. Peters, J. Pierre and E. Sørensen (2012), *Interactive Governance: Advancing the Paradigm* (Oxford: Oxford University Press).

Torres, L. (2004), Trajectories in Public Administration Reforms in European Continental Countries, *Australian Journal of Public Administration* 63, 99–112.

Torstendahl, R. (1991), *Bureaucratisation in Northwestern Europe 1880–1985* (London: Routledge).

Trägårdh, L. (2007), Introduction, in L. Trägårdh, ed., *State and Society in Northern Europe: The Swedish Model Reconsidered* (New York: Berghahn Books).

Treib, O. (2006), Implementing and Complying with EU Governance Outputs, *Living Review in European Governance* 1, 1–24.

Trompenaars, F. and C. Hampden-Turner (1993), *Riding the Wave of Culture: Understanding Cultural Diversity in Business* (London: Nicholas Brealy).

Trondal, J. (2010), *An Emergent European Executive Order* (Oxford: Oxford University Press).

Trondal, J. and B. G. Peters (2013), The Rise of the European Administrative Space: Lessons Learned, *Journal of European Public Policy* 20, 295–313.

Trondal, J., Z. Murdoch and B. Geys (2015), Representative Bureaucracy and the Role of Expertise in Politics, *Politics and Governance* 3, 26–36.

Tsebelis, G. (2002), *Veto Players: How Political Institutions Work* (Princeton, NJ: Princeton University Press).

Turner, E. (2011), *Political Parties and Public Policy in the German Länder: When Parties Matter* (London: Macmillan).

Umeh, O. J. and G. Andranovich (2005), *Culture, Development and Public Administration in Africa* (Bloomfield: CT: Kumarian Press).

Unger, B. and K. Heitzmann (2003), The Adjustment Path of the Austrian Welfare State: Back to Bismarck?, *Journal of European Social Policy* 13, 371–87.

USGAO (2019), *EPA Advisory Committees: Improvements Needed for Member Appointment Process* (GAO-19-280), July 8.

Van der Sprenkel, O. B. (1964), Max Weber on China, *History and Theory* 3, 348–70.

Van de Walle, S. (2007), Determinants of Confidence in the Civil Service: An International Comparison, in K. Schedler and I. Proeller, eds., *Cultural Aspects of Public Management Reform* (Amsterdam: JAI).

Van de Walle, S. (2018), Explaining Citizen Satisfaction and Dissatisfaction with Public Services, in E. Ongaro and S. Van Thiel, eds., *The Palgrave Handbook of Public Administration and Management in Europe* (London: Palgrave Macmillan).

Van der Meer, F. M., J. C. N. Raadschelders and T. A. J. Toonen (2015), *Comparative Civil Service Systems in the 21st Century* (London: Palgrave).

Van Ryzin, G. G. (2011), Outcomes, Process and Trust of Civil Servants, *Journal of Public Administration Research and Theory* 21, 745–60.

Van Waarden, F. (1995), Persistence of National Policy Styles, in B. Under and F. Van Waarden, eds., *Convergence or Diversity?: Internationalization and Economic Policy Response* (Aldershot: Avebury).

Vanagunas, S. (1995), The Influence of the *Nomenklatura* on Post-Soviet Administration, *International Journal of Public Administration* 18, 1815–39.

Vandenabeele, W. (2008), Government Calling: Public Service Motivation as an Element in Selecting Government as an Employer of Choice, *Public Administration* 86, 1089–105.

Vandenabeele, W., G. A. Brewer and A. Ritz (2014), Past, Present and Future of Public Service Motivation Research, *Public Administration* 92, 779–89.

Vandenabeele, W. and S. Van de Walle (2008), International Differences in Public Service Motivation: Comparing Regions Across the World, in J. L. Perry and A. Hondeghem, eds., *Motivation in Public Management: The Call of Public Service* (Oxford: Oxford University Press).

Vandenabeele, W., S. Scheepers and A. Hondeghem (2006), Public Service Motivation in International Comparative Perspective, *Public Policy and Administration* 21, 13–31.

Vansina, J. (2004), *How Societies Are Born: Governance in West Central Africa Before 1600* (Charlottesville: University of Virginia Press).

Veit, S. and S. Scholz (2016), Linking Administrative Career Patterns and Politicization: Signaling Effects in the Careers of Top Civil Servants in Germany, *International Review of Administrative Sciences* 82, 516–35.

Véliz, Claudio (1980), *The Centralist Tradition of Latin America* (Princeton, NJ: Princeton University Press).

Verheijen T. J. G. and A. Rabrenovic (2007), Civil Service Development in Central and Eastern Europe and the CIS: Swimming with the Tide?, in J. C. N. Raadschelders, T.A. J. Toonen and F. M. Van der Meer, eds., *The Civil Service in the 21st Century* (London: Palgrave Macmillan).

Verhoest, K., B. G. Peters, G. Bouckaert and B. Verschuere (2014), The Study of Organisational Autonomy: A Conceptual Review, Public Administration and Development 24, 101–18.

Verhoest, K., S. Vam Thiel, G. Bouckaert and P. Laegreid (2016), *Government Agencies: Practices and Lessons from 30 Countries* (London: Macmillan).

Vickers, G. (1968), Science and Appreciative Systems, *Human Relations* 21, 99–119.

Vibert, F. (2007), *The Rise of the Unelected: Democracy and the New Separation of Powers* (Cambridge: Cambridge University Press).

Viet, V. (1994), *Les Voltigeurs de la République: L'Inspection du travail en France* (Paris: CNRS).

Vogiatzis, N. (2018), *The European Ombudsman and Good Administration in Europe* (London: Macmillan).

Walsh, K. and J. Stewart (1992), Change in the Management of Public Services, *Public Administration* 70, 499–518.

Walsh, P. (1992), Henry Brooke's *Gustavus Adolpus*: The Ancient Constitution and the Example of Sweden, *Studia Neophilogica* 64, 63–79.

Warin, P. (2002), *Les dépanneurs de justice: Les petits fonctionnaires entre égalite et équite* (Paris: LGDJ).

Wayneberg, E. (2017), Framing en Belied, *Beliedsonderzoek Online* (September).

Wegrich, K. (2006), *Steuerung im Mehrenbenensystem der Länder* (Wiesbaden: Springer).

Weil, E. (1998), *Hegel and the State* (Baltimore, MD: Johns Hopkins University Press).

Weiss, L. M. (1999), *The Myth of the Powerless State* (Ithaca, NY: Cornell University Press).

White, L. B. (1948), *The Federalists: A Study in Administrative History* (New York: Macmillan).

Wildavsky, A. and A. Browne (1983), Should Evaluation Become Implementation?, *New Directions for Evaluation* 20, 101–3.

Wille, A. C. (2013), *The Normalization of the European Commission: Politics and Bureaucracy in the EU Executive* (Oxford: Oxford University Press).

Williams, G. (2005), Monomaniacs or Schizophrenics?: Responsible Governance and the EU's Executive Agencies, *Political Studies* 53, 82–99.

Wilson, G. (1994), The Westminster Model in Comparative Perspective, in I. Budge and D. H. McKay, eds., *Developing Democracy: Essays in Honour of J.FP. Blondel* (London: Sage).

Wilson, W. (1887), The Study of Administration, *Political Science Quarterly* 2, 197–222.

Woll, C. (2009), The Demise of Statism?: Associations and the Transformation of Interest Intermediation in France, in S. Brouard, A. M. Appleton and A. G. Mazur, eds., *The French Fifth Republic at Fifty* (Basingstoke: Macmillan).

Wollmann, H. (2001), Germany's Trajectory of Public Sector Modernization: Continuities and Discontinuities, *Policy & Politics* 29, 151–70.

Wonka, A. and S. Göbel (2016), Parliamentary Scrutiny and Partisan Conflict in the Euro Crisis: The Case of the German Bundestag, *Comparative European Politics* 14, 215–31.

Woodhouse, D. (1997), *In Pursuit of Good Administration: Ministers, Civil Servants and Judges* (Oxford: Clarendon Press).

Wünder, B. (1995), Les influences du "modèle" napoléonien d'administration sur l'organisation administrative des autres pays. *Cahiers d'Histoire de l'Administration n°4* (Brussels: Institut International des Sciences Administratives).

Yackee, S. W. (2006), Sweet-Talking the Fourth Branch: The Influence of Interest Group Comments on Federal Agency Rulemaking, *Journal of Public Administration Research and Theory* 16, 103–24.

Yang, L. and Z. van der Wal (2014), Rule of Morality vs. Rule of Law? An Explanatory Study of Civil Service Values in China and the Netherlands, *Public Integrity* 16, 187–206.

Yesilkagit, K. (2010), The Future of Administrative Tradition: Tradition as Ideas and Structures, in M. Painter and B. G. Peters, eds., *Tradition and Public Administration* (Basingstoke: Palgrave Macmillan).

Yesilkagit, K. and J. G. Christensen (2006), Institutional Design Within National Contexts: Agency Independence in Denmark, the Netherlands and Sweden (1945–2000), unpublished paper, University of Utrecht.

Zacka, B. (2017), *When the State Meets the Street: Public Services and Moral Agency* (Cambridge, MA: Harvard University Press).

Zafarullah, H. (2016), Public Administration and Bureaucracy, in A. Riaz and M. S. Rahman, eds., *Routledge Handbook of Contemporary Bangladesh* (London: Routledge).

Zariski, R. (1983), The Establishment of the Kingdom of Italy as a Unitary State, *Publius* 13, 1–19.

Ziblatt, D. (2006), *Structuring the State: The Formation of Italy and Germany and the Puzzle of Federalism* (Princeton, NJ: Princeton University Press).

Zypries, B. (2001), Der Anspruch an eine moderne, bürgernahe Verwaltung, in A. Picot and H. P. Quandt, eds., *Verwaltung ans Netz* (Berlin: Springer).

Index

For the benefit of digital users, indexed terms that span two pages (e.g., 52–53) may, on occasion, appear on only one of those pages

Aberbach, J. D. 5, 33, 215
Accountability 31, 161
Acemoglu, D. 189, 215
Adam, C. 86, 103, 215
Adams, P. S. 82, 215
Adelman, J. 26, 215, 244
Administrative change 24, 194, 196–199
Administrative culture 14, 16–20, 24,
    166, 169–170
  Dimensions 17–18
Administrative law 71, 90
Administrative persistence 194
Administrative reform 51, 59, 72–73,
    112–113, 134–136, 165, 195, 203–204
Administrative traditions
  Accountability 45–47, 70–72, 90–92,
    110, 132–134, 150–151
  Administration and politics 32–35
  Administration and
    service 35–38, 82–83
  Anglo-American 32, 47, 48, 50, 178,
    197, 205
  Behavioral 21–22
  Career 38–39, 67–68, 86–87,
    124–126, 150
  Confucian 4
  Germanic 48
  Hybrid 48–49, 180
  Ideational 21
  Institutional 21
  Islamic 4
  Law and management 30–32,
    58–60, 122–124
  Napoleonic 48, 50, 54–74
  Politics and administration 68–70,
    81–82, 126–129
  Scandinavian 48, 198, 205–206
  State 26–30, 57–58

State and society 39–42, 63–67,
    83–85, 118–122
  Uniformity 42–44, 60–63,
    88–90, 129–131
Advisory committees 40
Afghanistan 164
Adonis, A. 220
Afghanistan 164
Afonso, A. 84, 215
Africa 43, 44, 154, 179
Agency model 101–102, 150, 169, 207
Agh, A. 49, 215
Ahlbäck-Öberg, S. 95, 215
Ahn, B. M. 161, 215
Alcaras, J.-R. 60, 215
Alford, R. R. 244
Ahonen, P. 71, 75, 215, 222
Aja, E. 215
Akintoye, S. A. 187, 215
Alam, Q. 241
Alasuutari, P. 11, 215
Alba, C. R. 49, 59, 129, 215, 234, 239, 240
Alberts, S. 170, 215
Aliabadi, A. 163, 215
Allison, G. T. 126, 147, 215
Alou, M. T. 218
Andersen, J. G. 95, 216
Andersen, L. 164, 216
Anderson, C. W. 40, 216
Andrews, M. 183, 195, 216
Andranovich, G. 185, 245
Anechiarico, F. 16, 25, 216
Anell, A. 108, 216
Ankar, C. 179, 216
Ansell, C. 101, 165, 195, 210, 216
Anter, A. 6, 216
Appleton, A. M. 246
Arévalo, J. 225

Argentina 54
Argyris, C. 165, 216
Arifari, N. B. 218
Armstrong, J. A. 13, 38, 216
Arnold, P. 136, 216
Asia 36, 44, 179
Askim, J. 101, 105, 216
Athanasaw, Y. A. 36, 216
Auby, J.-B. 216
Aucoin, P. 195, 204, 216
Austerity 37, 84–85
Australia 47, 128
Austria 77, 79, 87
Austro-Hungarian Empire 49
Authoritarian regimes 4, 32
Authority 212
Auyero, J. 13, 216
Ayres, D. W. 50, 216

Bach, S. 124, 216
Bach, T. 85, 104, 217
Baczko, B. 57
Badie, B. 179, 217
Baksh, A. M. 17, 237
Bakvis, H. 216, 217
Balboa, C. M. 41, 217
Baldi, B. 217
Baldini, G. 217
Baldwin, R. 40, 124, 217
Balla, S. J. 1, 40, 217, 225
Ban, C. 52, 149, 151, 217
Banfield, E. C. 64, 217
Barbone, L. 236
Bardill, J. 180, 224
Barilari, A. 73
Bauer, M. 117, 149, 181, 217, 226, 243, 244
Bayart, J.-F. 184, 217
Beck, J. 18, 20, 24, 217, 224
Beck, U. 58, 217
Becker, S. 217, 226, 243, 244
Becker, S. O. 217
Beer, S. 121, 217
Bekker, A. J. G. H. 227, 232
Beland, D. 211, 217
Belgium 63
Bendixsen, S. 95, 217
Benin 184
Benz, A. 217
Berger, S. 244
Bergman, T. 105, 217

Berman, B. J. 185, 217
Bernhard, M. 189, 217
Bersch, K. 87, 217
Besancon, M. 1, 217
Best, H. 221
Betts, R. F. 182, 218
Bezes, P. 59, 72, 218
Bice, S. 223
Bickerton, J. J. 216
Biela, J. 103, 218
Bierschenk, T. 218
Binder, S. A. 227, 242
Binderkrantz, A. S. 40, 105, 218
Bjørna, H. 109, 218
Blais, A. 10, 218
Blake, S. P. 160, 218
Blau, P. M. 7, 218
Bleek, W. 216
Blomkamp, E. 232
Blundo, G. 14, 184, 185, 218, 236
Börzel, T. A. 145, 201, 218
Bochsler, D. 82, 218
Boda, S. 173, 226
Boeckh, K. 217
Börzel, T. A. 145, 201, 218
Bogason, P. 219
Bogdandy, A. 216
Bogdanor, V. 116
Bogedan, C. 242
Bogumil, J. 30, 75, 76, 218, 231, 235
Boin, A. 144
Boli, J. 234
Boone, C. 178, 181, 218
Booth, P. 62, 218
Boston, J. 2, 207, 218
Bothfeld, S. 242
Botswana 192
Bouchard, G. 124, 218
Bouckaert, G. 9, 11, 32, 45, 46, 134, 202,
    203, 218, 219, 223, 239, 244, 246
Bounded rationality 204
Bourmaud, D. 69, 219
Bousbah, K. S. 82, 218
Bouvier, M. 73
Bovens, M. A. P. 31, 45, 150, 219
Bowornwathana, B. 1, 154, 215, 219, 231
Bozeman, B. 46, 176, 219
Braendle, T. 33, 91, 219
Braibanti, R. 49, 181, 219
Branine, M. 163, 219

Brans, M. 1, 4, 214, 215, 219, 231
Braun, C. 40, 219
Brehm, J. 6, 10, 122, 219
Brewer, G. A. 245
Brewer, P. 20, 219
Brexit 133
Bringslid, M. B. 217
British East India Company 44, 160
Browne, A. 31, 246
Brouard, S. 246
Brunet, E. 45, 219
Brunn, F. 99, 219
Bruntiere, J.-R. 210, 219
Budge, I. 246
Buffat, A. 229
Bull, M. J. 228
Bullock, J. B. 110, 219
Bureaucracy 1
    Comparative 1–2, 3–4
    Performance 9
    Public confidence 15
    Representative 13
    Rewards 9–10
    Social background 13–14
    Trust-based 11
    Typologies 7
Bureaucratic authoritarianism 168
Bureaucratic autonomy 5
Bureaucratic behavior
    Citizens 14–16
    Formal-legal 6–9
    Individuals 13–14
    Institutionalism 11–13
    Politics 9–10
    Rationality 10–11
Bureaucrats and politicians 5
Burns, J. M. 181, 221
Burns, J. P. 1, 154, 215, 219, 231
Burton, M. 197, 219
Bussell, J. 49, 220
Bussmeyer, M. R. 78, 220
Butler, D. 130, 220

Cai, Y. 40, 220
Cairney, P. 50, 220
Callaghan, J. 113, 220
Calvert, R. 235
Cameralism 32
Campbell, C. 116, 220
Campbell, J. L. 233

Canada 32, 47, 112, 115, 128, 129
Capano, G. 6, 30, 172, 220
Caranta, R. 52
Carl, S. 91, 220
Carlsson, P. 108, 220
Carroll, B. W. 124, 218
Cassese, S. 216
Castles, F. G. 2, 220
Caulfield, J. 239
Causation 22
Central and Eastern Europe 155, 171–175,
    197, 202
Centralization 54–55
Cha, S. 157, 229
Chadwick, A. 198, 220
Chanlat, J.-F. 17, 220
Chapman, J. 2, 207, 220
Charter Rights and Freedoms 133
Cheung, A. B. L. 154, 220
Chevallier, J. 60, 220
China 158
Christensen, J. G. 40, 102, 104, 105, 106,
    218, 220, 226, 247
Christensen, P. M. 218, 240
Christensen, T. 2, 29, 45, 96, 97, 98, 99,
    104, 140, 143, 145, 220, 226
Christiansen, P. M. 140, 236
Chung, H. 216
Church, C. H. 77, 221
Cini, M. 146, 221
Civil society 96, 163–164
Clark, C. 78, 221
Clark, P. B. 213, 221
Clientelism 186
Clifford, C. 127, 221
Codato, A. 221
Cohn, M. 174, 221
Collaboration 195, 210
Collins, R. O. 181, 221
Colomer, J. M. 62, 242
Colonialism 26, 44, 54, 154, 155, 163, 168,
    178, 189
    Direct rule 182
    Indirect rule 181, 190
Comaroff, J. 223
Comaroff, J. L. 223
Commissions of inquiry 100
Common, R. 161, 221
Communism 155, 158, 171
Compliance 212–213

Compston, H. 244
Compton, M. 203, 244
Condrey, S. E. 225, 237
Confucian tradition 154–155,
    157–159, 161
Conklin, A. L. 49, 221
Connaughton, B. 52, 126, 221, 236
Connell, J. 51, 221
Consociationalism 145
Constitutions 29–20, 57
Convergence 175–176, 196, 199–201
Cook, B. J. 1, 221
Coordination 86, 103, 125, 142, 204
Copus, C. 130, 221
Corporatism 39–40, 65, 84, 97, 99–101,
    131, 169
Corruption 45, 186
Cotta, M. 33, 34, 69, 221
Cox, R. H. 211, 217
Craft, J. 128, 221
Cretu, G. 155, 221
Crook, R. 193, 221
Crossman, R. H. S. 5, 221
Crouch, C. 84, 221
Crowder, M. 181, 221
Crowther, W. 168, 221
Crozier, M. 199, 222
Culpepper, P. 56
Cutler, T. 200, 222
Cyert, R. 204, 222

d'Arcy, F. 129, 222
Dahl, R. A. 212, 222, 240
Dahlström, C. 87, 99, 104, 206, 222, 225
Dairokuno, N. 39, 235
Daly, G. 26, 222
Damaska, M. R. 136, 222
Darbon, D. 179, 180, 222
Davel, E. 220
Dávila, M. 215
Davis, J. 125, 222
Day, P. 45, 222
de Béchillon, D. 47, 244
De Graaf, G. 5, 222
De Herdt, T. 245
de Montricher, N. 59
de Waal, A. 180, 222
Debard, T. 226
Decentralization 9, 62, 66, 72–73,
    92–93, 184

Deconcentration 62
Delegation 45, 84
Della Porta, D. 243
Demmke, C. 226
Democratic backsliding 181
Denhardt, J. V. 38, 204, 222
Denhardt, R. B. 38, 204, 222
Denmark 102, 104
Derlien, H.-U. 95, 222, 236
Di Maschio, F. 73, 222
Diamant, A. 55, 222
Dienstag, J. F. 119, 222
Diez-Picazo, L. M. 71, 222
Dimaggio, P. 177, 180, 201, 204, 206,
    212, 222
Dion, S. 10, 218
Diouf, M. 182, 223
Domingos Costa, L. 221
Donahue, J. D. 41, 223
Double speak 154, 177, 186
Dorfman, P. W. 228
Dowding, K. 133, 223
Drechsler, W. 50, 155, 157, 163, 223
Dreyfus, F. 44, 55, 223
Drezner, D. 125, 223
Dubois, V. 13, 223
Duffy, D. P. 121, 223
Duncan, G. 2, 207, 220
Dunham, D. 20, 223
Dunlop, C. A. 192, 198, 223, 239
Dunn, W. N. 206, 223
Dupuis, J. P. 220
Duran, P. 65, 142, 223
Durant, R. F. 125
Duryea, S. 169, 223
Dwivedi, O. P. 227
Dwyer, P. 198, 223
Dysfunctional administration 185–188
Dyson, K. H. F. 2, 26, 223

E-government 198
Eastern Europe 35, 37, 50, 54
Ebbinghaus, B. 84, 223
Economics of affection 187–188
Ege 149
Egeberg, M. 7, 144, 146, 223
Eichbaum, C. 126, 223
Eisenberg, E. F. 229
Eisenstadt, S. N. 12, 36, 224
Ejersbo, N. 226

Ekiert, G. 171, 224, 231
Eliason, S. 4, 224
Elkins, D. J. 16, 224
Ellinas, A. 140, 151
Ellison, N. 198, 223
Engelstad, F. 236
Engida, T. G. 180, 224
Englebert, P. 224
Enjolras, B. 242
Equality 42
Erk, J. 90, 224
Erkillä, T. 46, 224
Esping-Andersen, G. 78, 95, 169, 224
Esplugas-Labatut, P. 60, 224
Estonia 94, 172, 202
Etzioni, A. 212, 213, 224
European Administrative State 152
European Union 10, 25, 50, 172, 201
    Directorate General 140
    Dossier system 148–149
    European Commission 139, 141
    Fragmentation 146–147, 151–153
Europeanization 52, 95, 152, 153,
    201–202, 210
Evans, M. 221
Evans, P. 1, 224
Eymeri-Douzans, J.-M. 38, 70, 105, 223,
    224, 227, 244

Fabbrini, S. 150
Fajertag, G. 85, 239
Falleti, T. 170, 224
Families of nations 2, 140, 156
Fan, R. 158, 224
Farazmand, A. 163, 224
Federalism 2, 43, 90
Feedback 213
Fenna, A. 44, 88, 130, 224, 229
Fenton, B. 5, 224
Filleule, O. 66, 224
Finke, B. 142
Finland 49, 94
Firmin-Sellers, K. 190, 224
Fisch, S. 17, 224
Fischer, M. 242
Fischer, M. E. 171, 224
Fisher, L. E. 55, 224
Fishman, S. 221
Fizot, S. 71, 225
Fleischer, J. 88, 225

Flinders, M. 150
Flores, G. 168, 221
Foa, R. 180, 184, 225
Fontaine, G. 216
Forest, V. 73, 225
Fournier, J. 50, 225
France 38, 191, 212
    Code law 56, 58–59, 70, 73–74
    Conseil d'État 46, 59, 61
    Consultation 66
    Corps des comptes 71
    ENA 38, 67
    Gilets jaunes 58, 60
    Globilization 95
    Grands corps 55, 59, 67–68
    Grands ecoles 59
    Inspectorate 71
    Jacobin tradition 58, 63
    LOLF 73
    Organizational membership 64
    Vichy Regime 57
France, P. 68
Frank, S. A. 10, 225
Freedman, J. O. 123, 225
Freeman, G. P. 206, 225
Freeman, S. 119, 225
Fried, R. C. 44, 61, 225
Fromont, J. C. 61, 236
Furlong, S. R. 124, 230

Gailmard, S. 10, 225
Gallego, R. 239
Gaman-Golutvina, O. 173, 225
Gandhi, J. 4, 225
Gargarella, R. 117, 225
Gash, A. 101, 165, 195, 210, 216
Gates, S. 6, 10, 122, 219
Gauthier, D. 119, 225
Gebrandy, A. 52
Genieys, W. 69
Germany 29, 38, 41, 44, 75, 98, 100,
    159, 205
    Administrative reform 79
    Bürgernähe 83
    Cameralism 77
    Corporatism 77
    Decentralization 78
    Kanzlerdemokratie 77
    Länder 85–86
    Neues Steuerungsmodell 76

Germany (*cont.*)
  Parliament 91
  Participation 79
  Proporzdemokratie 82, 83
  Ressortprinzip 78
  Reunification 75
  Schlanker Staat 79
  Staastssekretaer 82, 86
Gerring, D. 227
Gerring, J. 188, 189, 225
Gersen, J. E. 46, 225
Ghana 184
Gill, D. 2, 116, 207, 233
Gilley, B. 98, 225
Givan, R. K. 124, 216
Gleizal, J.-J. 236
GLOBE 17, 18
Go, J. 178, 225
Göbel, S. 91, 246
Goldfinch, S. 220
Goldsmith, S. 132
Goncharov, D. 225
Good governance 114, 158
Goodsell, C. T. 13, 19, 45, 144, 225
Goodin, R. E. 244
Gormley, W. T. 1, 225
Governance 1
Governance failure 188
Gravier, M. 148
Greece 54
Green, J. E. 226
Green, S. 230
Gregory, R. 2, 106, 226
Gremion, P. 43, 62, 226
Greve, C. 37, 226
Grindle, M. S. 14, 213, 226
Grohs, S. 231
Grønegård Christensen, J. 226
Grube, D. C. 115, 226
Gualmini, E. 17, 203, 226
Guichard, S. 70, 226
Gunlicks, A. B. 88, 226
Gupta, V. 14, 226, 228
Gutek, B. 230
Guyana 192

Hainz, C. 217
Hajnal, G. 173, 226
Hall, J. A. 221

Hall, P. 111, 226
Halligan, J. A. 46, 219, 226
Hammerschmid, G. 22, 226
Hampden-Turner, C. 17, 245
Hampton, J. 119, 226
Handy, C. B. 176, 226
Hanges, P. J. 228
Hansen, H. F. 111, 112, 226
Hansen, M. B. 226
Hanson, S. E. 171, 224, 231
Hardiman, N. 134, 227
Hargreaves, A. G. 54, 227
Hashmi, S. H. 165, 227
Hassel, A. 227
Hassenteufel, P. 69
Hattenhauer, H. 75, 227
Häusermann, S. 84, 227
Hay, C. 11, 227
Hayward, J. E. S. 57, 67, 227, 237
Hazareesingh, S. 43, 50, 227
Heady, F. 1, 7, 8, 227
Heider, D. S. 116, 227
Heider, J. T. 116, 227
Heisler, M. O. 3, 227
Heitzmann, K. 79, 245
Helmke, G. 173, 189, 190, 227
Henderson, K. M. 227
Hendrych, D. 155, 227
Hennl, A. 218
Hennessy, P. 128, 134, 227
Henriksen, J. B. 108, 227
Heper, M. 2, 7, 163, 164, 227, 228
Herbst, J. 3, 228
Herzfeld, M. 186, 228
Heskestad, A. 146
Heywood, P. 230
Hesse, J. J. 236, 238
Hicks, A. M. 244
Hill, J. A. 233
Hill, M. 229
Hinnebusch, R. 166, 228
Hirschl, R. 133
Historical institutionalism 117
Hjelmar, U. 109, 238
Hodgetts, J. E. 123, 228
Hoet, D. 219
Hofstede, G. 228
Hofstede, G. J. 17, 18, 19, 148, 157, 166, 167, 170, 175, 228

Hogwood, B. W. 130, 228
Hollibaugh, G. E. 127
Holmes, L. 185, 228
Holmgren, M. 87, 104, 222
Homburg, V. 198, 228
Hondeghem, A. 187, 228, 237, 245
Hong Kong 196
Hongbo, L. 110, 228
Hood, C. 4, 5, 14, 29, 32, 34, 71, 135, 140,
    176, 199, 201, 209, 211, 228, 235, 238
Hooge, L. 145
Hoque, N. 163, 226
Hoque, S. 226
Horton, S. 3, 36, 228
Houck, O. A. 31, 228
House, R. J. 17, 148, 228
Houston, D. J. 110, 229
Howard, C. 115, 226
Howlett, M. 16, 25, 229
Huber, J. G. 47, 216, 229
Hueglin, T. 44, 88, 130, 224, 229
Humphrey, C. 174, 229
Hungary 173
Huntington, S. P. 208, 222, 229
Hupe, P. 6, 15, 20, 36, 187, 229
Hurka, S. 215
Hurni, P. Y. 241
Hvinden, B. 216
Hyden, G. 4, 179, 184, 187, 188, 189, 229
Hysing, E. 100, 229

Ibarra, D. G. 240
Ibreck, R. 180, 222
Iceland 104, 110
Im, T. 36, 157, 229
Im, T. J. W. 229
Immergut, E. 229
Implementation 31, 141
Imported state 179
India 43, 159–160, 178, 189
Informal institutions 174–175, 189
Ingraham, P. W. 33, 127, 229
Institutional isomorphism 180,
    201, 206–207
Institutionalism 4
    Discursive 11
    Historical 2, 12, 117
    Logic of appropriateness 11
    Rational choice 12

Institutionalization 207–208
Interface bureaucracy 187
International Monetary Fund 29, 168
Inwood, G. J. 230
Ireland 116, 121
Islamic tradition 155, 163–166
Islands of excellence 183
Italy 40, 44, 63
Iyer, L. 188, 189, 190, 229

Jabbra, J. G. 227
Jacobs, H. 42, 75, 229
Jacobsson, B. 95, 229
Jäger, W. 229
James, O. 228
Jann, W. 4, 30, 52, 75, 79, 80, 218, 230
Janoski, T. 244
Jans, M. T. 63, 244
Japan 157, 159
Jarvis, M. 216, 217
Javidan, M. 228
Jenssen, S. 109, 218
Jerome-Forget, M. 131
Jessop, B. 29
Jewell, C. J. 83, 230
Jobert, B. 66, 230
Johns, C. M. 2, 230
Johnson, B. 32, 230
Johnson, J. J. 168, 230
Johnson, N. 121, 230
Johnson, S. 215
Johnston, K. 223
Johnston, M. 45, 230
Jones, G. W. 18, 228
Jones, M. L. 18
Jørgensen, O. 111, 230
Judge, D. 228
Judicialization 133
Justiemonopol 99

Kada, N. 73, 230, 236
Kagan, R. A. 123, 230
Kahn, R. L. 15, 230
Kaiser, A. 218
Kallis, A. 239
Kamisar, B. 129, 230
Kanyane, M. 230
Karlhofer, F. 100, 230
Kassim, H. 52, 142, 143, 146, 230

Katz, D. 230
Katzenstein, P. J. 29, 41, 77, 230
Kaufman, H. A. 211, 230
Keating, M. 233, 243
Keeler, J. T. S. 66, 230
Kenworthy, L. 66, 244
Keogh, D. 121, 230
Kerber, W. 89, 241
Kerwin, C. M. 1, 40, 47, 124, 230
Kettl, D. F. 50, 132, 230, 231
Khan, M. A. 226
Kickert, W. J. M. 2, 231
Kim, Y.-P. 157, 215, 231
King, D. S. 238
Kinglsey, J. D. 13, 231
Kiser, E. 56, 231
Kitschelt, H. 171, 231
Kittel, B. 77, 84, 244
Klein, R. 45, 222
Klemmensen, R. 226
Knapp, A. 62, 231
Knill, C. 25, 28, 52, 120, 152, 202, 214,
    215, 231
Kolltveit, K. 216
König, K. 149, 231
Kopecký, P. 173, 185, 231
Kopyciński, P. 35, 238
Korea 36
Kornai, J. 240
Kotchegura, A. 171, 172, 231
Kriesi, H. 80, 231
Kristinsson, G. H. 101, 104, 231
Kuhlmann, S. 75, 231
Kumlin, S. 96, 231

Laborde, C. 231
Laegreid, P. 2, 45, 95, 99, 140, 220, 226,
    231, 246
Lalenis, K. 54
Lane, J.-E. 236, 237
Lange, M. K. 43, 168, 188, 190, 192,
    232, 233
LaPalombara, J. 3, 40, 232
Latin America 26, 44, 117, 155,
    166–171, 210
Laver, M. 235
Lawrence, B. 232
Lawyers 99
Layering 207, 208–209
Le Gales, P. 73, 232

Le Grand, J. 6, 232
Le Lidec, P. 73, 232
Le Meur, P.-Y. 14, 184, 218, 236
Lee, Grace O. M. 228, 235
Lee, K.-H. 232
Lega, J. 242
Legacies 23, 26
Legalism 136, 149, 169, 173, 176, 205
Legay, M.-L. 44, 232
Lehmbruch, G. 82, 232
Lemarchand, R. 186, 232
Leruth, B. 216
Levitsky, S. 173, 189, 190, 227
Lewansky, R. 68, 232
Lewis, D. E. 127, 211, 232
Lewis, G. B. 10, 225
Lewis, J. M. 195, 232
Lichbach, M. I. 235
Lie, A. 220
Liebert, S. 225
Lietzman, H. J. 216
Light, P. C. 127, 232
Lijphart, A. 87, 104, 232
Lindenfeld, D. 77, 232
Linder, W. 89, 232
Lindström, A. 108, 242
Lindvall, J. 96, 97, 232
Ling, L. H. M. 158, 233
Lipsky, M. 6, 233
Lithuania 172
Little Tigers 121
Local government 108–109
Lodge, M. 2, 34, 116, 135, 207, 228, 233
Logic of appropriateness 151, 204
Longstreth, F. 243, 244
Lopes Ferreira, A. P. 221
Loriaux, M. 56, 233
Loughlin, J. 52, 61, 233
Louvaris, A. 71
Lu, X. 158, 233
Lugard, F. D. 181, 233
Lund, C. 154, 186, 233
Lundberg, E. 100, 229
Lynn, L. E. 204

MacCarthaigh, M. 134, 227
Mach, A. 227
Maddox, G. 181, 233
Madsen, P. K. 95, 233
Mahoney, J. 2, 12, 117, 207, 232, 233

Mair, P. 231
Mamdani, M. 235
Mann, M. 29, 233
Maor, M. 209, 233
March, J. G. 3, 11, 97, 144, 151, 200, 204, 208, 222, 233
Marchand, C. 215
Marin, A. 67, 234
Marin, B. 237
Marrel, G. 215
Martí-Henneberg, J. 49, 234
Martin, B. 159, 234
Martin, M. 233
Mashaw, J. L. 124, 234
Massey, A. 223, 228
Mastor, W. 57, 212, 234
Matei, L. 234
Mattson, I. 110, 234
Mavrot, C. 241
May, C. 198, 220
Mayntz, R. 234
Mazur, A. G. 246
Mazur, S. 35, 172, 234, 238
McConalogue, J. 133, 233
McConnell, G. 40, 233
McCourt, W. 192, 233
McFarland, A. S. 40, 233
McGann, M. 232
McGarvey, N. 50, 220
McKay, D. H. 246
McKenna, B. 63, 233
McSweeny, B. 18
McVicar, M. 228
Mead, W. R. 50, 234
Meininger, M. C. 67
Mendez, J. L. 4, 234
Menon, A. 237
Merit system 157, 159
Mesa-Lago, C. 169, 234
Meseguer, C. 234
Metzger, G. E. 24, 234
Mexico 168, 169
Meyer, J. 234
Meyer, J. W. 52, 200, 234
Meyer, R. E. 226
Meyer-Sahling, J.-H. 23, 49, 50, 172, 199, 234
Meyers, M. K. 6, 235
Migdal, J. S. 26, 96, 179, 235
Milanesi, A. 169, 240

Miller, D. Y. 206, 223
Minkov, M. 17, 18, 228, 235
Miorelli, R. 168
Mirow, M. C. 155, 235
Modeen, T. 244
Modernization 3, 179, 184–185
Moïse, N. 183, 235
Mogul Empire 160
Molina, O. 39, 66, 235
Montagnier, G. 226
Morabito, M. 216
Moreno, F. J. 155, 235
Moshonas, S. 183, 235
Mowla, M. M. 226
Moyo, J. M. 187, 235
Możdżen, M. 234
Muller, P. 66
Müller, W. C. 235
Müller-Rommel, F. 78, 235
Murtazashvili, J. B. 164, 235
Mustapha, A. R. 187, 235

Nagel, M. 145, 164, 211, 235, 238
Nakamura, A. 39, 235
Nakrosis, V. 219
Napoleonic tradition 155, 210
Naschold, F. 76, 235
Natalini, A. 73, 222
Nationality 2
Navarro, C. 49, 59, 215
Nef, J. 19, 221, 235
Nemec, J. 219
Neo-Weberian State 204
Netherlands 49, 54
Neto, J. V. 34, 235
Neuhold, C. 35, 69, 81, 235
Neutral competence 128, 135
New Public Governance 195, 204
New Public Management 2, 5, 31–32, 41, 45–46, 72, 75–76, 94, 101, 105, 109–110, 112–113, 116, 131, 156, 161, 175, 195, 201
New Zealand 124, 134, 207
Newbold, S. P. 123, 235
Newell, J. L. 228
Newman, P. 48
Niclauß, K. 236
Nielsen, V. L. 6, 235
Niklasson, B. 99, 222
Nishikawa, Y. 159, 236

Niskanen, W. 10, 236
Nonjon, M. 215
Nordlinger, E. 28, 236
Nordstrom, T. 217
Nørgaard, A. S. 21, 172, 236, 240
Nørgaard, O. 236
North Africa 191
Northern Ireland 129
Norton, P. 241
Norway 97–98, 102, 105–106
Nugent, N. 221
Nunberg, B. 156, 197, 236

Öberg, P. 97, 236
O'Connor, J. R. 199, 236
O'Donnell, G. 168, 236
O'Leary, R. 5, 126, 236
Oberdorff, H. 61, 236
Oleinik, A. 174, 236
Olgiati, A. 223
Oliver, C. 208, 236
Olivier de Sardan, J.-P. 179, 183, 185, 187,
    188, 193, 218, 236
Olsen, J. P. 3, 11, 97, 144, 151, 152, 172,
    196, 200, 208, 211, 233, 236
Olsson, J. 5, 122, 126, 236
Ombudsman 110–111
Ongaro, E. 32, 54, 236, 245
Ongur, H. O. 236
Oramus, M. 234
O'Reilly, P. L. 230
Organization theory 5
Organizational termination 211
Osborn, E. L. 232
Østerud, Ø. 97, 236
Ostrom, E. 12, 236
Ostrup, N. 226
Ott, J. S. 17, 237
Ottoman Empire 163, 164
Overeem, P. 221

Page, E. C. 1, 5, 6, 47, 75, 124, 202,
    235, 237
Painter, M. 6, 157, 159, 160, 183, 229,
    237, 247
Pakistan 160
Palermo, F. 73, 237
Palier, B. 223
Palme, J. H. 95, 237
Palonen, K. 75, 215, 222

Panama 168
Pandey, S. K. 37, 237
Panizza, F. 9, 14, 105, 168, 237
Pantouflage 39, 68
Papadopoulos, Y. 84, 215, 227
Pardo, I. 229
Parliament 33–34, 69–70
Parrado, S. 68, 72, 218
Participation 42, 206
Participatory management 165–166
Path dependency 12, 204–205
Patrimonialism 170
Patronage 14, 103–105, 173, 183, 213
Patterson, W. 230
Patty, J. W. 10, 225
Pedersen, O. K. 233
Pelgrims, C. 219
Pepinsky, T. B. 36
Performance management 46
Perrow, C. 7, 237
Perry, J. L. 187, 227, 228, 237, 245
Persistence 211–212
Persson, M. 110, 244
Peters, B. G. 1, 2, 4, 5, 6, 10, 11, 13, 16, 22,
    25, 27, 33, 35, 42, 46, 52, 69, 72, 81, 83,
    95, 99, 103, 104, 105, 117, 125, 126,
    135, 136, 142, 144, 145, 147, 150, 152,
    160, 164, 165, 173, 176, 183, 195, 199,
    203, 209, 211, 214, 215, 216, 217, 219,
    222, 223, 225, 226, 228, 229, 230, 231,
    233, 234, 235, 236, 237, 238, 239, 240,
    241, 243, 244, 245, 246, 247
Petersen, O. H. 109, 238
Philippines 51, 178
Picot, A. 247
Picot, G. 227
Pierre, J. 1, 10, 27, 29, 35, 42, 69, 81, 101,
    105, 117, 126, 215, 217, 222, 223, 225,
    226, 227, 229, 231, 234, 235, 236, 238,
    239, 241, 243, 244, 245
Pierson, P. 84, 204, 213, 239
Pinto, A. C. 66, 239
Pluralism 40, 131–132
Pochet, P. 85, 239
Poguntke, T. 4, 105, 133, 239
Poland 155, 173
Policy advice 31
Policy networks 144–145
Policy styles 25
Policy transfer 200

Policymaking 1, 142
Political culture 25, 137, 147–148
Political development 177
Political executives 2, 4
Politicization 34–35, 69, 81, 103–105,
   126, 173–174
Pollard, D. 163, 219
Pollitt, C. 1, 32, 45, 176, 192, 199, 203,
   219, 239
Poole, A. 223
Populism 113, 136
Powell, W. 177, 180, 201, 204, 206, 212, 222
Praça, S. 217
Pre-colonial governance 180
Prefects 43, 55–56, 61, 65, 109
Presidentialization 105, 133
Pressman, J. L. 31, 239
Principal-agent theory 10
Prismatic society 183, 193
Privilegism 187
Proeller, I. 226, 241, 245
Privilegism 187
Pronin, K. 97, 239
Przeworski, A. 10, 116
Public personnel 4
   Rewards 4
Public service motivation 14, 20, 36–37,
   110, 186
Public services 205–206
Punctuated equilibrium 198–199
Pye, L. 17, 239

Qazbir, H. 62, 239
Quandt, H. P. 247
Quitkatt, C. 142

Raadschelders, J. C. N. 232, 245, 246
Rabrenovic, A. 202, 246
Radaelli, C. M. 44, 198, 239
Rahman, M. S. 247
Rainey, H. G. 7, 219, 239
Ramio, C. 49, 239
Ramirez, F. O. 234
Ramirez, M. F. 118, 239
Ramos, C. 54, 169, 170, 215, 234, 237,
   239, 240
Randma-Liiv, T. 173, 240
Rauch, J. 1, 224
Rawls, J. 119, 240
Rechtsstaat 94, 98, 170

Reenock, C. 217
Reichard, C. 205, 240
Representative bureaucracy 164
Responsiveness 25
Revenue sources 88–89
Rhinard, M. 144
Rhodes, M. 39, 66, 235
Rhodes, R. A. W. 14, 116, 227, 228,
   240, 242
Riaz, A. 247
Richardson, J. J. 25, 240
Riggs, F. W. 154, 175, 177, 183, 186,
   193, 240
Ritz, A. 245
Roberts, M. 221
Roberts, R. 232
Robinson, J. A. 215
Rockman, B. A. 215, 227, 232, 242
Rodrik, D. 211, 240
Rokkan, S. 40, 41, 97, 100, 240
Roland, G. 117, 240
Roll, M. 183, 240
Romania 155
Rommetvedt, H. 100, 236, 240
Roness, P. 95, 231
Rootes, C. 224
Rosanvallon, P. 58, 240
Rose, R. 31, 66, 192, 199, 205, 240
Rose-Ackerman, S. 240
Rosenbloom, D. H. 123, 133, 235, 240
Rosser, C. 241
Roth, C. 148
Rothstein, B. 96, 97, 103, 111, 114, 231,
   232, 240
Rouban, L. 9, 39, 68, 222, 240, 241
Roux, C. 63
Rowan, B. 200, 234
Royal Commissions (Canada) 32, 123
Ruin, O. 96, 241
Russia 49, 155, 171–175
Rutake, P. 185, 241
Rykkja, L. 226

Saalfeld, T. 91, 220, 241
Saam, N. J. 89, 241
Sabbi, M. 187, 241
Saeidem, A. 164, 241
Sager, F. 47, 52, 156, 192, 199, 200, 209,
   221, 241
Salamon, L. M. 9, 241

Salminen, A. 94, 244
Salomonsen, H. H. 226
Salvador, M. 49, 239
Salvati, M. 241
Samaratunge, R. 241
Samier, E. 163, 165, 241
Sartori, G. 136, 241
Savoie, D. J. 4, 123, 126, 128, 135, 195, 197,
    200, 238, 241
Sbragia, A. M. 152
Scandinavia 37, 38, 43
Schachter, H. L. 112, 241
Schaffer, B. 135, 241
Scharpf, F. W. 234
Schedler, K. 226, 241, 245
Scheepers, S. 245
Schick, A. 194, 201, 241
Schiller, C. 79, 241
Schmidt, M. G. 78, 242
Schmidt, V. 11, 73, 242
Schmitter, P. C. 39, 242
Schön-Quinoivan, E. 146
Scholz, S. 82, 246
Schoyen, M. A. 216
Schröter, E. 230, 238
Schumacher, E. J. 184, 242
Schütz, H. 75, 242
Schwartz, M. A. 244
Sciarini, P. 84, 242
Scotland 129
Scott, C. 228
Scott, I. 196, 242
Scott, W. R. 7, 218
Seerden, R. 1, 242
Segrestin, D. 66, 242
Seibel, W. 75, 81, 242
Seidman, H. B. 5, 7, 242
Seigfried, A. 242
Self, P. 116, 242
Selle, P. 236, 242
Seller, J. M. 108, 242
Selznick, P. 11, 208, 213, 242
Semi-presidentialism 69
Sen, S. N. 160, 242
Sesselmeier, W. 242
Sharma, R. D. 19, 242
Sharpe, L. J. 242
Shaw, C. K. Y. 77, 242
Shaw, M. 242
Shaw, R. 126, 223

Shepsle, K. A. 12, 235, 242
Shih, C.-Y. 159, 233
Shipan, C. R. 47, 229
Shirikov, A. 225
Sieber, S. 242
Silberman, B. S. 2, 12, 139, 242
Simmie, J. 171, 243
Simeon, R. E. B. 16, 224
Sisson, C. H. 19, 243
Skelcher, C. 128, 243
Skocpol, T. 243
Skowronek, S. 29, 49, 120, 243
Smith, B. C. 243
Smith, E. 216
Smith, T. 189, 243
Smithey, S. I. 124, 243
Smullen, J. 239
Smyrl, M. E. 243
Sneath, D. 174, 229
Social mechanisms 211–214
Social pacts 66
Sørensen, E. 108, 195, 238, 243, 245
Solomon, P. H., Jr. 174, 243
Sootla, G. 236
Soros, G. 243
South Korea 157, 159, 161
Sovereignty 29, 41, 77
Soviet Union 172
Spain 43, 63, 68, 190
Spirova, M. 231
Spulbar, N. 243
Stack, L. 28, 243
Stacy, H. 27, 243
Staniland, M. 179, 243
State and society 27
    Communitarian 96
    Contractarian 27, 106, 118
    Organic 27–28, 106
State autonomy 28–29
State-building 43
Stazyk, E. C. 37, 237
Stegarescu, D. 89, 243
Steinbach, Y. 215
Steinbauer, P. 7, 239
Steinhorssen, R. S. 231
Steinmo, S. 12, 117, 204, 243, 244
Stephenson, M. 243
Stephenson, M. C. 46, 192, 225
Stewart, J. 42, 134, 246
Stilles, A. 56, 243

Stillman, R. 120, 243
Stoker, G. 197, 243
Stokes, S. C. 170, 244
Stone, L. 223
Streeck, W. 66, 244
Street-level bureaucrats 6, 13, 15, 36, 61,
    83, 144, 198
Stritch, J. M. 219
Strobel, B. 90, 244
Strøm, K. 46, 105, 217, 244
Strømsnes, K. 242
Stroink, F. 1, 242
Sturtzer, A. 91, 219
Stutzer, A. 33
Subirats, J. 239
Suleiman, E. N. 140, 151
Sullivan, H. 223
Sundström, G. 229
Super market state 97–98, 100
Super nationalism 143
Suvarierol, S. 148
Svensson, T. 236
Swanstrom, T. 244
Sweden 56, 106, 107, 111
Swenden, W. 63, 244
Swedish model 95
Switzerland 79, 89
Szanton, P. 241

't Hart, P. 203, 219, 244
Taiwan 158
Taagepera, R. 172, 244
Taggart, P. 244
Talbot, C. 239
Talos, E. 77, 84, 244
Tanguy, G. 43, 244
Tarschys, D. 102, 244
Tavares de Alameda, P. 33, 34, 221
Tayeb, M. R. 116
Taylor, M. M. 217
Taylor-Gooby, P. 216
Teicher, J. 241
Temmes, M. 49, 94, 244
Terneyre, P. 47, 244
Tettey, W. J. 185, 217
Teune, H. 116
Thatcher, Margaret 34
Thedieck, F. 217, 224, 244
Thelen, K. 2, 12, 117, 207, 233,
    243, 244

Thesen, G. 24, 236, 240
Thomas, G. M. 234
Thompson, J. R. 229
Thorallsson, B. 231
Thornley, A. 48
Thunman, E. 110, 244
Tignor, R. L. 168, 244
Tilly, C. 57, 65, 245
Titeca, K. 245
Toonen, T. A. J. 198, 227, 245, 246
Torfing, J. 1, 40, 195, 238, 243, 245
Torres, L. 2, 72, 245
Torstendahl, R. 3, 245
Tosun, J. 25, 229
Traber, D. 242
Trade unions 64–65, 98
Transparency 46, 111
Trägårdh, L. 96, 245
Travers, T. 220, 228
Treib, O. 149
Treschel, A. H. 80, 231
Trompenaars, F. 17, 245
Trondal, J. 141, 143, 144, 145, 152
Tsebelis, G. 12, 245
Tunney, S. 113, 220
Turkey 163
Turner, E. 88, 245

Umeh, O. J. 185, 245
Unger, B. 79, 245
Ungovernability 199–200
United Kingdom 30, 32, 128, 130, 160, 189,
    197, 202
United States 38, 90, 116, 119
    Administrative Procedures Act 123, 133
    Brownlow Committee 123, 136
    Senior Executive Service 127
Uruguay 54
USGAO 132, 245

Valenzuela, A. 215
Van de Walle, S. 15, 37, 245
Van der Meer, F. M. 4, 232, 245, 246
Van Der Sprenkel, O. B. 157
Van der Wal, Z. 158, 247
Van Gorp, J. 225
Van Ryzin, G. G. 245
Van Stolk, C. 199, 234
Van Thiel, S. 245, 246
Van Waarden, F. 25, 245

Vanagunas, S. 155, 245
Vandenabeele, W. 14, 20, 37, 83, 245
Vanhoonacker, S. 140, 235
Vansina, J. 180, 246
Varinard, A. 226
Vatter, A. 89, 232
Vauchez, A. 68
Veit, S. 82, 90, 104, 217, 244, 246
Véliz, C. 169, 246
Venaik, S. 20, 219
Verba, S. 239
Verhey, L. 235
Verheijen, T. J. G. 202, 231, 246
Verhoest, K. 5, 10, 101, 112, 219, 246
Verpeaux, L. 230
Verschuere, B. 246
Vibert, F. 128
Vickers, G. 16, 246
Viet, V. 71, 246
Vike, H. 217
Vintar, M. 223
Vizinat, N. 73, 232
Vogiatzis, N. 146
Vom Hau, M. 232, 233
Von Maravić, P. 238

Waine, B. 200, 222
Wall, R. 221
Wallis, J. 220
Walsh, K. 42, 134, 246
Walsh, P. 108, 246
Wanna, J. 240
Warin, P. 246
Watanuki, J. 222
Wayneberg, E. 151
Webb, P. 4, 105, 133, 239
Weber, Max 4, 6, 67, 75, 77, 78, 81, 92, 97, 124, 145
Wegrich, K. 79, 246
Weil, E. 76, 246
Weingast, B. R. 229
Weiss, L. M. 29, 246

Welfare state 78–79, 95, 107
Weller, P. 240
Westminster governance 115, 118
White, L. B. 120, 246
Wildavsky, A. 31, 239, 246
Wille, A. 150
Williams, G. 147
Wilson, A. 73, 237
Wilson, G. K. 115, 116, 220, 246
Wilson, J. W. 213, 221
Wilson, W. 6, 200, 246
Winding, S. S. 21, 172, 236
Witman, D. A. 229
Woessmann, L. 217
Woll, C. 246
Wollmann, H. 32, 230, 246
Wonka, A. 91, 246
Woo-Cumings, M. 233
Woodhouse, D. 50, 246
World Bank 168, 169
World Trade Organization 29
Wright, J. R. 40, 217
Wright, V. 67, 127, 221, 227, 230, 235
Wünder, B. 49, 246

Yackee, S. W. 41, 247
Yang, L. 158, 247
Yesilkagit, K. 102, 172, 183, 217, 226, 234, 243, 244, 247

Zacka, B. 6, 20, 83, 144, 247
Zafarullah, H. 155, 247
Zaretsky, R. 221
Zariski, R. 44, 247
Zeckhauser, R. J. 41, 223
Zelikow, P. 147
Ziblatt, D. 44, 225, 247
Zito, A. 145
Zohnhöfer, R. 220
Zombie ideas 211
Zypries, B. 83, 247
Zuckerman, A. S. 235